qur'an and cricket
Travels through the madrasahs of Asia
and other stories

Farish A Noor

SILVERFISH BOOKS
Kuala Lumpur

Published by Silverfish Books Sdn Bhd, 2009
www.silverfishbooks.com
email: info@silverfishbooks.com

Qur'an and Cricket ©Farish A Noor
Sketches and photographs © Farish A Noor

First Printing, Oct 2009
Second edition, Dec 2009

This book is sold subject to the condition that it shall not by way of trade or otherwise be lent, resold, hired out, or otherwise circulated without the publisher's consent in any form of binding or cover other than that in which it is published and without a similar condition including this condition being imposed on the subsequent purchaser.

Published by
Silverfish Books Sdn Bhd (483433-k)
58-1 Jalan Telawi, Bangsar Baru, 59100 Kuala Lumpur.
(Please refer to website for any changes in the street address)

Printed by Academe Art & Printing Services, S/B,
7 Jalan Rajawali 1A, Batu 8 Jalan Puchong, 47100 Selangor

Contents

The Nomad's Prayer	9
The Long Road to the Present	11
The Battle of Light and Darkness	19
Qur'an and Cricket: Touring the Madrasahs of Pakistan	32
Reign of the Kalashnikov	43
The Last Days of Empire	54
Welcome to FBI-stan	65
Kipling's Cat	76
Deoband, the Great	78
Vale of Tears	96
Forgotten Nation	105
Cold Turkey in Kandy	115
Fire and Brimstone	129
Santri: Another Look at the Pesantren al-Mukmin	143
The Merchant of Memories	157
In the Land of the Living Shadows	163
Rat Pancake	169
Saigon, The Devouring City	173
In the Shadow of Ataturk	186
A Dialogue in Hell	198
Silence	213
Another Country, Another Election	231
Land of Bleeding Smiles	245
That Quaint Little War Up North	255
Seeking Durga	273

Dedication

To Yusseri and Eddin;
brothers and fellow-travellers

qur'an and cricket
Travels through the madrasahs of Asia
and other stories

Farish A Noor

The Nomad's Prayer

Dear God,
I thank you for these feet, these eyes, these hands;
I pray that wherever I go I will be able to see you in the world around me,
and to always see honestly; let no sight be too terrible to bear;
let nothing and no-one be ugly;
I pray that whatever I touch will remind me of your eternal presence in all things;
let nothing be repugnant to me;
And I pray that with every step I take I will be getting closer to you;
God, take me home. And let my home be everywhere.

Farish A Noor
2009

The Long Road to the Present

On the night of fifteenth May in the year nineteen hundred and sixty-seven, my mother was lying on the bed in a the first floor ward of the Maternity Hospital in Georgetown, Penang. Half asleep and exhausted, she tried to rest after what was, after all, a rather tiresome ordeal that morning – giving birth to me. The records kept under the stairs of the hospital noted the circumstances of my birth thus: "8.45 am. Boy. Eight and a half pounds. Head circumference: thirteen and three-quarter inches. Big head."

Suddenly in the dead of night my mother noticed something a-stirring at the foot of the bed. In the gloomy darkness of the silent ward, the matron-midwife was pottering about my crib, torchlight in hand. My mother, who later admitted that she did not get along with the matron, who was fond of shouting at all the young mothers while they were in their labour pains, was examining my fingers one by one, torch in hand. "What are you doing? What are you looking at? Is my son all right?" she asked. To which the matron replied:

"Your son has got 'eyes' at the tips of all his fingers. Look! Each fingerprint is totally rounded, sealed like eyes. Every one of them. This one so rare, *lah*"

"What does that mean?" my mother enquired.

And the matron replied: "When your son grows up, he will talking-talking a lot. All the time, he will be talking. And travelling. He will travel all over the world, going to places you and I will never go to. But once he travels he will never stop. And he will not come back."

Needless to say, the matron's ill-chosen words were not welcomed by my mother who had, after all, just delivered her firstborn during the early hours of that morning. The thought that her son would leave her one day, never to return, spurred her to coddle her infant boy and keep him close to her bosom for as long as she could.

In time, and as soon as I was tall enough to wear a pair of shorts, I was despatched to St. John's Institution in Kuala Lumpur where I would be kept under the watchful eyes of Jesuits and prefects (until I became one of the latter myself) and forbidden to leave the sacred precincts of Bukit Nanas.

School was a life of routine and chores that were designed, primarily, to squeeze out what little trace of errant wanderlust boys had, so that they would eventually graduate into the ranks of respectable society and assume the role of merchant bankers or righteous bureaucrats. I pined for open fields and forlorn wastelands and the only consolation on offer were the dog-eared copies of National Geographic, whose pages had been judiciously mutilated by zealous missionaries to remove African nipples and other dangly bits.

Four decades later, I find myself assuming the avatar of the itinerant scholar, whose self-made career was as much the result of chance as it was of some degree of cunning. The tales that are contained herein are the results of the endless (though seldom pointless) wanderings that took me across the globe over the past two decades.

Does one take the road or does the road take one? My probationary stay in Western Europe – a hop-on, hop-off career of temporary posts and semi-sedentary stays in England, France, Holland and Germany – was but a prelude for something bigger that I had in mind. I had decided not to follow in the footsteps of my peers and contemporaries at school who chose the realm of commerce or politics. I chose academia instead, and a rather murky and dusty corner of academia at that. I gave up the life of business suits and sensible shoes for the backpack, camera and my beloved Arthur Jacobis – that I picked up in a flea market in Berlin and have been on my feet ever since.

Over the years my background in philosophy and literature served as the springboard for a move to politics, history and comparative area studies. Whether it was fate or chance that guided the steps I took I know not, but in the end my choice of research placed me in a situation where travel would be the order of the day; and where the nomadic life became my own: It was not unusual for me to spend half the year on fieldwork, and during those lonely sojourns to faraway places I had dreamt of travelling to as a child the sensation of isolation and loneliness was softened only by the bittersweet knowledge that I was living the life that I had dreamt of since childhood.

Not that travelling was easy, or even pleasant all the time, mind you: Luck played a part in keeping this weary body relatively intact and in presentable shape, and luck was in attendance on more than one occasion. In the northern frontier belt of Pakistan the choice of the midnight bus happened to be a propitious one for the simple reason that the bus that left in the morning was ambushed and shot to pieces, as was the one that left the following day.

Several near-crashes while flying have rendered me immune to fear of sudden death by flight. A late-night arrival in Morocco led to a rather unpleasant encounter with a knife that kissed my throat in the back alleys of Tangiers, and my sleep in several remote *madrasahs* was interrupted on more than one occasion by the curious sensation of a hand groping southwards in my sarong.

On at least one occasion a death by drowning was narrowly averted thanks to the helping hand of a passer-by whose own store of empathy was large enough for him to risk the same fate himself.

In fact, looking back at the years of travelling that this body has done (and the mileage has chalked up) I am stunned that the only harm that has ever befallen me was the sudden (and unglamorous) loss of a toenail that was rudely ripped off by a passing lorry while hanging precariously out of the door of a bus in Delhi. No bouts of bleeding malaria were suffered; nor long feverish nights gasping for breath in a humid tent. Ten years of travel with only the loss of a toenail is a bill that one would gladly pay with no complaints.

Along the way I also collected friends aplenty, who remain with me despite the relentless passing of water beneath the bridge. Some have been committed to posterity while many others remain as my constant companions in life: Christele, who first took me to the mosque of Wazir Khan in Lahore, and who taught me the beauty of silence there. Henry, with whom I mounted Lavinia, goose feathers and all. Shabab, who navigated us in and out of the dizzy lanes of Lucknow and Deoband, and whose culinary obsessions landed us in the filthiest eatery I have ever crawled into in my life, only to be rewarded by the best breads and mangoes that have ever passed my lips. Romo Toha, as we blazed our trail across all of Java, and who helped me escape the clutches of Umi Afida, the Madurese Jamu-seller. Jacque, who taught me that truth can be found in the pen as well as the keyboard. Margrit and her magic carpet. Cikgu Teacher, whose contempt for bad spelling kept us rolling on the floor with his imaginative grammar. Ustaz Fauzan, whose *jihad* for polygamy he explained to me while driving twice over the speeding limit. Amir Khan, whose green eyes were the most intense I have ever seen. Rasheed, who taught me the difference between a Russian-made Kalashnikov and a Chinese one. Robin, who taught me to accept contingency and contradictions as my friends and bed-fellows. Ustaz Meng, whose knack of avoiding road-blocks and landmines amazes me still. Danny Lim, whose consensus on the truly amazing taste of the half-boiled eggs in Kota Bharu assures me that I have yet to cross the frontier into insanity. Ibrahim who walked through the desert in the dead of night. The cat of Lahore that gave me the key to Kipling's genius. The Libyan desert that taught me how to keep still. Hang Tuah, who taught me that the world is home. They are all with me always, fellow-travellers on this journey we call life.

My academic colleagues are also among those whom I want to thank for these travels were hardly done without some foretaste of what I ought to expect. My seven years in Germany – five of which were spent at the Zentrum Moderner Orient – were among the most academically productive in my life, and I was thankful to be in the company of friends and peers who did – in one way or another – guide me and compel me to take to the road. In particular, thanks are due to my friends in Germany who were there for me before I left and when I returned, not least to share a round of drinks and stories. My thanks are due to Gudrun and Philip, Ulrike Freitag, Margrit Pernau, Dietrich Reetz, Dyala Hamzah, Baz leCoq, Sonja Hegasy, Britta Frede, Katarina Zoeller, Larissa Schmid and Chanfi Ahmed. I will always recall with fondness our story-telling by the lakeside as the sun was setting in a hot and humid summer, and how the narratives would flow as the barbeques simmered.

Thanks are also due to those who were appreciative of these travelogues and who thought that they ought to be shared with others. My gratitude goes to Jason Tan, editor, proof-reader and dear friend who was the first to have them published in Off the Edge magazine. It's been years since the very first travelogue on Pakistan appeared, but the novelty of seeing one's own words in print has not worn out. Thanks to Jason this academic was given the opportunity to try another form of writing that he had been secretly cultivating for years, and was too timid to share with others. That some of the travelogues have now been put together in the form of the book that you have in your hands is largely the result of his encouragement, and for that I can only say thank you, Jason.

Thanks are also due to my friends who stood by me and who were the ones with whom I shared many of the accounts of my journeys: Sophie, Yusseri, Jacque, Animah, Michelle, Eunice, Azmi, Imtiaz, Sym, Tricia, Bernice, Sue-Ann, Joe, Eddin, Lat, Haris, Huzir, Don, Dave, Anil, Zai, Ivy, Azril, Toha, Martin, Feisal, Amir, Pang, Baz – were all there to listen to this tired wanderer. Thanks are also due to Raman of course, and the crew of the good ship Silverfish who have helped to launch this academic's career as an aspiring wordsmith. To all of them, I would like to express my heartfelt gratitude for putting me right on course, and back on course whenever the compass went awry which it did, several times, I can tell you.

To the readers of these travelogues, the author has this to say: We live in the age of karaoke and mass tourism where a world that once kept its secrets from us is rapidly fading away. The internet, computer technology and digitalised imagery are the bane and poison to the imagination. As someone who was born an old fogey, this nomad is fearful of the prospects of quick and easy travel and what it will do the multiplicity of worlds that exist around us. Yet the places you will visit in this book are real; the temples were not generated by geeks in computer labs; the tastes were not artificially enhanced with additives; and the smells not rendered sweeter by perfume. Now, more than ever, there has to be such a thing as ethical travel – but first and foremost one has to travel, and travel truly.

The reader will note the personal tone of many of these travelogues; and that is hardly accidental. Travel is as much an internal process as it is external, and one could argue that one has never really travelled across the world unless and until one has travelled across oneself. This search for the limits of one's subjectivity, only to discover that there is no final frontier to the Self, was as much a motivation for me to pack and leave as it was the search for data and facts. If the roughly-hewn contours of my interior world seem somewhat broken and jagged at times, the author would beg the indulgence of the reader and the only defence I can muster at this point is to simply state that the writings here are as honest and open as they could be. My apologies are tendered, therefore, for my momentary lapses and journeys into the more convoluted passages of my interior self, but both modes of travel were undertaken simultaneously; and indeed, I cannot imagine another way to travel. Tried as I might, I could never escape myself.

Now if you would excuse me, I need to pack again.

The Battle of Light and Darkness
Zanzibar and Tanzania, 2002

The cabin lights dim as the plane begins its ground-ward plunge, the rickety kite of steel and fibreglass rocking and swaying from side to side as we cut through the layers of clouds. I rub my eyes as I force myself to wake up to savour the moment, for landfall is just minutes away and I am about to visit places I have always longed to for most of my adult life: Dar es Salam and Zanzibar.

Along with Tashkent, Archangel, Samarkhand, Jaisalmer, Anuradhapura and Tanjavur, Zanzibar has always been one of those legendary destinations I have been drawn to ever since I read *Corto Maltese*. And to be paid to go there for research is just that cherry on the cake that makes this trip all the more special.

Next to me is Laila, who seems just as excited as I am, and in the row in front of us sits Abdu, who is heading our team of academic-activists. We are here as part of a project to preach the values of universal rights and gender equality to Muslim scholars, preachers and students, and though the political aspect of our little jaunt is never entirely lost on me, I have to confess that romanticism has won the day, and I am semi-delirious at the prospect of walking through the alleys and lanes of Stonetown that I have read so much about. For an instant, I allow myself the luxury of obliviousness and neglect, and put aside questions of political correctness until breakfast, at least.

I look out of the window and am disappointed by what I see: the space around us is pitch-black. It is 4.00 am and there is nothing to greet the eye. All is dark, and I sense our disturbing proximity to the ground, as the great hand of the earth reaches up to grab us in one clammy grasp.

Then, for the briefest moment, a solitary white dot darts across the window, and is lost. My memory catches up with me a second later, and I realise what it was: a solitary crucifix; a white cross in neon light, standing somewhere out there in the middle of Dar es Salam that is otherwise bereft of anything that resembles street lighting. I pause and reflect: a solitary cross in white neon in a sea of darkness. It was as if a bold, if not poignant, statement was being made. But why, and why here?

Little do I realise that the land I am about to visit is in the middle of a turf war for the hearts, minds and souls of millions. Here in Tanzania, the battle of Light and Darkness is being waged in earnest in God's name, though it is unclear whose God, whose heaven, or whose salvation?

Merchants and slaves, missionaries and converts

One would have to be a tad dull-witted to remain aloof to the charms of Zanzibar and Dar es Salam. These are, after all, the fabled cities of Sindbad, and countless other adventurers who plied the waters between India and Africa for centuries. Zanzibar was historically one of the most important coastal cities of East Africa and home to the Sultans, Emirs, Princes and merchants of Oman. For centuries it was a bustling capital of trade where millions of merchants and itinerant scholars stopped on the way from Africa to Asia and beyond. The great

Chinese navigator Zheng He had paid a visit, and till today dedicated beach-combers are still rewarded with fragments of Chinese Ming dynasty porcelain that wash up along the shore. In Dar es Salam stands one of the oldest mosques of East Africa. Made of mud and stone, the Mihrab and windows are decorated with shards of Ming dynasty plates and bowls, worth a king's ransom at auctions at Sotheby's or Christie's.

Then came the Arabs and Indians, who likewise traded and bartered their way into the African heartland from their vantage point of Zanzibar. Ivory and gold were traded for cloth and spices; dinars, rials, rupees and what-nots were exchanged. Not that all of this trade was pleasant though, for Zanzibar was also the transhipment point for African slaves destined for the Arab kingdoms and principalities along the coast of the Hijaz.

Later still came the Europeans, and after almost all of Africa had been carved up, Tanganyika was summarily left to the Germans who were rather late in the scramble for the great continent. With colonialism came racialised capitalism, the imposition of secular commercial law and, of course, the missionaries – both Christian and Muslim.

As the winds of change blew across Africa in the wake of World War Two, the countries shook off the shackles of colonial rule, one by one. On 9th of December 1961, the East African state of Tanganyika attained independence under the leadership of the popular and charismatic Julius K. Nyerere who formed and led the Tanganyika African National Union (TANU). Later, on 16th of December 1963, the island of Zanzibar also became independent. On the 24th of April 1964, Tanganyika and Zanzibar were united through the creation of the Republic of Tanzania.

The taste of independence was not as sweet as it was hoped, though, for there remained long-standing debts to the past that had to be paid: during the anti-colonial struggle the Muslims of Tanzania played an important role in the resistance effort. But decades of German and British rule had helped to foment religious divisions within Tanzanian society, as Christian converts had been given preferential treatment by the colonial authorities. Both Catholic and Protestant groups had been allowed to convert locals and to open missionary schools all over the country. The Christian Tanzanians who were educated in the missionary schools enjoyed an obvious advantage over their Muslim counterparts, and were given better positions in the colonial civil service and business community. As a result, by 1961 the Muslims in Tanzania were noticebly under-represented in the fields of education, business and politics.

The secular Julius Nyerere's own political platform was based on his socialist leanings, and his political outlook was largely development-oriented. In 1961 Nyerere stated that ethnic and religious identities were no longer relevant and that henceforth the only identity that mattered was Tanzanian. Working within a secular constitutional framework, he hoped to de-emphasise ethnic and religious identities, declaring such primordial sentiments as regressive and un-patriotic. But the Muslims of the country felt that their own political and economic lot was made poorer as a result, and felt that their contribution towards the independence struggle was being down-played. In 1961, the Tanzanian Muslims organised the East African Muslim Organisation as an alternative political movement of their own. Nyerere's government responded by banning the movement and arresting its leaders – including the Ulama – a move that resulted in serious repercussions later. In 1970, Nyerere openly declared that he would do whatever was necessary to ensure that Tanzania's constitution remained secular, but allowed Roman Catholicism to grow in the country. Muslim aspirations were seen as secessionist and a threat to national unity, and more laws were introduced to suppress the expression of Muslim identity.

Things turned pear-shaped soon enough: by the 1980s Tanzania's Muslim community grew more radical and impatient with the slow process of change. Islamic schools were set up with funding from the local Muslim community, but funding from other Arab and Muslim states were discouraged and constantly monitored. In 1992 the Tanzanian government under Mwinyi signed a memorandum of understanding with the Tanzanian council of Churches to ensure that Christian schools would continue to receive state support, including financial support for the Christian universities. No such understanding was reached with the Muslim groups. A decade later, frustrated Muslims in the country turned abroad for succour and inspiration, and for a number of them, a new hero had emerged over the horizon whose mighty fist could crush the tanks and aircraft carriers of the 'Great Satan' America: Osama ben Laden. The bombing of the American embassy in Dar es Salam marked the next stage in the battle for God.

The accidental missionary

I think of my own place and role as I unpacked my meagre belongings on the hotel bed: the usual, bog-standard accoutrements – toothbrush and razor, mirror and comb, tight underpants and a supply of white shirts and linen trousers. The heaviest burden turns out to be my conscience that is still troubled by why I am here to preach the values of gender equality while the boys in Stonetown paint the walls of the streets and alleys with the slogan: 'Welcome to Osama Town'. Who am I kidding?

Walking through the streets of Dar es Salam I see plenty of evidence of the turf war (that has been going on since the 19th century). European buildings stand next to godowns and warehouses. There are mosques and churches aplenty. I pause for a rest and then realise that the building in front of me bears an uncanny resemblance to a theatre, and above its door is painted: 'Home of the Vedantic Church of the Arya Samaj of India'. God's missionaries continue to ply their trade here.

"Of course, you have to be here! Some Muslim men think that polygamy is normal and is acceptable in Islam and Islamic culture. What they forget is that these practices developed in the past under very specific circumstances, some of which no longer apply today. Moreover, to think that Islam gives all Muslim males the automatic right to marry more than one wife would be to oversimplify things, and to forget the other norms and regulations that restrict the scope and practice of polygamy in real life.

"We must not forget that no Islamic norm is based on impossible assumptions, or goes against God's natural laws. If we were to simply accept the concept of polygamy as defined in the Surah an-Nisa (Qur'an, 4:3) as the norm, then the ratio of men to women in society would have to be 1:4. This would mean that men would only make up twenty per cent of the human population! But, obviously that is not the case and the natural ratio of men to women is 1:1. This suggests that monogamy is the natural choice and norm, and that monogamy should be the normative practice in Islam."

Ustaz Abdurrahman Mwalongo is one of the heads of the Muslim Council of Tanzania and he doesn't seem to think that my coming to Tanzania is a problem. In fact, the more missionaries of gender equality, the better.

During the week Ustaz Mwalongo and his mates tell us about the state of things in the country and lament the turn that Tanzania has taken. "The young men seem so angry these days, and seem so easily led by any imam or ustaz who offers them any promise of salvation or simple solutions. They are frustrated, angry and demoralised, but instead of trying to understand their present state they take it out on the weakest members of society, and that is always the women. It is always the women who have to pay the price," he sighs.

I am struck by how progressive Ustaz Mwalongo himself is, and all the more after he informs me that he is a product of traditional religious education and not from some newfangled artsy post-modern lefty-pinko university like mine. "The Muslim woman is spiritually and morally equal to the Muslim man. This is based on the Qur'an itself, which categorically states that Muslim women who practice the principles of Islam deserve the same reward as Muslim men for their efforts. (Qur'an, 16:37, 49:3). But how many Muslim men here even understand or accept that?" Ustaz Mwalongo's smile is so sweet that his chubby cheeks make me think of hot chocolate laced with cinnamon. But things are not that sweet elsewhere in Tanzania today, and he warns me of how difficult the discussions will get on the morrow.

Soon, Abdu, Laila and I get to work and organise the workshops that we have been assigned to do. I am introduced to a host of magnificent Tanzanian women who all strike me as hilarious, jovial, welcoming, and who had nerves of steel to boot. Our discussions last all day and night, as we pour over texts and textual interpretations, Abdu leading the discussions. The ladies nod and murmur their approval and I am struck again by their formidable appearance and sheer presence, and wonder: how on earth can any man try to dominate women like them?

But under the measured tone of our discussion lies something deeper and more sinister than any of us would like to admit. Suspicion and deceit have found their way into paradise, and hidden in the shadows is the perpetual whisper of conspiracy and betrayal. We realise that the real issue is not gender equality per se, but rather the suspicion of what equality brings and what it might change in the future. At one point a young African imam breaks into the discussion and lays bare his soul.

"Why this? Why this? Why this? You come here from Europe, from Germany, from Holland, and you want to tell us to treat our women with equal respect. For what? Who are you working for? Who wants that equality here? Who? Who???"

Abdu and I look at each other across the table and realise that the moment has come when the cards have to be played. Better sooner than later, I think; and better played now than never.

The young imam continues: "I know about the West too. Here we see the West all the time; on TV, on the beaches, when the tourists come. They just come for fun, to play, but they do not care about us, about Tanzanians or about Muslims.

"I can tell you that they are trying to break our faith all the time. I see how they sell the prayer mats to the mosques. I look at the prayer mats closely, and you know what I see? I see crosses everywhere. Here, there, crosses and crosses everywhere. This is what they want, so that when we pray our heads will touch their crosses!

"And what is so good about the West? What is so modern about these people that they think they can teach us? They want freedom, but for what? I read that in the West you can do anything: a man can marry a man; a woman can marry a woman; and a man can even marry a dog!"

At the mention of the last — though not for reasons of any empathy with the canine species — Abdu finally steps in: "What do you mean you can marry a dog in the West? Where? Tell me where? Have you seen such a thing? Where did you read it? Let me tell you that such stories are lies. And brother, if we Muslims are angry and hurt whenever the media lies about us, whenever the media distorts Islam and Muslims, why are you not angry with such lies as well?"

While the exchange goes on, I sit back and sink into my chair and wonder: how many Christians here think that there are crescents surreptitiously smuggled into their Bibles?

Stalemate. Impasse. Our dialogue has met an obstacle that we have not accounted for. Subjectivity brings both sweetness and poison in equal doses, and I am struck by the emotion of the young imam whose anger is real, though its causes imaginary. And crosses on prayer mats? The battle of symbols, tropes and metaphors will never cease and there will never be a truce on any side.

'Come to the Light'

I walk around the dark streets of Dar es Salam to clear my head, and like the proverbial moth attracted to the flame, my feet are drawn to the light in the distance. Soon I see it: a spanking new church all lit up like a Christmas tree with a gigantic cross decked in blinding neon light. Below it reads the slogan: *Come to the Light.* The sound of singing emanates from within.

Just down the street is a humbler edifice, a mosque run by some local volunteers, who bemoan the fact that they do not possess a generator strong enough to match the blinding luminescence of the church down the road. "You see? That's what happens when the American missionaries come here. They have so much money, they can build such big churches with bright lights that look so clean and new. And they give you drinks too. If you go in, they will give you syrup to drink. And cakes. And Bibles. Then they will convert you!" the young Muslim with his stunted beard warns me.

"Have you ever stepped in there? Did they ever invite you? And have you ever invited them to visit your mosque?" I ask.

"Me? No! Never! We know what they want to do to us, so we keep away from them. But they are growing and spreading everywhere. George Bush sent them here to preach and then they want to make all of Africa Christian, like during the time of the Europeans. But we will resist them, Allah help us, we will resist them," he remains adamant.

I am tempted to enter the church to demonstrate in the most objective and scientific manner that drinking a plastic cup of syrup will not turn me into a Christian, even if George Bush himself serves it to me. But I am tired, and sceptical about what we are doing here in a country where mistrust has laid low all attempts at objective distance and impartiality. Browsing through the leaflets and books that are on sale in the Christian and Muslim bookshops I note that dialogue has ceased, and that God here speaks in dialects and the vernacular. All claims to universality have been thrown into the bin as each side claims truth for itself and denies it to the other, and in the midst of this battle of creeds and sects I wonder if I belong to one myself.

'Us' and 'them', 'we' and the 'other'. The battle-lines are drawn, as if I am standing in the front ranks at the great Bharatayuda, and the armies of the faithful are ready to launch themselves forth, headlong and hearts first, and sing their way to conquest and salvation. My own conviction in the equality of men and women pales in comparison. I realise that paradise and heavenly reward are not on the menu of my offer to them. I am no hero, and a missionary I ain't either.

Heroes and men

"Look Farish, the reality is that gender is relational and the problems faced by women are partly due to the problems faced by men. In developing countries like ours, women face a number of challenges. They are often uprooted from their villages and removed from traditional settings where they had more power and social standing. The young men of our societies are likewise dislocated. They lose contact with their families and get involved in all kinds of social ills like violence, drugs, sexual promiscuity, etc, which leads to other problems like domestic violence and AIDS. We cannot improve the condition of women unless we improve the condition of men as well. In developing societies, young men and women need positive role models. They need new heroes and heroines to emulate and not the usual types of gangsters and violent characters they see on TV or in cinemas."

Bibi Asmahani is the Regional Affairs Officer for South Kilimanjaro and works in the Social Services Department of the Tanzanian government. She is twice my size and I feel like Frodo the Hobbit. I marvel at how tough she is, and wonder what she has gone through to get to where she is. Above all, I am stunned by her good humour and the fact that she can still laugh about things: "You know, its funny to see how men here react to women once we begin to claim our equality with them. We still use phrases like *mtupeni* – throw the kid – and *mwokoteni* – pick up the kid – when we talk about girls. Nobody ever uses language like that for boys, but for girls you can say and do whatever you like!

"But in the end, education is the key, you see? In Indonesia and places like that girls make up half of the students in schools, colleges and universities. But here women are still largely illiterate, so of course they are victimised because they cannot even read the Qur'an to show that women are equal to men in Islam! But that will change soon, insha-Allah!"

I am touched that Bibi Asmahani still believes in the power of education and the role of the word. But, here in Tanzania, whose word will reign supreme in the end? That of the educationists, the teachers and lecturers who continue the long struggle to bring the miracle of the alphabet to those who have yet to unlock its hidden mysteries? Or the word of God, and if so, which God, and whose God? And on top of that, Tanzania has been re-designated as one of the 'problematic countries' by the hawks of Washington, spooked by the Osama ben Laden T-shirts in Stonetown. But they are less perturbed by the fact that in some parts of the country, like Mwanza, the illiteracy level has risen above fifty per cent? Washington's war on terror, the church and mosque's war for the soul of Africa, the war between men and women – all commingling in a heady mix of suspicion, conspiracy, deceit and betrayal. Tanzania's political landscape and social complexion seems as complex as the people I see around me, with the descendants of Africans, Arabs, Indian, Orientals and Europeans all mixed together in a kaleidoscope of colours and hues.

Home again, and resignation

The second week draws to a close and our little venture comes to its end. Abdu, Laila and I – we, too, a motley crew with intermingled ancestries and origins – potter about the streets and markets of Stonetown in Zanzibar for a last round of goodbyes and a hurried stop at the bazaar for souvenirs. Along the way I walk past the wharf to see a peculiar sight: Dozens and dozens of rickety tables made of bamboo and reeds line the beach, covered with what appears to be dried noodles. I have stumbled on the Chinese quarter of Stonetown and meet the descendants of Chinese merchants and travellers who visited Africa centuries ago, and here seem to be occupied with the singular task of making noodles by hand. I stop by a shop run by a Chinese man whose name is Abdullah, and whose family originated from Yunan, and who is Buddhist. He offers me the local offering of fusion food, *ala'* Zanzibar: noodles with bananas in banana gravy. It turns out to be the most adventurous dish I have ever had in my life…

The day wanes to a close and I sit alone at a local warong as Abdu and Laila make their way into the interior to do more work. As I while away the final hours before my midnight flight, the crowd around me begins to stir. Some of the older men stand up, agitated. Others shake their heads and sigh aloud. I wonder what is going on and turn around to see a tiny television propped up on a tumbleweed chair that seems to run on two AA batteries. The image is blurred but I recognise the figure on the screen. It is a CNN broadcast and the Prime Minister of Malaysia seems to be speaking to a crowd.

Someone shouts to the stall owner, "Turn it up! Turn it up! Turn up the volume!" And as I watch the image of a crying Mahathir on the dusty TV, the voice from the machine speaks: "… and in a surprising announcement today the Prime Minister of Malaysia, Dr Mahathir Mohamad, announced that he will step down from the post of Prime Minister and President of his party…" I am dumbstruck by the spectacle around me as the Tanzanians express their shock and disappointment over the news. "Why?" one of them asks. "It must be Bush," opines another.

The story takes on a life of its own, in the same way that crosses and crescents have the power to travel on their own volition. The narrative is animated; and though my eyes are tired my ears remain open, drinking in the sound of the crashing waves by the sea, the call of the sea-gulls, the chatter of the crowd, the din of the TV. In the distance I hear the sound of the muezzin's call to prayer. God is great. Come to the light. The sun sets, and I am back where I started.

Suddenly the though comes to me: I love this country.

Qur'an and Cricket:
Touring the Madrasahs of Pakistan
(Pakistan, 2004)

Part one of the author's Pakistan journal

Labelled as 'dens of ossified traditionalism' to '*jihad* factories', the *madrasahs* (religious seminaries) of the Muslim world have become the bugbear of Westernised liberals, Euro-centric secularists and the hawks of Washington. Summarily labelled as the bastion of religious conservatism, '*madrasah*' now stands like some dark forbidding metaphor for a normative expression of Islamic religiosity caught in a fateful confrontation with the West and all things western. The hype and hysteria that grips the world, thanks to the discourse on the 'war against terror', has not helped to calm the fears of the public; nor has it helped improve our understanding of the *madrasahs*.

It is against this backdrop of intrigue and paranoia that I find myself in Pakistan between February and March this year. My own research on the circulation of ideas and knowledge across the Indian Ocean compels me to spend time between the archives of Lahore situated in the majestic confines of the Tomb of Anarkali (the Moghul Courtesan, no less) and several *madrasahs* (*deeni madaris,* as they are referred to in Punjab).

But entering the *madrasahs* of Pakistan – not to mention living in them – is not exactly the easiest thing to do these days.

For a start, one has to transcend a gulf of suspicion and fear. Since the 11th of September 2001, the *madrasahs* of Pakistan have been labelled by many self-professed 'security experts' as laboratories for an Islamist experiment gone badly wrong. Before making my trip to Pakistan I had heard and read stories of how students as young as seven were made to watch videos of killings, decapitation and dismemberment of Westerners in order to prepare them for the great *jihad* against the infidels. My academic colleagues were not too keen on me going to these places, much less live there for whatever reason.

But those who have heard these stories should realise that there is a multiplicity of Pakistans, as would be the case in any other country. It is true that Pakistan has had a history of bloody, unrestrained violence, and that the notorious 'AK-47 culture' that thrived and prospered during the period of martial law under General Zia-ul-Haq, and the Afghan war, has yet to breathe its last. It is also true that Pakistan was the breeding ground of the infamous Taliban, who were armed, trained, financed and protected by a succession of Pakistani politicians, Pakistan intelligence agencies, as well as its erstwhile ally, the United States of America. Pakistan ain't no picnic ground – a trip to the Afghan refugee camps in the tribal areas of the north will quickly disabuse anyone of any such illusion, but more of that later.

Being a political scientist and historian, I needed to prove that there is another side to the *madrasah* culture of Pakistan, and that this other side has a story that deserves to be told. What emerges in the end is a story far more complicated than I had originally anticipated; a sordid tale of machiavellian intrigues laced with deception and exploitation, of naïve youths being used and manipulated by mercenary interests, and of young lives being sacrificed at the altar of *realpolitik*. But what sets me on the right track – or so I hope – is my visit to one of the more prominent *madrasahs* of Lahore, the Syed Maudoodi International Islamic Educational Institute (SMII).

Qur'an and Cricket

"Come on, we want to show you our football trophy," the boys say to me on my second day in the *madrasah*. The Syed Maudoodi Institute has won its fair share of sporting trophies: last year the *madrasah's* team was placed second in the all-Punjab football competition for boys, and there is the cup in the cabinet to prove it – shining, as if it had just been polished an hour ago. The trophy cupboard at the *madrasah* is impressive indeed, filled with medals and cups won for many different sports and activities, ranging from cricket and football to debating. I wonder how people would react if I told them that sports is a compulsory activity in this *madrasah*?

I am the guest of the Jamaat-e-Islami party, Pakistan's equivalent of PAS, though with a more complex history and a wider transnational network of supporters and members. The *madrasah* is named after the founder of the party, Syed Abul Alaa Maudoodi, who founded it in India, opposed the partition of India and the creation of Pakistan, but who later migrated when the division of the Indian subcontinent proved inevitable. As their guest I find myself staying at their guesthouse, which is located in their political headquarters compound, the Mansoora complex, that is just off Multan Road, in a run-down part of Lahore.

Mansoora is a self-contained, though not self-supporting, community set within an enclave of its own. Established in 1974, it stands as a bold statement of how the Jamaat-e-Islami would like to see the rest of Pakistan governed. Around 500 people (all party members) live in 150 houses covering 400 *kanals*. Individuals own 200 *kanals* of land, while the other 200 is owned and let-out by the Majlis-i-Ahya-Ul-Islam. The complex is linked to the Syed Maudoodi Institute as well as the Islamic Research Academy, the Markaz Ulum-al-Islamia, the Mansoorah Model Schools and College, and the Jamiat-ul-Muhsinat. Medical facilities are provided for both residents and non-residents at the 80-bed Mansoorah Hospital. Security is maintained by an armed, private, Jamaat-run security force.

The main feature that dominates the landscape is the mosque, the minaret of which towers above all else. Sitting on the grassy lawn one gets the impression that life in this micro-universe is idyllic, compared to the rest of Pakistan where the water can give you dysentery and power failures make it impossible for you to work. But the idyllic impression is soon dispelled when you are told that the lawn is named after a martyr of the Jamaat, Hafeez Muhammad Yusuf, who was killed just outside the gates during a protest against the government of Nawaz Sharif in 1998.

"We haven't done anything wrong."

Living in the *madrasah* as an outsider means that I am bombarded with questions all the time. The principal of the *madrasah*, the retired Brigadier Professor Omar Farooq Dogar, is worried about the fate of his students whose numbers have diminished drastically when compared to my last visit a couple of years ago. "Why are they targeting us? We have done nothing wrong. All the boys are good students, they work hard and study hard, they haven't done anything illegal. Their – the foreign students' – papers are in order and they came to Pakistan with the knowledge of their own governments," he assures me time and again. At one point Prof Omar takes out a copy of the official certificate of recognition issued by the Pakistani government, to show that his *madrasah* is recognised as an institution on par with the Punjab university, no less.

But Prof Omar has good reasons to be concerned. In September 2003 nearly two dozen students from Malaysia, Indonesia and Burma were arrested and taken from their *madrasahs* in Karachi on the grounds that they were engaged in militant training and terrorist-related activities. After the initial fiasco of denials and counter-accusations (notably between the Pakistani and Indonesian governments, with the latter insisting that it did not order the arrest of the Indonesian students), the hapless students were sent back to their own countries to an unknown fate. Many have since been detained without trial under anti-terror laws, and the public is none the wiser about their fate.

Instead, the public is fed all manner of news about how these *madrasahs* are being used for political indoctrination (something that most of them admit) and how they serve as recruitment centres for future militants and *jihadis* who are then sent to early deaths fighting in places like Kashmir, Chechnya and Mindanao. While it is impossible to deny that some of the *madrasahs* are used by militant groups as recruitment centres, it would be wrong to conclude that making bombs and shooting automatic rifles are part of the standard curriculum in all of them.

If anything, the curriculum of the Syed Maudoodi Institute would put to shame most government-run colleges in Pakistan (or any other country, for that matter). For a start, after a revision and modernisation of its syllabus, the *madrasah* now teaches subjects like political science, sociology, psychology, history and geography – in English. It also offers the standard fare of religious subjects ranging from Qur'an and Hadith, Qur'anic exegesis, religious law (*fiqh*), ethics and morality – in

Arabic. Language teaching is central at this *madrasah*, which comes equipped with its own centre (complete with audio-visual equipment) and computer lab.

Sports and extra-curricular activities like debates and quizzes are compulsory for the students, and Southeast Asian students seem to be particularly good at badminton. I ask them if they had tried their hand at cricket. "The ball comes at you too fast, we don't know how to catch it properly," is the reply I get. But that's the point of the game! I think. Most of all the boys are bored out of their minds, and fed up with having to eat chapattis every day. "We take turns cooking for the whole group," they tell me, and I in turn hope that their cooking is better than their cricket.

But inevitably our discussion returns to the topic of what will happen to them when they get home. One of them, a Kelantanese lad named Mohammad Amin, is lucid enough to have some inkling of what is going on outside the walls of their *madrasah*: "These days, the whole world thinks that we *madrasah* students are terrorists. Every time there is a report on *madrasahs* on TV all you see are images of the Taliban; and now everyone thinks we are all the same. It's just not true, but our parents are afraid, and so are we. We don't know what the future will bring." In resignation I admit that I cannot predict what will happen to them either.

Victims of superpower politics?

My stay at Mansoora convinces me that not all the *madrasahs* of Pakistan are involved in militant training or terrorist activities. Though it is impossible to conduct a proper survey of all the *madrasahs* in Pakistan – there are more than 20,000 of them in the country, with thousands more that don't even look like proper schools – local analysts contend that the overwhelming majority of them are engaged in nothing more than basic religious education. If they are to be faulted at all, it would be for their relatively poor standard of service and facilities, but this would also be the case for most government schools.

Why were those Malaysian and Indonesian students detained in Karachi, and under whose orders? Here my own research takes a decidedly murky turn. I spoke to someone who (I thought) would know, Ahmed Rashid, the author of the book on the Taliban movement and the only researcher who has lived with and studied the Taliban from their origins in the 1990s.

Ahmed Rashid says that many of the older *madrasahs,* with links to established Islamist organisations, are actually well-run schools that offer a balanced, rounded education, including social and 'hard' science subjects. "Some of them even offer courses in comparative politics, literature, comparative religion, and so on – and even allow their students to read Western philosophers like Marx. The *madrasahs* run by more established parties like the Jamaat-e-Islami provide much better education than government schools. Their curriculum may be conservative, but that is not the same as saying they are *jihad*-oriented. They produce real religious scholars and priests, just like theology schools in the West produce Christian priests," he noted.

But the Southeast Asian students arrested in Karachi were picked up in *madrasahs* linked to the Jama'at-ul Dawa, the civilian front of a militant group called the Lashkar-e-Taiba, which has been responsible for the deaths of hundreds in Kashmir. After the Presidential ban on six militant *jihadi* groups in January 2002, the Lashkar-e-Taiba was forced to disband in Pakistan and transfer its activities to Indian Kashmir. Its leaders then re-emerged in the Jama'at-ul Dawa, complete with their combustible rhetoric: I witnessed a demonstration by the group in central Lahore where the leader of the Jama'at-ul Dawa, Faeez Saeed, openly called for an all-out *jihad* against India.

This brazen display of martial defiance raises the most obvious question of all: if the Malaysian and Indonesian students were arrested on the grounds that they were involved in clandestine militant activities organised by the Jama'at-ul Dawa, why are the movement's leaders allowed to roam freely around the country, recruiting followers, potential *jihadis*, and calling for war against India?

"These *jihadi* groups have been working with and have been protected by elements within the Pakistani government and its intelligence agencies all along," argues Ahmed Rashid. "During the 1980s, when the Cold War was at its height and the *jihad* against the Soviets was in full swing, the Americans, Pakistanis and their allies actively campaigned to create an international Islamic brigade that trained in camps and *madrasahs* along the Afghan-Pak border, to be sent over to fight the Russians in Afghanistan. But after the Afghan conflict, the Americans abandoned Pakistan (yet again) and let the local regional players sort things out among themselves. Many of these militant groups then lent their support to the Taliban, while others turned their attention to Indian Kashmir." In the case of the latter, the *jihadi* groups were protected by elements within the Pakistani army and the intelligence that regarded these militants as part of the 'unconventional force' to weaken Indian power in Kashmir.

In the course of my research I have come across numerous examples of propaganda material distributed openly by the *jihadi* groups openly. Apart from having their donation boxes dotting the urban landscapes of Lahore, Karachi, Quetta and Peshawar, these groups are still recruiting followers openly – an observation confirmed by Ahmed Rashid. "The militant groups are good at recruitment and marketing their services. They recruit extensively and intensively, and produce a lot of propaganda material promoting their services to Muslims. The sophistication of the radicals lies in the way they manage to disguise their real agenda. They never tell you what they really expect of you, what they want to do with you, and what they expect you to do for them in return. The boys, once caught in their grip, are indoctrinated and trained to become hardline *jihadis*, without them realising that their training is far more radical and dangerous than that offered at mainstream *madrasahs*."

The fate of the Southeast Asian students in *madrasahs* therefore hangs in the balance, and depends on the vicissitudes of Pakistani politics, which is unpredictable at the best of times. The crackdown on the *madrasahs* of Karachi is widely seen as a cosmetic gesture on the part of President Musharraf's government, to show that something is being done to control the hardcore militants. Now that the tide has turned and the liberal conscience of the West is troubled by the menacing spectre of Osama ben Laden – another American ally turned enemy – the militants, who were partly funded and protected by the Pakistani government and its Western allies, have become an embarrassment.

The solution to the problem has become a case of pragmatism at its most vicious and hypocritical, as Ahmed Rashid argues, "The arrest of the foreign students (in Karachi) is really a token offering, a way of satisfying Washington and other foreign governments, to show that something is being done. It is a way of making it look as if these militant groups are being brought under control, when we know that is not really the case. But the foreign students, like the ones from Malaysia and Indonesia, are really the weakest and most vulnerable. They are foreigners; they don't understand what is happening; they have no idea what they are being used for and whose special interests they are serving; and they are the least important and the least protected. In all my years of research I have hardly ever come across boys who know what they are getting into before enrolling into these schools. Most Pakistani boys go to these *madrasahs* because they offer cheap Islamic education, and that is probably the only education they may ever get."

Of all my discoveries during my research trip to Pakistan, this is the most troubling of all. Having visited and lived in the *madrasahs* and even taught there, I cannot help but feel like a trespasser who can only deliver bad tidings. As I leave the compound of the Maudoodi *madrasah* I catch a glimpse of Malaysian, Thai and Indonesian students playing *sepak takraw* – ASEAN's contribution to the sporting culture in Pakistan, albeit within the walls of this micro-universe. But what will happen to these boys when they leave, and what will their fate be? I board my rickshaw as if the burden of responsibility is all mine.

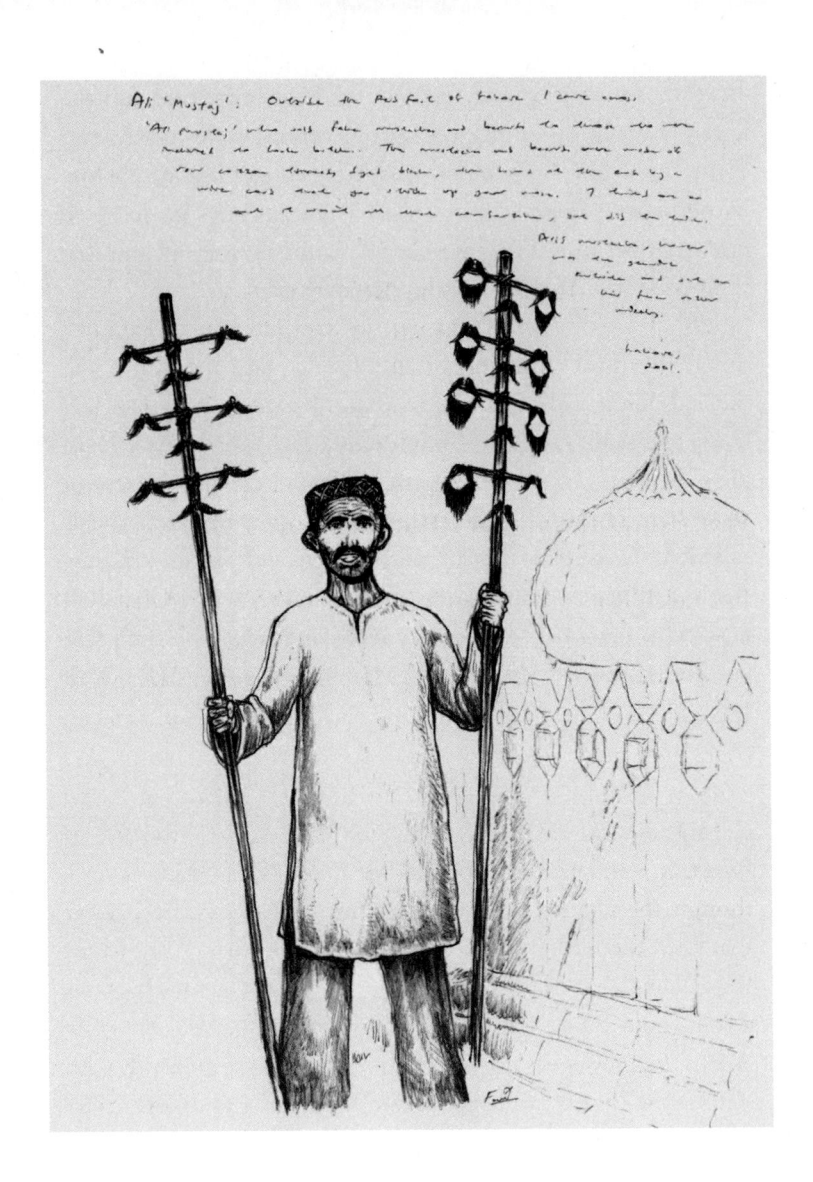

Ali 'Mustaj' selling fake moustaches in Lahore
(Sketch from Farish Noor's journal)

Reign of the Kalashnikov
(Pakistan, 2004)

Part two of the author's Pakistan journal

Ihsanullah Khan is, without a doubt, one of the most beautiful men I have ever seen: his fine features – dark eyebrows that come close to touching one another, reminiscent of images in Iranian paintings of the Qajar period; jet-black hair combed back; grey-green eyes that stare with a cold penetrating gaze – all set against a fine black silk *sherwani*. He is handsome and elegant. He sits on a shaky wooden chair – an overlord in his twenties – in the shade of the verandah of his *chaikana*; and though the chairs are loosely arranged in a circle, it is clear that he is the leader of the group and it is he who is in charge. Ihsanullah Khan does not speak much, nor does he have to: a solid-gold Rolex on his wrist does all the talking for him. And if the message is not abundantly clear, his bodyguards who stand close by, with Russian-made AK-47 Kalashnikovs ready, add emphasis to any point he makes.

"Welcome to my bazaar, I am happy to see you. My tribe welcomes you," he says to me. I reply with the usual formula of time-tested courtesies.

Ihsanullah nods in reply, and signals for *kava* to be brought – a fine sweet green tea that is served in the northern region of Pakistan. When the tea comes it is poured out for all, but everyone declines the first sip — a normal display of modesty and good manners in these parts.

Then, one by one, we sip our tea, staring at the flies as they dart across the space between us, and count the minutes as they pass. Little is said, for Ihsanullah Khan isn't one for idle chat, and his coterie of followers are certainly not about to break the ice. The air is thick with the scent of freshly cooked hashish, for I am at the smuggler's bazaar in the tribal areas of the North-West Frontier Province, and here Ihsanullah's word is law, and the Kalashnikov the final arbiter in any dispute.

The romance of the Great Game

I find myself at the bazaar of Ihsanullah Khan thanks to my guide Sohail, whom I met in Peshawar, and who seems to know every nook and cranny of the fabled medieval city of the mountains, as well as the tribal regions around it. I was in Peshawar to complete my research on Islamic seminaries — *madrasahs* — in Pakistan, and had been told that somewhere out there, in the midst of the tribal area (designated 'Federally-Administered Tribal Areas', FATA, by the government) is a certain *madrasah* set up by Southeast Asians for Afghan refugee children. I have come to look for this *madrasah*, and to visit the Afghan refugee centre that is run by the Malaysian Islamic Youth Movement (ABIM).

Travelling around the north of Pakistan is not an easy thing to do these days. The North-West Frontier Province (NWFP) can be described as a laboratory where an international social experiment has gone badly wrong. Following the Soviet invasion of Afghanistan in 1979, the NWFP became the buffer zone that absorbed hundreds of thousands of Afghan refugees fleeing south. With them came tens of thousands of young boys – most of them poor, illiterate and inexperienced – orphaned by the conflict and traumatised by the cruelty of war.

Soon these boys were picked up and crammed into hastily-constructed *madrasahs* funded by the Pakistan government, the army, and a host of Pakistani religious parties, as well as foreign backers and NGOs from the United States and Saudi Arabia. In these *madrasahs* the young boys from Afghanistan were given the most rudimentary form of Islamic education – in some cases the schools did not even have tables or books – and trained to use the infamous AK-47 Kalashnikov to fight the Soviet army and the Soviet-backed regime in Kabul. Thus was formed the *mujahideen* movement, an army of homeless orphans sent to throw themselves against the might of the Soviet juggernaut.

At the peak of the fighting in the 1980s, the Pakistan government and its Western allies proudly proclaimed to the world that they had created an 'International Islamic Brigade' to fight against the evil of Communism. At that time, Washington was less concerned about errant Islamists, who could use their US-funded weapons for other causes, than the Soviets. All that mattered was providing the *jihadi* war-machine with enough young bodies to be laid on the bloody altar of *realpolitik,* and the Cold War. Pakistan, and a host of other Muslim nations from Sudan to Indonesia, promptly gave up their young to be killed fighting Washington's dirty war in the barren mountains and passes of Afghanistan. While the 'Great Game' of the superpowers continued, the Muslim countries involved continued to bleed, and thousands of young men were shocked and brutalised. After the Soviet retreat and the collapse of Communism, the Americans walked away from the scene, abandoning Pakistan and allowing the situation in Central Asia to spiral out of control.

Soon the *mujahideen* were at one another's throats, and the tribal conflicts of the past erupted after the ghosts of the Soviets flittered away. In the midst of this chaos and confusion emerged a new movement called the Taliban – funded, as before, by elements within the Pakistani government and countries like Saudi Arabia and the USA. The Taliban managed to put an end to the internecine conflicts among the *mujahideen*, but imposed their own conservative Wahabbi-Salafiyya interpretation of Islam that was both medieval and barbaric in its form and content, and effectively sent Afghanistan back to the dark ages.

Since then, the northern regions of Pakistan have become the home of the Kalashnikov, in the hands of rival tribes. Indeed, the North-West Frontier Province has never been governed by a central power, before or since independence. When my guide Sohail offered to take me to the tribal areas just outside Peshawar, I jumped at the chance. But the going was not easy and the tension in the air was palpable. Further to the West, in the region of Waziristan, tribesmen were engaged in an all-out battle with Pakistani armed forces as the latter tried to break through their mountain strongholds in search of al-Qaeda suspects. In the week that I was to take the bus to Peshawar, another bus was shot to pieces by armed bandits near Quetta, while another was hit by a rocket in the tribal zones. I wisely opted for Sohail's motorbike instead of the bus: a flashy sleek black number that looked as if it just came out of the box.

"Where did you get that?" I ask him.

"Aaaah ... to know the answer to that question you have to come with me, and I will show you, my friend," he smiles.

"Why you don't like guns, my friend?"

It is with the help of Sohail that I soon find myself in the bazaar of the Shahwari tribe where Ihsanullah Khan is lord and master. We drive past several checkpoints and border controls, but at no point are we stopped. I ask Sohail if I need permission to go there. "Normally you do, but you can pass off easily as an Uzbek," he tells me, as we race at well beyond the speed limit. A nice compliment, I think, as my shawl flutters in the wind and I try to keep my *chitral* cap on my head.

The smuggler's bazaar of the Shahwari is a veritable emporium, choc-a-bloc with all manner of goods: in one space enclosed by walls and bolted doors we find rows of brand-new four-wheel drives, Pajeros and Jeeps. In another storehouse piled high, right up to the ceiling, are shiny TVs and videos; in a third, a mountain of gleaming fridges and kitchen equipment. In yet another, air-conditioners still in their plastic wrappers. "Where do all these things come from?" I ask Sohail. "They come from Dubai and the Arab free ports," he tells me. "Then they are smuggled to Iraq, brought through Iran and Afghanistan, and finally here. Here you can buy anything you want. It's all brand-new! This is where I bought my motorbike. Look – it's so new it doesn't even have a number plate!"

That would be the least of our worries, I think. I am more concerned about the open cooking and smoking of hash nearby. "The smuggler's market is known for its hash. We have the best hashish money can buy from Afghanistan. Come, come, I show you," Sohail beckons as he drags me to the nearest drug den.

Reza's drug den looks as if it is straight out of a 1970s hippy movie set: the walls are festooned with images of busty sari-clad Bollywood actresses. It is a riot of colours, interspersed with labels of whisky from all over the world. "You want hash, brother? Whisky? Gin? Vodka?" asks Reza, the proprietor of the drug den. Reza also comes from Sohail's tribe, and they all belong to their master's, Ihsanullah Khan's, sub-clan.

There is no need to worry, they assure me. They have a special understanding with the local police, and in the tribal areas Federal law does not apply. "Are you a Muslim?" Reza asks me. "I thought you were Uzbek, dressed like that." A second compliment in one day. I like this country more and more, I think. "In that case, as you are a Muslim brother, we offer you hashish number one, first class! Only the best for you, brother. We sell the bad stuff to foreigners. The *ferenggi* (Westerners) can't tell the difference anyway!" Everyone in the den laughs out loud; rising above us spiralling clouds of bluish hashish smoke dance circles against the dark ceiling.

Sohail is itching to show me his Kalashnikov. "Here, touch and see: Russian made, a good one. Not like the fake copies the Afridi tribesmen make at Darra," he assures me. Darra is a small town in the north where they specialise in making all types of weapons, and was a known tourist-trap in those days when tourists still came to Pakistan. At Darra, the Afridi gunsmiths can make you any type of weapon: from pencil-pens to rocket launchers, complete with bullets or rockets, as long as you had the cash to pay for it.

I decline Sohail's kind offer to caress his beloved semi-automatic rifle, even if it is the bona fide article from Russia. "Why you don't like guns, my friend?" Sohail asks, bemused by my apparent coyness. "You remember when you told me you hate snakes, Sohail?" I reply. "Well, it's the same thing for me. You don't like snakes, I don't like guns. It's just like that." I am not sure if Sohail is persuaded by my argument, as he doesn't seem to be the sort who takes to relativism easily. It is estimated that in the tribal areas, there is a Kalashnikov or its equivalent for every adult male. In the bazaar every man has his own Kalashnikov or pistol, with the exception of their leader Ihsanullah Khan. But then again, Ihsanullah has a solid-gold Rolex, and even Sohail cannot match that.

"The Americans have destroyed our country."

The next day I find myself in the Kachageri refugee camp for the Afghans that is just an hour away from University town, Peshawar. Sohail's motorbike proves to be an invaluable asset as it winds its way through the alleys and drains that criss-cross between the mud houses. They say there are eighty thousand refugees in this camp, yet I see only one working tap that spits out brownish water. The 'river' nearby seems to be the only other source of water, and one can smell the garbage and sewage from a kilometer away. While talking to the refugees I accept their offer of *kava* tea, and for the next few days I lie in bed with food poisoning as a result.

After the 1980s, Peshawar transformed into an Afghan settlement with hundreds of thousands of Pashtuns and other ethnic groups – Uzbeks, Tajiks and the myriad of peoples of Central Asia – flooding into the city until it is bursting at its seams. The Pakistani government and foreign aid agencies have set up numerous refugee camps, which in turn have been pounced upon by local and foreign *jihadi* organisations and militant groups who regard them as rich for recruitment. In the camp I come across an ex-Taliban member who has been 'rehabilitated' after the American invasion of Afghanistan in 2002. He has an excited look about him, and is keen to tell me about the visit of an Australian medical team to the camp the week before. The highlight of the trip was the parting ceremony, where the ex-Taliban was given the honour of shaking a nurse's hand. "It was the second time in my life that I touched the skin of a woman," he beams. He is 26 years old.

I cannot find the *madrasah* I am looking for. After blasting Afghanistan back to the middle-ages the Western powers have summarily declared the conflict over, and that it is safe for the refugees to return. Soon the bulldozers moved in and half of the camp is levelled to the ground. The refugees are packed onto trucks and sent back to an unknown fate. One of the men in the camp comes up to me and asks me if I am a journalist. I answer in the negative, pointing out that I am an academic who has taken to writing by accident. "Whoever you are, you need to tell the truth to your people back home. Look at our miserable condition here. We have hardly anything here. The schools are closed down, the NGOs have left. Now they want us to go back to our country. But the Americans have destroyed my country. What can I return to? I come from Jalalabad, and a few months ago some families from Jalalabad were sent back. We heard that when they arrived there was nothing left of their village but a pile of rocks. Do they want us to go back to that? Do they want to kill us all? Why has the world forgotten us?" he asks, again and again.

Around us a crowd of excited children begin to gather. They are covered with flies and all seem to be suffering from malnutrition. Heaven knows what these kids have gone through, and what the future holds for them. But the world does not care and Washington assures us that everything is being done to win the war on terror.

But the war on terror would not have been necessary in the first place, had it not been for the meddling of the superpowers in Central Asia, and the introduction of the culture of the Kalashnikov during the Afghan conflict. This is a land scarred by the gun, drowning in a crisis not of its own making. Since time immemorial the northern tribal areas of Pakistan have been ruled by laws and moral codes of their own. Yet the complex moral universe of the Pashtun people and their ethical code known as Pashtunwali has been abused by a succession of foreign interlopers, spies, maverick mercenaries and clueless securocrats who only saw Pakistan and Central Asia as a gameboard to play the Great Game. Pakistan, and the rest of the region, needs peace above all else. Peace, to let the region and its people heal their wounds; peace, to let the painful memories of the past die; peace, to let the children enjoy the fleeting moments of childhood. But peace is a luxury that remains forever beyond their reach.

Walking around the camp and talking to its hapless denizens I once again feel like an intrusive outsider burdened by my own privileges and status as a foreigner. In the following week I will be on a plane to Berlin, and then on to Paris, where I will work as a visiting professor. But for the children of Kachageri camp, such an option simply does not exist: sooner or later the bulldozers will come to their doorsteps, and they will be packed on board trucks to be sent on a journey home to a land devastated by nearly three decades of incessant warfare.

Life will go on for the rest of the folk in the tribal areas: the smuggled Pajeros and air-conditioners will be hauled over the mountain passes to the smuggler's bazaar, to be bought by rich Pakistanis and expatriates. The tribal areas will remain lawless and ungovernable, and this will serve the interests of everyone – the local politicians, the army, the *jihadi* groups and even the Americans and their Western allies. The doors of the laboratory that produced the *mujahideen* and the Taliban will also remain open for a host of other dark experiments. Hobbes' infernal vision of the malignant state of human nature has come to roost in the North-West Frontier Province, where might is right and the Kalashnikov reigns supreme. I stare at my own shadow on the shifting ground as we ride back to Peshawar on Sohail's bike, too ashamed to admit to what I have witnessed.

Reza chilling out in his opium den, Hyattabad

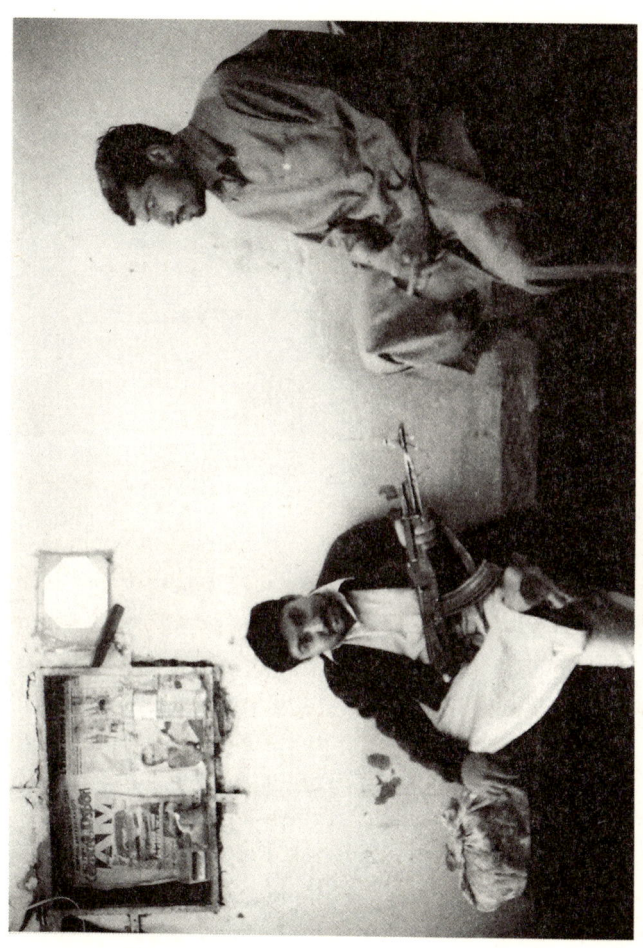

Tribal area: Sohail plays with his beloved AK-47 in the opium dens of Hyattabad

The Last Days of Empire
(Pakistan, 2004)

Part three of the author's Pakistan journal

While standing in line at the Central Post Office on Mall Road in Central Lahore, I find myself staring at a somewhat obscure yet fascinating portrait that hangs on the wall. The face that stares back at me wears an expression that is a mixture of indifference and boredom, coloured somewhat by the patina of a humdrum daily existence. It is the face of an ordinary man, dressed in an ordinary shirt, set against a background that is likewise ordinary, in keeping with the mood of the painting.

Sensing that the queue is heading nowhere fast, I break ranks and decide to give up on my mission to send off the twenty kilos of books I had bought yesterday. Stepping out of the stagnant line – the gap is immediately filled by bored-looking office boys likewise driven to distraction by the endless queuing – I decide to take a few steps towards the portrait on the wall. It is clear that the painting has not been cleaned for some time and, with casual neglect, has been left tilted slightly to the left. Upon closer inspection, the face in the picture appears no less ordinary than it did a moment ago. Then I notice a small brass plate affixed to the base of the frame. The sign reads:

> "Abdul Rehman (Shaheed), martyr of the Post Office – Hero of the postal service (d. 3. 8. 2002), martyred to save the public exchequer showing valour while resisting the Dacoits at Baghbanpura Post Office."

I am staring at the face of Abdul Rehman, a hero apparently – a hero of the Pakistani Postal Service, no less.

Pakistan is an amazing country, a land overflowing with heroes and martyrs, villains and despots, mystics and madmen. Seeking to find its centre of gravity, its quotidian and equator, one finds only excess and hyperbole. A myriad of competing and antagonistic tendencies pull this nation in all directions, and the outsider is often caught in this whirlwind of centrifugal forces, leaving him or her disoriented and in search of some mental compass.

I am not exaggerating when I say that I truly love this country and its people – nowhere else have I come across a nation more welcoming and open, more friendly and genuinely curious to learn more about the Other. Being of part-Indian descent myself, I cannot help but feel that I am at home here, and Pakistan is indeed a country where even social misfits like me can find a niche to call his own.

Pakistan doesn't need to advertise its hospitality: during the Afghan conflict it absorbed more Afghan refugees than any other country in the world, and that, in a country that is already suffering from chronic uneven development, corruption, abuse of power and endemic sectarian violence. The Cold War left Pakistan with hundreds of thousands of refugees and a culture of routine violence, with the legacy of the Kalashnikov and the International Mujahideen Brigade.

Yet Pakistan endures, and this is a land that still produces heroes and martyrs, even in the postal service. I leave the Central

Post Office with renewed respect for the underpaid denizens of that bureaucratic asylum. Outside the air is hot and smoky, and by the gates *shalwar khameez*-clad Punjabis squat and wait for customers who bring them books and other things to pack for posting abroad. A gleaming white Mercedes Benz sits – fat and imperious – waiting by the gate with its tinted glass windows wound up, hiding its occupants and keeping them cool with air-conditioning.

"May Allah give His vengeance to the rich!"

"We are good people, mister. We are good Muslims, honest people. You look at me – I work all day, all night. I have six children and I drive foreigners like you all over Pakistan. I love my beautiful country, I take you all over to see beautiful Kashmir, beautiful Swat valley, all the way up to beautiful Murree hills. I work and work, but who gets the money? My boss, he keeps eighty percent of the money you pay me. The rest, I keep, but I have to pay for petrol, for repair of car. What is left? How can I pay for my family's food? My son is now ten years old, my daughter eight. Both go to school – but who pays for their uniforms, their books? And what of my other children? When I complain to my boss, he say to me 'Take the money, or quit. I can find other drivers anytime.' What can I do? Every night I pray to Allah almighty, may Allah bless my work, save my family from harm, and give his vengeance to the rich!"

Muhammad the driver is sharing his sorrows with me as we drive through the backlanes of Lahore. I am looking for *madrasahs* as part of my research work because that is the reason I am in Pakistan; and during the ride I play the role of amateur psychoanalyst and counsellor, offering comfort to strangers for free. Muhammad declines my offer of a cigarette but lets me smoke in his taxi, fouling the air in the car as the windows don't work properly. His Qur'an is propped up on the dashboard, next to a tiny sticker of the People's Party of Pakistan.

Muhammad's story is typical of the stories that I hear daily. He is just one among millions of Pakistanis whose labour and endurance has kept the country going for decades, though their sacrifices are unrecorded. Nor is he exaggerating when he recounts the endless tales of abuse and corruption in his country. Once our taxi is stopped by the police. A Punjabi officer comes sauntering up to the car, a cartoon-like figure with a bloated belly and handle-bar moustache which he tweaks intermittently with his fat fingers. After grilling poor Muhammad for some minutes, Sergeant Moustache walks over to my side of the car and takes a good look at me. Fuzzy moustache in his fingers, he asks me with a greasy smile, "Hello mister foreigner, welcome to my country. Have you got a present for me? A little, little present for good mister policeman?"

"No, I haven't brought you a gifts, I'm sorry" I say to him.

The question is repeated and I offer the same reply. And again. And yet again. Finally Sergeant Moustache realises this dialogue is not going to lead to an exchange of money, and turns his attention back to Muhammad. After a brief *tête-à-tête* we are allowed to drive off. But not before Muhammad coughs up fifty Rupees for Pakistan's finest. When he tells me what transpired, I feel guilty and pay Muhammad the fifty he lost. The sum is paltry, but it is probably Mohammad's income for the day – for me, a packet of cigarettes. But, what I cannot dismiss as easily is the casual victimisation of the man in the street.

Kings and beggars

Throughout my Lilliputian voyage, I come across tales of kings and beggars. Pakistanis love their country. I have never met a people more in love with their nation, although that nation exists in their minds only. Muhammad, like many other Pakistanis, waxes lyrical about the glory days of the past. As we drive through Lahore he points out the noteworthy features of the cityscape.

We drive to the Badshahi mosque that was built during the time of Emperor Aurangzeb, the 'Great Defender of Islam' whose contribution to Moghul history was to wipe out all traces of accommodation and inter-religious dialogue that had been painstakingly built by his ancestors, Emperors Akbar the Great and Jahangir.

Badshahi mosque stands smack in the middle of Hira Mandi, the red-light district, whose prostitutes and courtesans, in the past, were women of learning, culture and erudition in all forms of the arts. Today their descendants are, black *hijab*-clad Shia women whose brothels bear the sign of the hand of Fatima who refused to 'work' during Muharram (and thus leaving the men of Lahore to fend for themselves for a while).

Badshahi mosque stands mighty and tall, an imperious, overblown statement of power and the will to exercise it. Aurangzeb is still revered by the more conservative Islamists in Pakistan as the Moghul ruler who restored the pride of Muslims – but at what cost? He was responsible for the destruction of numerous Hindu temples. And, by the time his reign was over, Hindu-Muslim relations in the Indian subcontinent was so bad that many Hindu states rose up in revolt.

Close to the entrance of Badshahi mosque stands the tiny marble mausoleum of Maulana Muhammad Iqbal, the great philosopher-poet who is still regarded as the spiritual father of Pakistan (Muhammad Ali Jinnah, the Quaid-e Azam, great leader, being regarded as Pakistan's political father). During his time Iqbal wrote about the need for the spiritual, intellectual and political reconstruction of Muslims, and in his writings he engaged with the works of Western thinkers, from Nietzsche to the modern rationalists. Yet, today his mausoleum is dwarfed by the military grandeur of Badshahi mosque, and the Islamists overlook the liberal thrust of his writings and ideas. During an earlier visit to the mosque in 2001, I participated in the Friday *juma'ah* prayers there. The imam delivered his *khutbah* in Urdu which I barely understood, but when he began to talk about the need for Muslims to take their *jihad* to India and to kill the '*kafir* Hindus and Jews', I could not stomach it any longer. I simply walked out.

Muhammad is indifferent to these swings and shifts of history. As he shows me around Badshahi mosque and the tomb of Jahangir, his otherwise despondent and forlorn look gives way to a sort of muted ecstasy. Even the poorest beggars in Pakistan share this sense of collective pride as they partake in this popular nostalgia that seems infinitely more sweet than the present. "We were great once," he reminds me and himself. "If only we Muslims could unite and use our nuclear weapons against our enemies, we will be strong again, and the rest of the world will beg at our feet." I feel like reminding Muhammad that had he lived during the time of Aurangzeb or Akbar, it is likely that he too would be cringing before the sandalled feet of the Moghul rulers. But for once I decide to shut up. If Pakistan is a question, then the answer cannot be found here. I have to look elsewhere to figure out how a country like this can remain static for so long.

Fashion models and liberal intellectuals

"You cannot imagine what it was like – we felt we were roasted alive during the day, and at night our butts froze. Worse of all, all of us ended up suffering from piles from having to take a dump in the mountains!"

Najam Sethi laughs out loud as he recounts his days as a guerrilla fighter in the mountains of Baluchistan. Seated next to him are Ahmed Rashid, the world-famous journalist who wrote the first study of the Taliban, and Rashid Rehman, former editor of the *Frontier Post* (until the office of the paper was burnt down by a mob of Islamists a few years ago). All three of them were students at Oxbridge in England in the late 1960s. When Zulfikar Ali Bhutto came to power in the 1970s, one of the first things he did to extend his grip on the country was to sack thousands of bureaucrats (including judges) whom he though were obstacles in his path. In time, the region of Baluchistan rose in revolt, and Western-educated Pakistani students like Najam Sethi, Rashid Rehman and Ahmed Rashid smuggled themselves back to Pakistan (after abandoning their studies) to join in the Baluchi uprising on the side of the tribesmen who declared themselves Marxist revolutionaries.

With the helping hand of America, and an arsenal of American-made weapons that included attack helicopters, Zulfikar Ali Bhutto put down the Baluchistan revolt. Tens of thousands of Baluchistanis were killed or displaced as a result of the fighting, and those who took their side were declared enemies of the state. It might have been the end for Najam Sethi, Ahmed Rashid and Rashid Rehman, had it not been for the timely fall and subsequent execution of Zulfikar Ali Bhutto at the hands of General Zia-ul-Haq who came to power through a coup. Following the killing of Bhutto, General Zia (then a favoured ally of the West and a close friend of Washington) pardoned the men and allowed them to re-enter Pakistani society. Today, all three are noted public intellectuals and writers, Najam Sethi being the editor of the *Pakistan Daily Times* while Ahmed Rashid is making a name for himself as the world's foremost expert on the Taliban.

All three remain progressive, modern, rational liberals and democrats at heart. Through their writing – most of it courageous and polemic – they have been fighting to defend the civil liberties of Pakistanis for the past 30 years. Yet, little has changed and today the army is still the *de facto* ruler of the country.

"To change Pakistan for the better is no easy task. You must understand that the country's history is steeped in feudalism and militarism, and this was made worse during the British colonial era when the Brits decided that we Punjabis, Baloch and Pathans were the 'martial races' they needed to recruit to keep their colonies in check. Pakistan was really a frontier region for them, a bulwark against the Afghans and the Russians. Unlike in India, the British never really laid the foundations for a civil democracy here. So how can one expect things to change when there are so many invested interests hell bent on keeping things the way they are?" Najam says. I can only nod in agreement and stare into my glass.

Here lies the contradiction that is, in a sense, the dilemma of the entire developing world: all over the developing South there has emerged a disjuncture between the ruling elite (which includes the liberal educated classes) and the masses. The well-intentioned liberals of Pakistan may wish to improve the lot of their fellow citizens, but the fact is that they are closer in their values and ideas to their counterparts in New York, London or Paris, rather than poor old Muhammad driving his taxi in Lahore. The military elite are happy to keep things as they are, knowing that a human resource crisis is precisely what is required to ensure that there is always a surplus of manpower that can be called up to fight, kill and die for whatever cause the politicians dream up. The liberals write, and God knows how much has been written already, but who reads them? In parts of Baluchistan today, illiteracy among women and girls is as high as 80 per cent. A fat lot of good that would do for liberal columnists in the Pakistani Anglophone press, I think. (What more, in a country where only two per cent of the population read English.)

On my final night in Lahore I am invited to a fashion show in a new urban development project called Bahria town. The town is located way out of the city, so the rich and famous who live there don't have to crawl through the traffic and pollution of Lahore as they rush to their clubs.

Local gossip has it that Bahria town's owner and developer is a Pakistani multi-millionaire who made it big thanks to his cut from a submarine deal with the French. (Hmm … I've heard that story many times, I think.) As we drive to Bahria town at night, we speed along Multan Road, which looks like a rally track for some kind of extreme sport, with potholes and pools of mud all along the way. But suddenly, as we reach the outer parameters of Bahria town, the road transforms itself into a spanking new super highway, well lit for miles and miles. I feel as if I am in a different country, and indeed Bahria town is a different country compared to Lahore.

The compound of the plush mansion where the fashion show is to be held is guarded by Mister Bahria Town's private army, dressed in paratrooper fatigues and carrying state-of-art automatic machine guns that even the Pakistani army don't have. After some inspection to ensure that we have the right invitation cards and passes, we are allowed to go through and park in front of the mansion.

The mansion itself is totally 'out-of-this-world' (a favourite phrase among the bright and young of Pakistan). Someone points out to me that the curtains are by Giorgio Armani and the chandeliers have been specially flown in from Europe. But as the rest of the new urban settlement is not complete, the toilets are not ready and the men have to take a leak in a shed in the back garden.

By 11.00 pm the fashion show begins and I find myself strategically seated right at the end of the catwalk, just so that each model ends up standing right in front of me. Fieldwork has never been more difficult, but I endure for the sake of academic research. The models who walk up look like luminous butterflies, lit up in a riot of colours. The first collection, we are told, "is inspired by the vales and hills of Kashmir, with pastel shades of pink, pistachio, aquamarine and turquoise." Oddly, shades of pastel do not come to my mind when I think of Kashmir – I can only visualise the images of bearded members of the Lashkar-e-Taiba on a killing rampage.

Watching the fashion show from my seat, I am once again reminded of my status as an outsider in this land. The contradictions are clear, yet I am powerless to affect any change. Condemned as a passive witness, my thoughts drift back to Muhammad in his taxi, who prays that one day, "May Allah give his vengeance to the rich." Yet here they are: the rich, beautiful, educated and well-connected among the Pakistani elite. If I ask, I am sure that all of them will tell me how they really want to do something for the poor and downtrodden amongst their people. But the structural inequalities and differentials in power remain, and shall remain as long as the army, the feudal elite and the religious bigots remain in power. To top it all the cruel and petty tyrannies of Pakistani life are made worse by the intervention of Big Brother USA, who now rules the roost and is orchestrating the 'war on terror'.

"What is to be done?" rings through my mind – the perennial question of the great revolutionary remains unanswered. Watching the fashion show from afar, I feel myself shrinking into my private world of worries and concerns for Pakistan's future and the friends I have here. This is, as I have said, a country that I truly love. Yet it is not my home and never shall I be part of it. From the time of the Moghuls to the British colonial epoch, right up to the age of Pax Americana, Pakistan has been the stage for a pageant of kings and beggars. These are the last days of Empire, but the empire remains, obstinate and unmoving. And all of us – kings and beggars and errant scholars alike – are caught in its suffocating grip. The model smiles in my direction, but I realise that it's the camera behind me she is looking at. I am invisible.

Welcome to FBI-stan
(Pakistan, 2004)

Part four of the author's Pakistan journal

Close to midnight, in the back-streets of the old quarter of Peshawar, in the North-West Frontier Province (NWFP) of Pakistan: I am huddled in the back seat of a three-wheeled motorised trishaw, speeding through dark lanes back to the old Khan's Club where I am staying. My shawl is wrapped around me and the mottled plastic curtains of the trishaw's freezing cabin flutter wildly, trying in vain to keep out the cold as the temperature plummets in the northern mountains, as they often do at night.

Suddenly the trishaw comes to an abrupt halt and the curtains cease their shambolic dance. Cooped up in the rear cabin of the trishaw I try to peer out to see what's going on. A piercing beam of light greets my eye, blinding me temporarily as voices are raised and questions and answers bartered. As my eyes adjust to the glare, I make out three upright figures approaching the trishaw. Amidst their silhouettes I discern the familiar outlines of sticks and guns. Suddenly, the flap of the curtain is pulled apart and a grubby hand reaches into the cabin.

A low voice, with a heavy accent, demands, "What are you? You are Talibani? Where your passport? Come, show me now."

I peer into the gloom and make out the face of a policeman, possibly from the Pakistani Frontier Constabulary (FC). It's too dark for me to make out the colour and details of his uniform, but I know the FCs have been posted in the Northern mountains for some time. These days the FCs have their hands full trying to monitor the movement of alleged terrorists, Islamist *jihadis,* al-Qaeda supporters and remnants of the Taliban who continue to filter through the porous border with Afghanistan. It's a thankless job at the best of times, and thus far, it has incurred a heavy cost, in human terms as well. Needless to say, the FCs are not inclined to let good manners get in the way of their work.

For a second I wonder about the question that had just been thrown in my direction. "Talibani? Me? I collect old post cards and drink Earl Grey, for heaven's sake!" Then I remember that my beard is nearly three inches long and that the *chitral* cap on my head and the khaki shawl around my shoulders do make me look like an Uzbek. Some days ago, this fancy dress helped me cross into the tribal zone as I went in search of *madrasahs* and drug dens in the mountain ranges. Now, it is payback time.

I try my best to sound polite and confident, no mean feat in the dead of night in the middle of nowhere, lost in the bowels of Peshawar. I tell the policeman that I am a Malaysian academic, and that I am heading back to Khan's Club where my passport is safely stored (or at least I hope) in my luggage. I am expecting a heated argument, but am surprised when the faceless officer simply says, "Okay, go back then. It's late now, don't stay up so long, and carry your passport with you next time!"

It doesn't take much prompting for the trishaw driver to rev up his motor and take us as far away from the cops as possible.

If trishaws could fly, this one would have hit the stratospheres at the speed it went. It is my last week in Pakistan, and my fifth encounter with the police; by far the most pleasant and least expensive. But the police have been with me since day one, and for visitors to Pakistan these days, the presence of Big Brother (whose address is both Washington and Islamabad) is everywhere. Welcome to the Panopticon state, invented by the FBI.

Panopticon revisited

Upon arrival at Islamabad International Airport, one is met by the eye of the security camera, like a cyclops, mounted on the immigration officer's counter. As the yawning officer fingers my passport indifferently, I stare into the camera, waiting to hear it click. No sound is emitted, and my passport is handed back to me. "Okay, you are welcomed to Islamic Republic of Pakistan," the officer says as he rubs his tired eyes. It is dawn and I enter the country wondering if my photo was taken.

Like a lanky cyclops, mounted on a flexible silver-grey stilt, the camera is a silent yet attentive herald of more to come. For in the wake of 11 September 2001 and following the US-led invasion of Afghanistan in 2002, Pakistan has been designated a major strategic 'non-NATO ally' by the Bush administration. Welcome to the front row seat in the so-called 'war on terror'. Those with beards can step into the interrogation room on the left.

The flexi-cam is the latest toy presented to the Pakistani security forces by the United States, along with a myriad of other surveillance systems and technologies. America's involvement in Pakistani domestic politics and security has led to a powerful and visible backlash from local opposition groups, mainly in the Islamist front. The only thing that has saved the country from falling into the hands of the Islamists is the fact that they are unable to agree on anything themselves (save restricting the rights of women and keeping them under lock and key for their 'own good').

But American meddling in Pakistani domestic affairs has incurred other costs as well. An indirect result of US intervention has been the relative marginalisation of the Pakistani Inter-Services Intelligence agency (ISI), which is linked to the Pakistani armed forces, and the promotion of the Pakistani Federal Intelligence Agency (FIA) in its stead. The former was strongly supported by the American Central Intelligence Agency (CIA) in the 1980s and 1990s when the Cold War was at its height, while the latter is now being strongly supported, trained and financed by the American Federal Bureau of Investigation (FBI).

This battle for influence and hegemony in the hotly contested terrain of Pakistani security affairs has led to the creation of an unevenly developed state; with hi-tech security systems in place at the country's airports while the schools remain bereft of books and teachers, power failures are a daily occurrence, and the water in cities like Karachi remains undrinkable. The Americans have 'persuaded' the Pakistani authorities to accept the introduction of the Transaction Tracking Server (TTS) system installed in its major airports and entry points. All visitors are photographed by the flexi-cam, and their passports are sifted through an on-line database. Visitors to Pakistan are immediately photographed and their personal records logged into an integrated national database. The TTS is in turn linked to the Pakistani National Database Registration Authority (Nadra), the FBI database and the Interpol database by satellite.

Though the TTS system is directed primarily at monitoring the entry and exit of foreigners, local analysts argue that the FBI and Pakistani government is also using the Nadra system to produce a national database of every Pakistani citizen. The TTS system has been criticised by local opposition parties and NGOs in Pakistan because it allows the US government and its agencies, like the FBI, to keep track of every citizen and keep a record on all Pakistanis through the back-up Personal Identification Secure, Comparison and Evaluation System (or PIECES) which allows them to monitor the movement and activities of any foreign citizen wanted by the US government. But the database may also contain the particulars of political opponents, NGO activists, independent civil society actors and anyone suspected of having anti-American sympathies or opposed to further US intervention in Pakistani politics.

The entire operation is housed in the offices of the Pakistani Intelligence Bureau (IB) based in Islamabad and its sub-office in Karachi. Both offices are manned by local Pakistani IB personnel with the help and supervision of the FBI. The TTS and PIECES system are supported by local Pakistani agencies like the Pakistani Federal Investigations Agency (FIA) that has been directed to provide a local database of known Pakistani criminals and suspected terrorists. The FIA headquarters in Islamabad houses the Pakistani National Automated Fingerprinting System (AFIS), with the database being shared with the FBI.

"The Americans have simply used us."

Somehow, I do not feel any safer when I learn of America's clumsy handling of Pakistani politics and its intervention in Pakistani security affairs.

For a start, I am in Pakistan to do research on the historical link between Islamic educational centres in the Indian subcontinent and Southeast Asia. This means that I have to work in the numerous religious seminaries (*madrasahs*) that dot the landscape – not an easy thing to do considering the hype and negative propaganda about them since 11 September (though it started even before that) and the hysterical global media adding more fuel to the fire with their spurious claims that these institutions of learning are fundamentally '*jihad* factories'.

During my visit to the Syed Maudoodi Islamic Educational Institute in Lahore, the students I meet are mostly fearful of the future. The principle asks me why his institution and his students were being monitored by the security services. 'Why don't you ask the plain-clothes policeman in the bright orange *shalwar khameez* who follows me whenever I sneak out of the *madrasah* for a smoke?' I think.

Resentment against American intervention in Pakistani affairs is even more palpable when I meet some of the leaders of some Islamist movements and parties in the country. During my interview with Syed Munawar Hassan, Secretary-General of the Jamaat-e-Islami party at their headquarters in Mansoora, Lahore, the Islamist leader does not mince his words:

"Things in Pakistan are getting from bad to worse, because this country's political elite are playing into the hands of our so-called Western allies. Our relationship with the US is particularly problematic at the moment. Pakistan has always tried to be on the side of the US. We were a member of SEATO, CENTO, and have always been on the same side as the Americans. During the Afghan conflict when Afghanistan was invaded by the Soviets, we were the frontline state and we bore the brunt of the Soviet invasion. And it is well known that during the recent US-led invasion of Afghanistan, the Americans would not have succeeded without Pakistani assistance. It was Pakistan that offered them the air bases and logistical support. But where has this got Pakistan? The American government has always been close to Pakistan's military dictators – from General Ayub Khan to General Yahya Khan to General Zia, and now

General Musharraf. Whenever an elected government and democracy comes to Pakistan, the US has conspired to bring it down by working with the army and authoritarian elements in the country. Today, with their so-called 'war on terror', the US government is doing the same thing. Values like democracy, civil society, rule of law and etcetera, are not terms that offer any comfort to us. The Americans have simply used us."

So evident is the Secretary-General's sense of outrage that I cannot sip my tea or grab a bite of the dry biscuits on offer. Concentric ripples wave across the surface of my tea cup, like in that scene in Jurassic Park when the dinosaur is about to have the team of scientists for breakfast. Even the plastic flowers in the china vase on the table seem to tremble.

The 'glass house' revisited

It would appear as if Pakistan has become an enormous 'glass house', as depicted in the novel *Rumah Kaca* by the Indonesian writer Pramoedya Ananta Toer. Pram's landmark novel about the rise of Indonesian nationalism during Dutch rule, describes how the colonial power attempted to create a complex and totalising surveillance state where the government's reach extended to the most intimate and private affairs of their conquered subjects. In Pakistan too, the all-seeing eye of the Big Brother can be discerned everywhere.

Indeed, for a dysfunctional state that cannot even provide the most basic health and educational facilities for its subjects, the Pakistani state seems over-developed in other areas, particularly in surveillance and policing. The Pakistani Inter-Services Intelligence (ISI) agency started actively monitoring local communication (both by land-line and satellite) well before 2001. Nationwide bugging by the ISI began in October 1999, and after 11 September 2001 they have been simply forwarding transcripts of suspected telephone calls and faxes to their FBI counterparts.

Once again, ordinary Pakistanis have Uncle Sam to thank for the routinised policing of their daily lives. To further consolidate its hold on the local intelligence network and its operations, the FBI and other services initiated the creation of the Spider Group, a modern hi-tech surveillance and espionage network based in the four major provincial cities of Islamabad, Lahore, Karachi, and Peshawar, as well as the Afghan-Pak border areas (NWFP, Baluchistan). The Spider Group's immediate objective is to accelerate the process of identifying, locating and neutralising elements of al-Qaeda and Taliban working in Pakistan, as well as any local anti-American movement or militant organisation. Made up of retired or senior army and intelligence commanders and operatives originally established to support the *mujahideen* (and, later, create and support the Taliban), the Pakistani component of the Spider Group helps the American authorities identify, locate and neutralise these insurgents.

In return for allowing former Pakistani military operatives to work with the US-led Spider Group, the American government increased its aid and training programmes for Pakistani active service intelligence personnel. Between November 2003 to February 2004 an estimated 100 Pakistani intelligence and military personnel were sent to the US for intelligence training and upgrading. These trainees were in turn expected to form the nucleus of the new Pakistani Special Investigations Group (SIG), with the status of an intelligence agency distinct from other agencies like the ISI, FIA or IB. The Bush administration has also released an emergency grant to Pakistan for the purpose of improving border controls and policing along the Afghan-Pak border.

Friends in need, friends in deed

Being friends with the world's only remaining superpower is not always easy. Pakistan remains a client state beholden to the interests of its patron-protector, the USA, which in turn has used and abandoned the country repeatedly. Despite the sweet sound-bites and talk of 'mutual assistance and partnership', it is clear that the power differentials between the two countries are painfully real.

In some cases it is not clear if the Americans are working for or against Pakistani interests. For instance, on 3 January 2004 an American Remote Pilot Vehicle (RPV) or airborne spy probe, either crashed or was shot down by Pakistani air defence forces in the Dalbundeen area of Changi, 10 kilometres from the Pakistani nuclear test site. The aircraft was said to be flying over the Changi hills on its way back from a spying mission over Iranian airspace, but local critics have raised questions about its flight path and why it was flying so close to the Pakistani nuclear test site. According to American accounts, the RPV crashed against a mountainside, while Pakistani sources claim that it was shot down. But, both the American and Pakistani governments have been quick to cover up the incident and local officials have refused to speak or comment to journalists.

During the course of my stay in Pakistan it quickly dawned on me that most ordinary Pakistanis are not overly enthusiastic about America's unsolicited presence in their country. "This is not Pakistan anymore. You can call us 'FBI-stan' instead!" a bearded member of the Jami'at-ul Tuleba-e Islam (JUI) tells me as he hands out anti-government leaflets in the streets. He is not alone in his condemnation of his government's policies. As I watch a demonstration by the conservative Jama'at-ul-Dawa movement at the Mall in Lahore, I note the numerous posters and banners denouncing President Musharraf, the Bush government and the USA as the 'Great Satan' in league with that other arch-nemesis of the Islamist radicals, Israel. And I wonder if the FBI operatives back in Islamabad are monitoring this?

The following week I push my luck as I try to get an interview with one of the leaders of the Jama'at-ul-Dawa. My earlier attempts were fruitless, as the movement's leaders decided to keep mum after the Presidential ban on their sister organisation, the radical Lashkar-e-Taiba. For decades the Lashkar has caused havoc and mayhem in Indian Kashmir and has been responsible for the deaths of scores of Indian soldiers and Kashmiri civilians. Today, the Lashkar has transferred its activities to India while the rest of the group's leaders have moved to its civilian front, the Jama'at-ul-Dawa. From the pulpit they preach against the government, and call for an all-out *jihad* against India and the 'enemies of Islam'.

Finally, after much coaxing, the official spokesman for the group, Yahya Mujahid, consents to an interview via the phone and email. Coyness aside, he is quite open about the group's agenda and their contempt for the government and its American ally. "They (the Pakistani security forces) are watching us and trying to keep tabs on us. But we know they are being pressured to do so by the government and the United States, and we keep our distance. But they have never really come for us because they know that our activities are really directed at Indian Kashmir. In Pakistan we simply recruit and train our members and fighters, but we have never caused any sectarian conflict in the country. We are not hypocrites; we have never hidden our agenda and everyone knows what we are doing. We have never hidden that from others, or apologised for our stand. We have been open about our *jihad* to liberate Kashmir from India all along."

Here, then, lies the crux of the problem: Pakistan today is forced to deal with the Americans because the country is in dire need of aid and development assistance. After suffering the tremendous costs of the Afghan conflict, Pakistan was abandoned and cast aside by its erstwhile allies in the West, only to be rediscovered yet again when Washington decided to embark on its latest folly, the 'war against terror'. Yet American aid to Pakistan has been lopsided and uneven to say the least. While the country's educational system is allowed to rot and basic social services remain under-funded and neglected, the radical Islamists have been allowed to jump into the void created by the state's absence. The Americans in turn hope that Pakistan can somehow be 'domesticated' and brought back to the fold of democracy, but their methods have only served to bolster anti-democracy in the country. Elsewhere, America, by its conduct overseas (notably in its support for Israel), has squandered what little respect it had left in the Muslim world. The rest is simple arithmetic: it doesn't take a political scientist like me to see where this will all end.

As I stand in line at the immigration counter at Islamabad airport on my last day in Pakistan, the words of the Jama'at-e- Islami's Secretary-General echo in my head: "Now the Americans have come and they are trying to do something the British imperialists failed to do after two centuries of occupation. How can they ever succeed? They don't understand us, they don't understand this country, nor do they understand Islam. American power may be strong today, but it will not last forever." That may be, but for now Uncle Sam is here and he looks like he intends to stay.

The immigration officer stamps my passport and hands it back to me, with the parting words, "Come back soon." As I walk away towards my flight, I again fail to note if the cyclops-camera on the flexi stand has snapped a picture of me.

Kipling's Cat
(From the author's Pakistan diary)

What, if I may be so bold as to ask, are you looking for in this patinated city, dear fellow?

You see me sitting here, my whiskers having seen better days and my fur somewhat faded by the cloak of dust that has become my mantle in this forlorn city.

Perhaps you are wondering why I, a mere cat – tabby variety, no less – seem quite happy to rest at this spot;
At the crossroads of the city you've heard and read so much about.
The traffic around me does not bother me the least;
And the trucks and wagons rush past with little fanfare to me, the metalled beasts.

I have, you see, been here since time immemorial; and those who care to pause for a while as you are doing now might perhaps catch a glimpse of me – this tiny bag of fur animated by a thimble-sized pulse of life – in the midst of this din and chaos.
You wonder how a tiny heart such as the one I possess can remain beating amidst this noise; and how, over the passing of time, I can remain here at all, of course.

I'll let you into a little secret that little hearts like mine possess:
Great men and great conquerors come and go, their armies shuttling along this very same great trunk road, you know.
I witnessed them all, from Alexander to Ghauri, Babar to Akbar; yet I alone remain. Great men are consumed by their own greatness; history snatches their names before they die, without refrain.

But all greatness requires a witness, and that is why I, the cat, will stay.

So let the kings and emperors conquer and plunder as they will. I, immortal cat, will choose to be still.
And what need I of armies, kingdoms, wealth or more?
I am the eternal cat, and my yawn is as good as a roar!

Deoband, the Great
(Uttar Pradesh, North India, Jun–Aug 2005)

At 3.45 am I am woken up by the sound of the gong.

Shabab is lying next to me, snoring loudly. On the other side of my face are the smelly calloused feet of Muhammad 1, who in turn is lying next to Muhammad 2, who in turn is lying next to Muhammad 3.

In the gloomy darkness of the room I slowly rise from a much-disturbed sleep to a cacophony of snoring, belching, grunting and farting emitted by my motley company of thirteen boys; all in their mid to late-teens, faces pockmarked by zits and spots of various shapes, sizes and stages of eruption. The faint sickly-sweet scent of mangoes lingers in the cold morning air, a reminder of the binge we had the night before. The mixed cocktail of stale sweat, humid feet and ripe fruit in this warren of exploding hormones leaves me dizzy.

In the darkness I make out the shuffling silhouette of young Nawab who is, again, the first to rise. He wraps his shawl around his thin shoulders and lifts his nimble frame upwards and outwards, heading to the door in search of water to boil for tea.

A cock announces the coming of dawn, and through the door-frame I see the first streaks of pink and orange that herald the start of a new day.

For a moment, I wonder where I am.

And then it comes to me:

I am lying on the floor in one of the rooms on the second floor of the southern dormitory, in the southern wing facing the quadrangle, and across from the Naudara, 'the great hall of the nine doors'. I am lying on the floor surrounded by boys who are students of the *madrasah* I have come to study: the great Dar'ul Uloom of Deoband, Uttar Pradesh, India.

One by one the boys get up and, in the first few minutes of the morning, there is a curious exercise in mutual indifference and deference. Nobody says anything. Nobody looks at anyone else. We stretch our limbs and yawn aloud, as if the first sound that has to be issued at daybreak is a primordial grunt that announces our masculinity.

Nawab comes back into the room and lights a fire with matches. The Bunsen burner ignites and the smell of gas fills the room. Mango skins are scooped up by the handful and thrown into a plastic bag that serves as the dustbin. Our gummy eyes want to remain shut, while some of the boys (Muhammad 1, 2 and 3, in particular) nurse their erections under their *shalwars* with the casual indifference of young men. Fairuz, the fair-skinned Kashmiri with his grey-green eyes, picks his nose with such intensity and determination that one is almost prepared to forgive him for the rude act that despoils his otherwise near-perfect countenance. Kaseem, the dark one, picks his toes, then smells his fingers. The company is rude, crude, poor and honest in their lack of guile and mannerism. They are boys about to become men, and from men to scholars; and scholars of Deoband, no less. One does not need finery and genteel manners when one is about to join the ranks of savant-hood.

Finally it is Shabab, my research assistant, who breaks the silence with a question I have come to expect from him every morning, "What's there to eat? I'm hungry!"

Nawab, forever soft-spoken and whose words are always chosen carefully, calculated to attain the maximum effect through a combination of politeness and brevity, answers, "Nothing. This morning *chai* only. Apologies, Ustaz Noor."

"*Chai* is fine, Nawab. It is more than welcomed. We can have lunch in a few hours, anyway," I reply. In the corner of my eye I can see Shabab wincing at the thought of having to wait six hours – a quarter of a day – for the first piece of chapatti that he will wolf down. The boys smile, thankful that their guests are not too demanding. I remind Shabab that there are mangoes for sale outside, and that all will be well. Faith is restored, and we sit together in a circle to sip our tea in silence. Outside, the gong sounds again. Classes will begin in fifteen minutes.

I am living and working in the bowels of the great Dar'ul Uloom Deoband (sometimes referred to as the Deoband college), that was founded in the town of the same name in Uttar Pradesh, eighty miles to the north-east of Delhi. The institution, whose name is almost legendary, was set up in 1867, one decade after the failed Indian Mutiny. The two major figures behind the founding of the Deoband college, Maulana Muhammad Qasim Nanotawi and Maulana Rashid Ahmad Gangohi, both came from prominent Ulama families and went through normal conservative as well as Sufi-inspired forms of education.

Nanotawi and Gangohi both played a part in the anti-British uprising of 1857, as commanders of Indian forces based at Shamli, near Delhi. In 1867 they chose to settle at the town of Doad and opened a *madrasah* at the Chattah Masjid. This was the nucleus of the Deobandi school. At the time, both Muhammad Qasim and Rashid Ahmad had progressive ideas about improving the standards of Islamic education. Their *madrasah* was cut off from the mosque complex, and the school was established in 1879, funded by contributions from the public rather than on a *waqf*. The college borrowed techniques and methods of the government colleges, with a rector, principal and salaried teachers. But it also had a mufti who supervised the issuing of *fatwas*.

The Deobandis were a rather conservative bunch who rejected many Sufi practices and customs on the grounds that they were contaminated by Hindu and pre-Islamic elements. Thus, the Deobandi school became famous for its strict adherence to Qur'an, Hadith and Sunnah in its zeal to purify Islam of Hindu, Hellenic, Persian and pre-Islamic elements. Students resided at the *madrasah,* and the teaching periods ranged from six to ten years. During this time, the students developed close bonds and ultimately the school produced a network of Deobandi Ulama who shared a similar outlook and approach to Islam. The Deobandi Ulama were known for their uncompromising and confrontational approach. The school issued more than two hundred thousand *fatwas* in its first hundred years, and its Ulama engaged in many polemics against Hindu and Christian missionary movements.

Being strict adherents of Islamic orthodoxy, the Wahabi-inspired founders and teachers of the Deobandi school were thoroughly anti-rationalist in their outlook. For them, the philosophical and rationalist approach of modernist schools was dangerously close to the positivistic trends of the West, which they labelled as *nechari* (naturalist) and materialist. They preferred instead the approach of the Asharites, who argued that the crisis in the Muslim world was due to the lack of faith among Muslims themselves. So great was their hostility towards rationalist philosophy and logic that Maulana Rashid Ahmad Gangohi once wrote, "I think that this *falsafah* (philosophy) is a useless discipline (which) is misleading ... It mars the proper understanding of the Shariah and under its sordid influence, men are led to express heretical views. This devilish art, therefore, has to be banished from the *madrasahs.*"

Small comfort for me, being the product of just such a secular Western philosophical tradition.

For years I have been studying the networks of itinerant scholars who travelled across the world in search of knowledge, and with the passing of time the analyst became one with his subject. I am in Deoband, for it happens to be the *madrasah* with the oldest link to Malaysia, and among the alumni of the great institution is none other than Tok Guru Nik Aziz Nik Mat, the spiritual leader of the Pan-Malaysian Islamic Party (PAS). I relished the opportunity to check out Tok Guru's school records to see if he was ever canned for coming late to class. In the wake of the attacks on the United States on 11 September 2001, Deoband became a focus of attention, but for decidedly less pleasant reasons: among the leaders of the Taliban then safely embedded in the caves of Afghanistan were ten Deobandi graduates.

Shabab and I take our leave and walk down the stairs to the quadrangle before making our way to the great Western gate, the towering presence of which lends the distinct impression of a medieval fortress. Deoband's redbrick walls stand tall, rising well above forty feet, and the monumental edifice dwarfs everything else in the tiny muddy town that survives on the meagre income of sugar-cane and wheat farmers.

We are, in fact, not supposed to be sleeping in the *madrasah,* for we have been given guest accommodation at the *madrasah's* modest guesthouse just outside the gate. But, our interviews with the students – plus the bout of mango-devouring frenzy that we all succumbed to the night before – meant that Shabab and I were unceremoniously locked in when the gates were bolted at midnight.

We walk up to the gates just in time to see the gatekeeper removing his rusty old key for the lock. He grunts and smiles at us and we return his grunt and smile. But as soon as the gate is open, a stream of boys — all clad in the same uniform white *shalwar khameeze*s and skullcaps — come darting into the compound, running at full speed, as if in fear for their lives. The gatekeeper shouts at them as they scatter in all directions, "Hoi! You there! Abdul! Hakeem! Muraad! I saw you! You stayed out late to watch those evil Hindi flicks at the cinema house, ya? Wait till I get my hands on you! Come back here, you rascal!!!!"

My concern for the plight of taut young bottoms being caned mercilessly is tempered somewhat by the realisation that some boys might actually enjoy it, and that a jolly good whipping after a night of sinful debauchery at the local filmhouse may actually be the cherry on top of the cake for some. In any case, Shabab is no longer able to conceal his hunger, which seems to be on the verge of killing him, and so we tarry no longer and make our way to the guesthouse where toothbrushes and towels await our return. The heat is beginning to rise and, at its zenith, the sun will blaze upon our heads at a searing 48 degrees centigrade. This will be another long day.

I have come to Deoband and to the famous Dar'ul Uloom *madrasah* for a number of reasons: to trace the historical links between South and Southeast Asia as part of a project to map out the networks of itinerant scholars and students who had crisscrossed the globe long before Western colonial rule compartmentalised Asia and imposed upon its peoples the regime of passports and identity cards; to look at its curriculum and to ascertain what impact it had in the development of Muslim intellectual thought in Southeast Asia; and to see just how and why Muslim boys from all over the world will come all the way to India, to settle in this medieval fortress of knowledge and learning, while the computer engineers and the chartered accountants are the heroes of the modern world. Why, in short, would anyone want to come here?

My assistant Shabab, himself a student at the decidedly more upmarket and respectable Jamia Milia University of Delhi, is convinced that I've gone bonkers and that I happen to be one of those wandering scholars who probably took to the road after one too many late nights out. He is not entirely off the mark, but I entertain his questions nonetheless.

"What is so special about Deoband that you want to come here, Farish Bhai? There is nothing here. Look, here's a cow, there's a cow, there's another cow. Only cows and *madrasah* boys. Nothing else," he rightfully observes.

"Yes, but I want to know why they keep coming here, Shabab. You study at Jamia (Milia), right? You want to be a professor like me one day, right? But these boys, what can they do? Where will they go from here? There is only one English class for forty in a *madrasah* of almost six thousand students. How about the rest of them? How will they cope with the world around them when they graduate? That's what I need to understand."

The day is spent roaming about the compound of the grand *madrasah* and it feels like taking a walk through the pages of Umberto Eco's *The Name of the Rose*. Boys and teachers all dressed in white, their *shalwar khameezes* crisp and pristine in a town where cow dung seems to be splattered everywhere, and where the blazing sun keeps me occupied by making me drink four litres of water a day. How do they do it, I wonder? Just keeping my clothes clean seems like a near-miracle to me.

Shabab and I take a break as we walk around the parimeter of the great wall that surrounds the *madrasah*, only to end up at Kareem's tea-house, situated strategically at the very corner where the walls veer off at right angles. Shabab's eyes devour the mangoes as I pay for them, and we saunter into Kareem's dimly lit grotto that looks like a set-piece from the Tatooine in *Star Wars*. There is a giant cauldron brimming with boiling water and teapots aplenty. *"Do chai!"* we order, and sit ourselves down on the bench as we wait for the students to end their first class.

The boys who are in between classes are already there, whispering and giggling like virgins whose cherries have yet to be popped and wondering who the stranger in town is. With faltering English they attempt to make contact, and the standard questions spill forth. "Ustaz, where you from? Ustaz what your name? Ustaz, why you come here?" To which the same standard replies are given, buying me time to pause for a moment and for Shabab to get through his third mango. Then in the distance I spy Muhammad 2 and 3, rushing to us as we sit on the bench outside Kareem's.

"Ustaz! Ustaz! We have friends coming from England! They coming from England to Deoband. They wanting to talk with you!" the boys cry out.

Between Muhammad 2 and 3, two other boys squeeze their way through, their teenage faces marred by what appear to be tufts of fuzz, juvenile attempts at growing a beard. Goggle-eyed and mouths open, they stare at me for a second and then one of them asks, "You speak English, mate?"

"Why yes, evidently. And yourself?" I reply.

"Blimey, thank God! At last! Someone who speaks English in this friggin' place! We were going stark raving bonkers, mate! I mean, how on earth do they expect us to learn Arabic, Hindi, Urdu and Farsi, and read the Qur'an at the same time???"

Muhammad (no. 4) and Nasrullah (*Naz* for short) are two hapless lads who seem to have been despatched to Deoband by their well-meaning parents whose piety and love of Islam meant that they don't want their boys to grow up in that den of sin and vice second only to Sodom and Gomorrah – Manchester. The pair make an odd couple – one a head and shoulder above the other – and both of them seem to display the nervous excitement of boys that, on my better days, would be greeted with a smile. On a bad day, it would be met with a stiff knock on their heads. They chatter simultaneously, and I sit back while trying to decipher their little operetta. In the midst of the din and static, I make out sounds that resemble words and sentences.

"I mean, what's up with our parents, mate? I mean, what did they think, sending us here to study? I mean, like we've never left England all our lives, right? Like, the closest we ever got to India was watching *The Far Pavillion* thingy drama whotsit on telly, right? And what did they expect? Like, we would just come here and then at the airport them blokes would just come runnin' up to us and like, hug us and kiss us, and them would just go all lovey-dovey and, like, say 'welcome back home to India' and like? I mean, like, I'm from Machester me, and me mate is from Leeds. Like, what do we know about India, mate? They wont even let us watch the telly here. In fact, there ain't no bleeding telly in the first place!"

After venting their spleen at an unjust world that has marooned them in this corner of South Asia, Muhammad 4 and Naz settle down and we chat in the middle of a small but attentive crowd of boys who are curiously listening to this exchange between three itinerant scholars. The two of them seem lost against the backdrop of an institution whose history is as long as it is grand, and their pining for a television set to catch up on episodes of *Coronation Street* and *Neighbours*. It is touching, to say the least. I ask them how they have managed to keep themselves sane in the face of cultural dislocation and alienation, to which they reply by pointing out that the miracle of hand-phones, the God-sent instrument that keeps them in touch with each other and with other boys from Blighty who are scattered all over the Indian subcontinent. Their references and asides strike me as familiar as they calm themselves down, and some degree of composure is restored. I am struck by the fact that both of them – despite all appearances – are so clearly *British*.

It is mid-day by now, and the heat is overpowering. The sun has clearly gotten to me for I order yet another glass of hot, sweet milky tea – my fourth for the morning – and the boys follow suit. There are smiles all round as we gulp down the next round of *chai*, and then young Naseem comes to collect the orders for the shops down the road.

Naseem is all of ten years old, a street-wise kid whose job it is to deliver cups of tea to the shopkeepers down the streets and alleys of Deoband who can't get enough of Kareem's home brew. His diminutive stature means that he is invariably the butt of everyone's jokes, and the boys cry out as they see him approach, "Hey shorty! *Ek chai! Do chai! Tin chai!*"

The touting and baiting doesn't seem to get to Naseem however, and as he leaves he turns around for a second and fires off his own salvo, "Listen boys, you may all be students at your great *madrasah*, but you are just boys, still at school. Me, I'm a man now. I'm the one who is taking care of my mother and my brothers and sisters, understand? Understand, boys?" And with that, he darts off, the trail of dust he leaves behind pierced by arrows of insults and jeers from the boys in their white *shalwar khameezes*.

Naseem, the ten-year-old man, who cares for his mother and siblings, and the 'boys' who dream of becoming Ustazs and Imams one day. Boys to men; in this forest of male stalks I feel like the gardener. I suddenly realise that I have been here for two weeks, and have yet to see the face of a woman or a girl.

When the time comes for *zuhur* prayers I walk to the main mosque – a rather garish and overstated number built of marble and stone that stands out of place against the older patinated crumbling form of the Dar'ul Uloom whose red bricks, white mortar and plaster strike a resonant chord with my own anglophile leanings for Mameluke revivalism and Anglo-Moorish architecture.

Book in hand, my own steps measured and paced, I feel like some don walking through the quadrangle, but the memory that comes to mind is of my very own school, St John's on Bukit Nanas, with its redbrick walls and long corridors.

It is as if I am back at school again, surrounded by the boyish faces of my childhood, in a homo-social environment that is curiously gendered and yet at the same time genderless, for want of a dialectical other. Not a single female face or voice has been seen or heard in two weeks. And the boys who live and study here have probably not seen a girl or a woman in months, if not years, I realise.

After *asr* prayers Shabab and I are dead tired and forced to concede defeat to the sweltering heat of Uttar Pradesh. We return, forlorn and despondent, to our guest quarters while entertaining the faint hope that the electricity won't be cut again and that the fan might be coaxed to work. No such luck. The bedroom is even hotter than the street outside, so we resign ourselves to our sad fate and I use the last litre of water I have to douse myself as the taps have run dry as well.

Then there is a knock on the door, and it is young Naseem again, from the teashop around the corner. "Ustaz Sahab, the rector wants you to dine with him at his house tonight, after *isha* prayers. Don't forget! And shave first!"

As the day winds to a close, Shabab and I count the cash we have left and decide that it's time for us to treat ourselves, not that there is much to splurge on in Deoband. The area around the great *madrasah* is surrounded by narrow alleys and walkways where there seems to be nothing but teashops, sweetshops, bookshops and more bookshops, paltry concessions to the vices of schoolboys. The hotspot in town (and the place to be seen, if there ever was one) is the barber's shop that is tucked between two Qur'anic bookshops. Shabab and I stand in line and wait for our turn to be sheared.

Finally, it is my turn to subject myself to the whim of the barber, who takes one look at me and decides what I need to have. "Ustaz, you must go all the way. Haircut, shave and facial." The mention of the last sent shivers down my spine with the thought of what a facial in Deoband might feel like, and what I might look like afterwards. The barber takes out what appears to be a giant tub of pinkish chewing gum, which he assures me is a 'special cream' for delicate skin like mine. He slaps a bucketful of the toxic matter on my face and tells me it will sting a little. As he works the mysterious substance all over my face, I worry that the skin of my face is being scrubbed off with Fab or Breeze, or some industrial-strength detergent.

Finally, the ordeal is almost over, and I am allowed to open my eyes. Upon doing so I am relieved to discover that my face is still where I left it, and that I have not changed colour.

While the barber does his work and applies the finishing touches, I spy a young lad who has come for a shave. His appointment does not take too long, though the other barber is kind enough to spend at least five full minutes trimming off what must have been at least three whiskers on his chin. Having been lathered, shaved, massaged, trimmed and perfumed, the young gent gets off his rickety seat, picks up his books, and slowly walks to the door with a purposeful gait. Then – and I have never forgotten this scene over the years – the lad slowly turns around, mutters a soft word of thanks, reaches into the pocket of his *khameez* and takes out a coin, which he flips through the air and onto the waiting palm of the satisfied barber.

Poise.

Elegance.

Panache.

The boy from Deoband has learnt the one thing that books cannot teach you: dignity of purpose and self-worth. After two weeks in Deoband, I am finally getting close to answering my question: Why are these boys here, and what do they hope to achieve?

Dinner at the home of the rector is a quiet affair, with all of us seated cross-legged on the floor around a giant platter that is crowded with a small stack of chapattis. I sit beside the aged savant and he plies me with questions while I stuff my mouth with chapattis. "What do you think of our *madrasah*?" he asks. "And your boys from Indonesia and Malaysia, have you met them? Are they good?" Before I can offer an answer he answers the questions himself, "They are very good, the Malaysian and Indonesian boys. They learn Arabic faster than any of the others, and they are the best behaved. No problems from any of them. First in class, last to leave. And they keep themselves clean, too."

I ask the rector's permission to bring my camera along and take some photos of the place, to which he concedes but with a condition, "Take your camera if you have to, but don't photo the boys when they are studying. We don't want them to be vain here. Boys must be men, not behave like girls or women. We can't have them preening about with make-up just to look pretty for your research, understand?"

Close to midnight, Shabab and I find ourselves downing our tenth cup of tea in front of Kareem's tea-house, which seems to be run by a legion of possessed *chai-wallas* who cannot stop making the tea, and seem to be addicted to it too. I am joined by Nawab, Fairuz, Kaseem and Muhammads 1, 2 and 3. We laugh and joke and I am struck by the simple, innocent humour the boys are capable of before they cross the threshold into adulthood and discover the mysterious world of women. Some of them, perhaps, may never really cross that threshold entirely, and would remain along that contested territory where love, both platonic and carnal, can be found. Their humour is boisterous and jolly, the laughter rambunctious and hearty. In the years to come I wonder how many of them will go further, and cry the clarion call for *jihad* and the great war against Shaitan from the pulpit of their mosques.

Then – and this is the second incident that has remained burned in my memory ever since – a curious encounter takes place. While the boys of Deoband in their white *shalwar khameezes* drink and laugh at Kareem's, there come from around the corner a band of lusty lads from the college of business studies nearby. Their light blue shirts standing out in contrast to their black trousers, the lads appear to be on their way to some late-night rendezvous where no *madrasah* boy is allowed to venture. For an instant I feel as if Shabab and I are trapped between two wolf packs. The boys of Deoband standing proud and tall, confronted by their rivals, the boys from the business college downtown.

All is silent. The boys eye each other with unbridled contempt. For a whole minute the air is still and even young Naseem is cowering in the corner. Then, with the slightest feint of hand, the most imperceptible gesture, the boys from the business college give way and concede their ground.

They scuffle passes silently, their heads bowed, their walk hurried, but not too fast as to give the impression of a troop in retreat.

I sit on my bench and take it all in, and then realise. that this is it; this is what Deoband does for you. For while the boys of the business college will one day join the ranks of the commercial classes in India, and while their future seems bright as long as the forces of global capital decide that India is the place to park your investments, the boys of Deoband have one thing that no business degree or diploma in communications technology, accountancy, computer engineering can give you: cultural capital.

It is the knowledge that despite their humble beginning and their meagre prospects in the future, the boys of Deoband will one day graduate and join the ranks of the learned Ulama that gives them the self-confidence, dignity and sense of purpose that makes them what they are: gentleman-scholars who hold the keys to Islam's patrimony and theology. Even Harvard cannot do that for you.

"Hell, yes! That's why our parents sent us here!" chips in Naz from Manchester. "Who do they think they're toying with? We are Deoband, mate! This is the Oxford of *madrasahs!*"

Thank you, Naz, that will go into my paper.

Past midnight, Shabab and I make one last foray into the bowels of the Dar'ul Uloom in search of leftover chapattis so that I don't have to listen to my companion's plaintive wailing until dawn. Deep in the heart of the Dar'ul Uloom, the kitchens are working around the clock, milling flour, pounding spices, rolling dough.

The contraptions that pound, stir and gyrate in the semi-darkness of the cavernous kitchen work all day long, for every single day there are thousands of mouths to feed, with the army of ulamas-to-be marching on its stomach. We bag a sackful of chapattis and make good our escape, thankful to pass through the great Western gate just in time, lest we get locked in again.

As we walk down the darkened alley back to our gueshouse, I hear the sound of the machines in the kitchen pounding and thumping: thud-thud-thud-thud-thud ...

Night has fallen, but Deoband never sleeps.

Postscript:

I have maintained regular correspondence with many of the boys of Deoband long after I left the *madrasah*. One year later, some of the photos that I took were put on display at the Rotterdam Museum of Ethnology where I also presented a lecture entitled *'A Day in the Life of Deoband'*. Later, I wrote to one of the boys, Nawab, and informed him thus:

Dear Nawab,
You will be pleased to know that last week I was in Rotterdam, which is a city in the Netherlands, and I gave a talk about your school. I showed them the photos I took, including the one I took of you, me, Shabab Bhai, Fairuz and Muhammad. They were very pleased with the exhibition and I hope you will be proud to know that your photo is hanging on display in a museum in Europe.

Days passed, and then weeks. Finally, I received a reply from Nawab, who wrote thus:

Dearest respected and beloved Ustaz Fareesh al-Muhammad al-Noor, May Allah bless you and guide you in your work, and may Allah always protect you in your travels.

My friends and I are happy to hear that your research has been published and one day we hope that Allah will help us visit you in German (sic). Sadly I do not have a photo of you to remember by, but Allah is kind. Whenever I need to think of you, I close my eyes, and I see you again.

Then my heart swells with love; and my eyes, they drown in tears. Your most respectful student,

Nawab

There are those who think that travel today entails being strapped in some Russian tin can and shot into space. Never mind that. I have travelled to life-worlds that many have never visited, and probably never will. The heavens cannot contain all the wonders as there are here on earth, and that is enough for me.

Naseem, the 10-year-old man

Kareem's tea-house

Inside the great Deoband *madrasah*

Vale of Tears
(Kashmir, 2006)

I stink.

It has been four days since I last washed myself and I have been working and sleeping in the same clothes since I got here. A tent has become my home, albeit temporarily; and for a week I have been camping out in army fatigues, and smelling rather butch at that.

I am in the village of Ambor, just outside the town of Muzaffarabad, capital of Pakistan-administered Kashmir, and I am here to help with the relief efforts in the wake of the most devastating earthquake that has hit South Asia in recent years. In the course of my work I interview the survivors of the quake, and one night a young man by the name of Yasir Khan walks into my tent for a chat.

Yasir pauses for a moment as he searches for the right words.

Then he begins to recount his story, "The earthquake happened during the month of Ramadhan, and I was fasting. I woke up early to eat before dawn, but then I could not get back to sleep. In my heart I felt that something was wrong, something bad was going to happen. I went to the kitchen and found my mother there, preparing the spices for the dinner later when we would break our fast at dusk. I said to my mother, 'Ama, I cannot sleep. Something bad is going to happen.' She told me that I was playing too much, and that I should be studying instead; so I went into my room. I could not work, could not read. I sat down by my desk and felt like listening to some music. My radio was just next to me. Just as I pressed the button, the earth shook. Suddenly there was a terrible noise, the whole house started shaking. The ceiling was cracking and falling all around me. I did not know what was going on. I ran to the kitchen and called out to my mother: 'Ama, Ama! Run, run!' I ran out of the house and when I was outside I realised that my mother was still inside; so scared, she was. I ran back in and pulled her out though she was crying. We ran, but by then the walls were collapsing. I could not see anything, the corridor was moving from side to side. I closed my eyes because of the dust and had to feel my way out. Then we fell to the ground in the garden and our house collapsed behind us. I thought to myself: 'Allah, what sin have we committed against you, for you to do this to us? We are good people, honest people. Why do you punish us like this?' I felt so small, like a little chicken with its mother. My mother and I held on to each other. Everywhere around us houses were falling, people screaming, children crying. Someone performed the *adzan* (call for prayer). We were all crying to God, begging him to stop. Then suddenly it stopped. Our village was destroyed and there was chaos everywhere."

I sit quietly before Yasir and he looks out, his eyes seem to be staring at something in the distance.

The tent above our heads – Chinese-made and olive-green in colour, more suited for an army field camp than to shelter a family – is the only thing that is keeping us warm in the cold climate. Yasir and his family have been living in their tent since October last, when a massive earthquake hit the region of

Muzaffarabad and destroyed the livelihood of thousands, while killing an untold number.

One is tempted to describe the victims of the Kashmiri earthquake as 'innocent', yet there exists an irony that is all too obvious in this. How can the victims of any natural disaster be innocent? For, would that not imply a culpability of sorts, an element of agency in an event where agency is totally absent? Accidents claim victims, innocent or otherwise, without discrimination. Yet, somehow, the survivors invariably feel a sense of responsibility for the event itself. And along with the relief there comes the thought of being spared, and an even more uncomfortable sense of guilt for having survived.

Yasir's discomfort gnaws at him as he continues his story. "You know sir, I felt very bad after that. You know why? My aunty was staying in the middle of the city and there was no-one to look after her. Right after the quake stopped, I told my mother to calm down and I ran all the way to Muzaffarabad to see if my aunty was all right. As I went, I ran past so many houses with people trapped in them. They cried out, 'Help us, help us, please – we are trapped in here.' But I could not stop. I had to rescue my aunty in the city. I cried all the way as I ran. But when I got there, it was too late. My aunty's house had collapsed completely and she was crushed. Still, whenever I am alone, I hear the voices of those people asking me to help them. I keep hearing them. They won't stop crying."

Yasir's story is one of many. The area around Muzaffarabad today is a surreal landscape of destroyed houses, cracked roads, broken bridges and expansive tent-camps where thousands of peoples' lives have been put on hold. Like a nomadic settlement existence, it remains on probation (the authorities repeatedly threaten to close down the tent-camps and force the people to go back to rebuild their houses in the villages or the mountains) with an all-pervading sense of temporality and contingency hanging in the air. The earth still shakes and the mountains tremble, occasionally. One can no longer have faith in the solidity of things when even the earth moves beneath one's feet.

Life here has been turned inside-out. Stumbling through the rubble and ruins of houses, one comes across their contents laid out in the streets, as if the houses were performing some kind of macabre strip-tease, exposing the lives of its inhabitants. I look around and find odds and ends everywhere; obscure and seemingly unimportant objects that have been abandoned in haste and which now are laden with meaning. I spy a solitary shoe and wonder where the other one is. A child's notebook lies open with an unfinished sentence hanging in mid-page, as if inviting me to complete it. There is a radio that has lost its outer casing but still works, remarkably. I hear music and then realise that the song is a recent hit by the rock-band Korn, *Twisted Transistor*. It is too surreal for comfort.

As I walk among the ruins of Muzaffarabad, I bear witness to humankind's enduring will to survive and overcome: ramshackle schools made of tents and tin-sheets have been set up here and there, and the kids are back at work. Though a handful of schools are still left standing, the children refuse to go into them for fear that another earthquake would bring these down too. Many of the children have witnessed the deaths of their schoolmates, for the quake hit in the early hours of the morning, just when the first classes had begun. With gestures both poignant and defiant, the kids gambol and play amidst the ruins, as if they are conscious of the fact that they have survived the onslaught of some great unseen beast, and are now dancing on its shattered carcass.

For the elders, however, the pain of loss and the trauma that came afterwards is more agonising and difficult to accept.

A wizened old Kashmiri, his dusty shawl wrapped over lean, bony shoulders, shrugs as he speaks, "What can we do? It's all gone now. Every family has lost someone. None of us were spared. I saw my friend, as old as me, go crazy as he put together the pieces of his child after the body was dragged out of the ruins. We were in hell. It was everyone for himself. Nobody could help you because everyone had to look after his own, and what was left. My friend was left with no-one. His child was dead and he wanted to bury the boy, but he had no tools. Not even a shovel. So he dug the grave with a spoon. It took him two days to dig the grave as the ground was hard. He cried throughout. When it was over he could not cry anymore, he had nothing left in him. Now, he hardly speaks to anyone. A part of him died that day."

Here lies the real tragedy of the earthquake: the ground cracked and the mountains split open, throwing Jurassic boulders into the sky, crushing human lives in an instant. No statistical study can account for the dehumanising effects of such a calamity, nor the scale of the pain that it spread. Houses can be rebuilt, bridges repaired, roads reconstructed. But no degree of aid can erase memories of desperation, and primordial horrors unleashed by the quake's violence.

Young Yasir has his share of memories that will not go away. His eyes light up suddenly, animated by some mysterious need to share. "You know what, sir?" he says, half-smiling. "One week after the earthquake, if you had put a piece of human flesh, chicken flesh and other animal flesh next to one another in front of me, I could have told you which one was human. For more than one week, that was the only thing we could smell. Bodies everywhere, sir, you cannot imagine. It was too much terrible, too much terrible. Too much."

Calamity to excess, excess to overdetermination. The earthquake has become a signifier for a plethora of anxieties and fears, some collective, others private. One cannot explain it. 'Why?' Is the question on everyone's lips, 'Why us? Why here? Why now?' The geologists collate their data, but numbers do not and cannot foreclose radical contingency. The politicians make their promises, but they cannot undo the past or bring the dead back to life. But there are those whose narrow logic offers a straight path that is best walked with blinkers: the *jihadis*.

"They were bad Muslims and they did not implement the Shariah, that is why God has smitten them and brought them down." Hafeez Saeed's words sound a tad too well-choreographed, like a hackneyed script memorised. But his lack of originality is made up for by his accoutrements and style: black fluffy beard overflowing, his dark-set eyes framed by heavy brows that look decidedly unfamiliar in these parts. He is not a local Kashmiri, but a Pathan from the North-West Frontier Province, and he is here along with the other Islamist groups who were once the biggest suppliers of martyrs for the *jihad* against India. Kashmir was their battleground. And Muzaffarabad was once the main supply depot, training centre and rallying point for a myriad of *jihadi* organisations with fiery names that befitted their combustible nature: Hizbul Mujahideen, Lashkar-e-Taiba, etcetera. Up to 2003, it would not have been unusual to meet Hafeez in the streets with a Kalashnikov in hand and perhaps a rocket-propelled grenade or two. Today he wears an armband signalling his membership of an Islamist relief group.

The Islamists have descended upon Muzaffarabad in full force, though in a sense they never really left. Today the gun-totting militants of a not-too-distant past have opted for a new look, that of relief workers, NGO activists, medical aid practitioners and rescuers. But their discourse and vocabulary still bear traces of their previous avatars.

Picking up the leaflets dropped over the town by the Islamist groups, one sees the trite skewed logic of the Islamists. Some pamphlets allege that the earthquake was the result of an underground nuclear explosion detonated by ever-nefarious India next door. Others claim that the quake was God's judgement on the sinful people of Kashmir who had not embraced the *jihadi* with open arms. The Islamists are there to provide the truth and the way out: *jihad* against India and the creation of the Islamic state of Jammu and Kashmir, as part of the global Muslim Caliphate.

The powers-that-be in Islamabad bemoan that even an earthquake the scale of the one last October could not dislodge the *jihadis* from their Kashmiri stronghold. But nobody can deny the fact that the Islamists were the first on the scene, and that their activists were the bravest, toughest and most committed among the rescuers. Stories abound of how Islamist activists threw themselves into the rubble of Muzaffarabad and dug the victims out, with tooth and nail. Armed with little more than their faith in their struggle, they scaled the mountains of Kashmir and were the first to reach the most isolated villages in the upper regions. They were the first to use donkeys and mules to get to villages that were cut off by broken roads. They were the first to construct their own makeshift rafts and to transport much needed medicine and supplies to villages upriver, braving the glacial waters of the great Jheelum and Kishan Ganga rivers that run through the valley.

As I walk through the tent-camps I come across the familiar flags of the Islamist groups: the Jamaat-e-Islami are there, as are the Jama'at-ul-Dawa. The blue and green pennants flutter over their tents like in medieval military campsites, with different armies next to one another. Make no mistake about it: this is a turf war being fought in earnest. The Islamists may be united in their common hatred of India and all things Western, but this is matched only by their rivalry against each other. The Jamaat'-e-Islami have set up a food distribution centre where *chapattis* and *rotis* are distributed along with Jama'at-related propaganda material. Right across the road is a Jamaat-ul-Dawa field clinic with equipment so modern that even the government's own relief camps and field hospitals seem backward in comparison. After the catastrophe, the real battle for hearts and minds has begun. Western donor agencies like Medicins San Frontiers, Diakonie and the Red Cross are there too, but they cannot offer the salvation and heavenly reward promised by the Mullahs.

In the midst of this, I am left bewildered. Where is the state? What is the Pakistani government doing? I am told that a Pakistani army relief camp is in the neighbouring district of Chikar, and that I can visit it by jeep if I want. Eager to see what the Pakistani army is up to, I accept the offer.

The road to Chikar takes one all the way to Srinagar and runs parallel to the great Jheelum river, with its icy waters, running down in angry torrents. What was once a two-lane mountain road is now reduced to a narrow path with huge chunks ripped off the mountainside and fed to the river below. The driver shouts to me as he speeds on at close to 90 km an hour. "We are sorry that our roads are so bad! The earthquake destroyed our roads and everything is broken. How are the roads in Malaysia?" he asks me. "Don't worry," I answer. "Malaysian roads break apart even without earthquakes." "*Acha*?" the driver replies. "Very special country, Malaysia!"

The remains of a school that was destroyed by the Kashmiri earthquake in Chikar.

Forgotten Nation
(Kashmir, 2006)

With morbid fascination, the pornography of death entices us.
The crowd sits agitated, waiting for the moment of collapse, to re-witness the end of the world. The ground shakes.
Buildings fall apart.
Death descends and claims the lives of innocents and the guilty alike.
They clap. Some take pictures.
I stare at my own shadow on the ground, embarrassed by this public spectacle of voyeurism.

I am standing on what used to be the grounds of Muzaffarabad University that was levelled by the earthquake in the month of Ramadhan last year. It looks like a giant parking lot, and cluttered around this space are makeshift tent-camps where refugees from the villages nearby have taken shelter. I am in Pakistan-administered Kashmir to help with post-earthquake relief efforts, and for the past ten days I have been on a staple diet of death warmed up.

Earlier today, a huge tent was erected by the local council of Muzaffarabad. We are here to witness the demonstration of earthquake-proof houses that the United Nations and other international aid agencies wish to see built in the area, in case another earthquake of the same magnitude hits the region. It grows hotter by the hour and soon we are all perspiring. At one end of the tent are rows of chairs set up for the dignitaries: UN representatives, local politicians, representatives of the army and police, NGO directors, aid workers, the foreign press and the wives of local leaders, overdressed and bored out of their minds. Around the tent are more rows of chairs for the local villagers, shepherd and farmers, who have come to watch two model houses — about the size of large crates, set up on two ping-pong tables — undergo the earthquake test. A Japanese earthquake expert speaks into the microphone and explains that one of the houses is a model of a typical Kashmiri house, while the other model is built according to the new standards approved by earthquake experts, with reinforced ceilings and pliable steel joints that bend rather than break, should the earth tremble. The crowd, who are mostly non-English speakers, keep whispering to one another, "What is he saying, what is he saying?"

Then the moment arrives when the Japanese expert gives the signal for the tables to be shaken violently. The first house — the normal Kashmiri one — breaks up and falls apart. The door falls off the front, the walls crack, and by the third jolt the ceiling collapses. The second house, however, is less worn by the shaking of the tables, and though it doesn't look like anything one would invest in for one's retirement, at least the ceiling still holds, and the second floor remains where it is supposed to be: above the first.

The crowd claps and howls of approval issue forth. The Japanese expert thanks them for their attention and then an overweight politician reminds the crowd to vote for him at the next election. The show is over; four hours of waiting for thirty seconds of macabre entertainment. Kids scream for ice cream and the politicians' wives look as bored as they were an hour ago.

I pick up my camera and head for the jeep that is going to take me to the village of Chikar in the mountains. Apparently, the earthquake's epicentre was close to the area and many of the outlying villages were totally destroyed. Along the way our jeep manoeuvres its way between huge cracks that have opened up on the road, like gigantic maws waiting to devour errant vehicles and their hapless passengers. We pass caravans of donkeys and mules and the odd bullock-cart transporting contents of households: broken furniture, twisted lamps, unrecognisable contents of homes and piles of clothes wrapped in bundles, with the ubiquitous grandmother and her grandchildren sitting on top of the heap, trying to keep their balance.

Then in the middle of nowhere, there is a traffic jam. Our jeep is stuck in a queue of lorries and buses, and a crowd gathers. The road is narrow and we are hemmed in between a mountain on our right and the Jheelum river to our left. Drivers come down from their lorries and buses to see what is going on.

Young Yasir Khan, the boy who was in my tent a few nights ago, comes running towards our jeep. "Don't look, don't look!" he shouts at us. Apparently, one of the boys from Yasir's village was run over while riding his motorbike round the slippery bend. His passenger had been thrown off into the valley below. The motorcyclist – Yasir's neighbour's son – was instantly crushed and his brains are now all over the road. The boy's uncle was called to identify the body, but broke down as soon as he recognised his nephew's shirt. He is in a state of shock, and insists on looking at the victim's face, only there is no face. In fact, there is no head even. Blood mingles with mud, and the crowd is shaken. In the bus in front of our jeep someone has left the radio on. I recognise the tune. It is Eminem singing 'Ass like that'. None of us know what to say, and in the distance we hear the uncle crying.

The rest of the journey proceeds in silence, with the exchange of a few lame jokes and insults being the only semblance of a conversation. In the distance the snow-covered peaks of the Makra mountains look down upon us sternly. We feel like ants clinging on to the feet of an elephant.

Our jeep suddenly lurches to the side as the driver tries to avoid an old man squatting in the middle of the road. We come to a screeching halt and get out, but the man appears unmoved by his recent close encounter with death. One more road accident today will be too much for me, and I thank the stars that our jeep did not add yet another casualty to the toll. My guide walks up to the man and asks him who he is and what he is doing. His name is Mousa and apparently he is one of the survivors of the village of Naida.

The guide explains, "The old man is here staring at the remains of his village which was across the valley, right there." I follow the direction of his forefinger and try to see what he is pointing at, but can only see a lake in the middle of the valley. "That was the village of Naida; and that is what is left of it." On the day of the earthquake the men of the village had left to tend to their sheep and goats that they had left grazing along the hillsides the night before, leaving the women and children in the village. When the quake struck, the avalanche of boulders and rocks from the top of the mountain swept the entire village into the valley below. Two thousand women and children were crushed in an instant, with the rubble coming to rest in the valley where a mountain stream runs.

The men raced back to their village only to find it all gone. Then they ran all the way down to the bottom of the valley to dig out their families. But the rubble had created a dam across the stream. Within hours the water rose. The men kept on digging but they could not dig fast enough. Soon the water collected into a lake. If there were survivors, they were trapped and could not be rescued in time. They probably drowned. Within a day whatever was left of Naida was buried under that lake.

An estimated two thousand bodies remain under the water, along with the contents of homes and lives. The men of the village have been reduced to mute zombies ever since. They come to the lake and stare at it in disbelief. Old man Mousa is soon joined by another aged villager, Hassan, who speaks to us in his broken voice. "I am nearly ninety years old now. I have seen wars, invasions, the deaths of so many. But never in my life have I seen anything like this. I prayed that God would let me die peacefully surrounded by my family. But instead, it is I who have outlived them and when I die there will be no-one to bury or remember me. I have nothing but these clothes I wear." He squats by the cliff's edge, maintaining his vigil for the family he has lost. Again our words mean little. We say goodbye and move on to Chikar.

The road to Chikar is littered with more broken houses. I see the remains of buildings swept off the roadside and into the valley below, their pillars still standing, like circus acrobats who have lost the rubber balls they are juggling. The driver says to me, "There used to be a good resthouse there, just where the white pillars are. They served good tea and *briani* rice. It's such a pity. I do feel hungry now."

Our jeep winds through the narrow alleys of Chikar town and we finally make our way to the army camp with a helicopter base at its flat plateau in the centre. Our jeep is stopped by some soldiers in camouflage fatigues and berets. The badge on their lapels and caps carry the title 'Baluchistan Division'. I've come to Chikar to see what the Pakistani government – or rather the army – has been doing in the relief effort and I ask to meet the commanding officer. The sergeant does the obligatory salute and clicks his heels, despite the fact that his muddied boots don't click all that well. We walk into the camp compound, to a khaki-green briefing tent and are served sweet milky tea in plastic imitation china cups. There is a laminated drawing-board that has been set up in one corner with a map of the Chikar region. Next to the map is an impressive display of statistics recording the number of victims, their family names, the amounts paid out to those who have lost their relatives, to those who have been injured, and to those who have been maimed for life.

In steps Lieutenant Abdullah, a smart-looking young officer, both handsome and flawlessly courteous. He clicks his heels but his boots are not muddied so the sound effects do work. I resist the temptation to salute back and remind myself that I've never been a soldier despite all the war movies I had watched as a kid. Lieutenant Abdullah tells me that their division was moved to the Chikar region two weeks after the quake and each village now has one company of troops to maintain law and order and to provide whatever assistance necessary. Later he shows me the field hospital that they have set up, pointing out to me the cleanliness of their toilets in particular. I peep behind one of the tents and express calculated amazement at the cleanliness of the loo, and the lieutenant beams. "Was it difficult to co-ordinate the relief efforts by so many international organisations?" I ask him. "Not really," he says. "They are all very, very co-operative and they even compete amongst one another to show off how much they are willing to do. The only difficulty is having to keep the American and Cuban aid workers apart."

The conversation gets complicated when I ask the lieutenant about the activities of the militant *jihadi* groups. I pointed out that the city of Muzaffarabad is now full of militants who have only dropped their Kalashnikovs for the moment, and have taken to giving out medical care. "They, too, are trying to help, so we don't stop them as we need all the help we can get," Lieutenant Abdullah assures me. But I wonder how long this uneasy alliance between the Pakistani army, the militant groups and the foreign powers will last. Already there is talk of closing down the tent-camps and sending the refugees back to rebuild their villages, despite the fact that none of the promised aid money has materialised in any concrete form. The lieutenant does not seem all that convinced with his explanation, and he seems to feel my own unease as well. While waiting for the jeep to pick me up, we both stare at each other's shoes.

"The army cannot do anything, and the international community doesn't care about us anymore. All that you've seen on the TV is false and, in fact, things have not improved at all," says Professor Khaleeque.

I find myself back in Muzaffarabad and am sitting in what was once the living room of Professor Khaleeque's house before it collapsed last year. We are joined by Farooq Niazi, who heads the Human Rights Movement of Kashmir, and we settle down to tea, which comes with a sweet desert made of yoghurt and nuts. Then comes something which is spuriously called 'Chinese soup' that looks and tastes like Cantonese noodles but without noodles.

Professor Khaleeque stares outside the window and launches into a long lecture about the politics of Kashmir. "My dear friend, you are now in Kashmir. Remember that. This is not Pakistan, nor India. This is Kashmir. We are a separate nation, with our own history, our own language, our own culture. That's why this part of Kashmir is called Pakistan-administered Kashmir. That is not an accident. We are a nation of our own that is administered by another country; just in the same way that Indian-occupied Kashmir is occupied by India. The whole world wants to help us, but they don't know how to do it because they don't understand the issues."

For Professor Khaleeque the root of the problem has been the lack of recognition of Jammu and Kashmir's own past and identity as a nation in its own right. The division of Kashmir into Pakistan and Indian-administrated zones has only made things worse. "Look at where we are now. The Pakistani government wants us to rebuild, but they complain about the costs of reconstruction. Don't the officials in Islamabad realise that it would be much easier for us here in Muzaffarabad to go down the road to Srinagar and buy our building materials from there? No, they want us to buy our materials from the Pakistani side, but something as basic as a sheet of tin roofing from Pakistan costs ten times more than the same thing in Srinagar. What logic is that? We Kashmiris want to help each other, but we are prevented from doing so by the governments of India and Pakistan that keep us apart. Who imposed these borders and check-points on us? Do you see Kashmiris manning these guardposts? No, what you see are Pakistani and Indian soldiers. We don't even have a currency of our own. In fact, parts of our old nation, like the provinces of Gilgit, Hunza, Ladakh, have even been carved out of our map and identified as part of Pakistan or India instead."

The human rights activist in Farooq Niazi chips in at this point, "We are a people who cannot even move in our own homeland. Why should a Kashmiri from one part of Kashmir have to apply for a passport and visa to visit his family in another part? Who gave them – the Pakistanis and Indians – the right to divide us like this? This has been our tragedy since 1947. The world has forgotten us, and when it tries to remember, it can only think of us in terms of the Pakistan-India dispute. But Kashmiris have never been in dispute with one another, you see?" I note down his point as I stare into the mysterious Chinese soup that seems to be turning into a kind of jelly.

Our talk turns to the role of the army and the militant groups now operating in the region. "For a start, the army is despised here because of their role in keeping down the free-Kashmiri movement. They were the ones who have been suppressing our freedom struggle all along, and who keep up the myth that we Kashmiris are happy to be part of Pakistan; so it's no wonder that despite their help, people here still don't trust them. The militant groups like Lashkar-e-Taiba and Hizbul Mujahideen, on the other hand, are a different kind of menace altogether. They are the ones who brought the ideology of *jihad* against India, to be fought out in Indian-occupied Kashmir. Where is the logic in that? They wanted us Kashmiris to support their *jihad* against India but what this means is we Kashmiris supporting them in their terrorist attacks against fellow Kashmiris who are our brothers and sisters. Most of these militant groups are made up of Pakistanis – Punjabis and Pathans, or even Arabs and foreigners, not Kashmiris."

For men like Professor Khaleeque and Farooq Niazi, the earthquake of 2005 merely exposed the tip of an iceberg. It highlighted the plight of the Kashmiris who remain among the poorest people of the country and whose region remains one of the most under-developed. The international community's response was fast, but in many ways counter-productive, as it merely lent further legitimacy to the occupation and foreign administration of a nation divided and robbed of its own political identity, will and agency.

What is to be done? I found myself asking the same question time and again. For the militant Islamists, the answer is clear: the imposition of Shariah law and the commitment to all-out *jihad* against the infidel state of India. For the army, the solution lies in law and order and the perpetuation of Pakistani rule. The local politicians promise miracles at the price of a vote. For the international aid agencies, the remedy is in handing out bandages and tents to a people whose scars run much deeper than what is visible. But no-one inquires about what the Kashmiris want. The answer is there, but the question has yet to be asked.

I lay down my pen and join Professor Khaleeque as he stares out at the mountains in the distance. It is beautiful here.

Cold Turkey in Kandy
(Sri Lanka, 2006)

The moustachioed sergeant grabs a handful of my balls, weighs them, warms them up by gingerly rolling them, and then looks up at me and asks with a smile, "Are you Sinhalese?"

"Er … No, I'm not Sinhalese," is the only reply I can give, and a rather lame one at that.

His hands then reach for my butt and I have the distinct impression that this man in uniform is well acquainted with the tactile subtleties of the male bottom. He grabs them with both hands, draws them close, reaches for the crevice between the cheeks and grips hard in anticipation of the clenching of the muscles that follows. Satisfied that my butt meet his discerning standards, his hands then go back to my front and assail my balls, again. Once more the same question is put to me: "Are you Sinhalese?"

"No, I'm sure I'm not Sinhalese," is my second – equally lame – reply.

After a quick and random probe up and down my legs it becomes clear where the focus of his attention really is. For the third time my balls are the subject of his nimble enquiry, and as he grabs them yet again, the now-familiar inspection routine is repeated, "Are you sure you are not Sinhalese?"

"No, I'm telling you. I'm not Sinhalese. I'm sure of that."

It feels as if I had unwittingly entered some gonad race-identification parade, as if one could tell one's ethnicity by the shape of one's testicles. But just as I am preparing myself for an even more intrusive search of my person, up comes a strapping young lad who looks far more Sinhalese than me, who stands behind me in the queue. The sergeant is clearly pleased by this fortunate turn of events, and suddenly his ardent desire to determine the nationality of my testicles abate somewhat, much to my relief. "Okay, you can pass," he says, as he waves me through the green curtain that offers what little privacy there is in the frisking booth of the guard house.

I step through the curtain and find myself in a long garden, and there before me is what I have come to see: the fabled Temple of Tooth, holding the tooth relic of the Buddha. I am in Kandy, up in the central mountains of Sri Lanka, and I have not touched a cigarette for four-and-twenty hours now.

Cold turkey in Kandy

When one travels by moving and removing one's body from one place to another, and one travels within oneself as well, moving from one state of mind to another. I am, and have been, a traveller almost all my life and over the past 20 years I can say that I have lived in at least thirty-five different places (if one regards a stay of at least three months anywhere as enough to count as a 'stay'). Looking at the map I can trace my life in terms of long stretches of erratic, sometimes meandering movement. This body, now at the verge of forty, has grown somewhat tired of travelling. It's gravity that I now seek.

Much of my travels have been the result of work. Travelling across Asia in search of *madrasahs* and following the footsteps of itinerant religious scholars and mystics has been my business for the past few years, and my work has taken me to some of the most fascinating, wonderful, dingy and horrific places I have ever had the fortune (or misfortune) to visit.

But there are times when one travels simply because a change of scenery is needed to affect a deeper change in oneself. This jaunt to Sri Lanka was one such episode.

After a chance encounter with three rather surly and uncouth skinheads in the middle of the park in Berlin (who appeared not to take too kindly to meeting a bespectacled Asian academic sitting on the bench reading the *Times Literary Supplement*) my life changed somewhat. A two-day spell convalescing is hospital does things to you: you suddenly realise that you are more fortunate than you perhaps deserve to be, and wonder what might have happened if the first skinhead who strangled you from behind had a knife in his hands. You wonder how and why your life has changed in the way it has. You look again at the trail of failed marriages, broken relationships, lost loves and hopes. You wonder why the woman you love doesn't love you back. And you wonder why you can't stop smoking to save your life.

And so, as soon as the painkillers wore off and I was well enough to stumble on the pavement with a walking stick in hand, I hobbled off to the travel agents and picked the first destination I saw on the advertising board. So, Sri Lanka it is.

I have come to Sri Lanka to find myself. Again. Odd, some might think. Why someone would need to travel so far to find oneself. Surely a look in the mirror would suffice, and wouldn't that be cheaper too? But the mirror lies, and the eyes that do the looking conspire too. Travel to the unknown robs one of the comfort of the familiar. It forces one to look into oneself anew and find a way of explaining things a tad clearer. The underside to this sort of cathartic travel is that the place one travels to is often reduced to a convenient backdrop for the staging of a personal drama of sorts, and all else becomes little more than scenery. Thus even before boarding the Condor flight to Colombo, I scribbled a note to myself in my head, "Don't forget to pack your morals."

Sri Lanka is a place I have longed to visit for years, no, decades. Perhaps, I had hoped to find bits of me there that I had lost somewhere along my travels. I pray that the country I am about to visit will be a kind host to this personal quest, and that the usual hassles I have grown familiar with over the years – military check-points, demands for bribes, the Kalashnikov pointed in my face, etcetera – would not hinder my train of thoughts or my travels. But just a week before I leave, things begin to go pear-shaped all of a sudden: a coastal assault by the Tamil Tigers leaves scores dead in villages up north, the short-lived ceasefire has broken down. After that comes a car bomb that blows away a senior commanding officer and some of his bodyguards. Sri Lanka is getting hotter all of a sudden. Cold comfort for someone trying to de-stress and give up smoking.

The only thing I take with me, apart from my nicotine patches, toothbrush and camera, is the first volume of S. Radhakrishnan's *History of Indian Philosophy*. By chance, as I board the plane to Colombo, I turn the page and start reading the chapter on Buddhism. Fate seems to be smiling.

S. Radhakrishnan was one of the greatest philosophers of the 20th century, and his two-volume treatise on the history of Indian thought still ranks as the greatest exposition on the subject ever attempted by anyone. The chapter on Buddhism is still the best introduction to the subject. And for a burnt-out wandering academic seeking solace in stillness and quietude, it is a soothing balm indeed. As I take the train up into the mountains heading for Kandy, admiring the rolling hills – dotted as they are by idyllic tea plantations, straight out of some postcard – Radhakrishnan is the only company I keep.

"Individual existence is itself evil, and desire is merely the outer expression of it," Radhakrishnan writes. "The false sense of 'I' is the central support of individual being, it is the bearer of karma and its breeder. Buddha asks us to face facts, yet it is ignorance consisting of assuming as real what is not, that produces the craving for life; it impels us to live and enjoy the world." I ponder upon this idea that is so central to Buddhism, as I try my best to keep my distance from the smiling cigarette-sellers on the road. I have come here to find myself again, but is this perhaps the wrong path? I wonder if the denial of one's ego makes sense at all, when the desire to save my 'Self' is the fundamental error that has got me into the mess that I call my life in the first place?

As I try to begin the painful process of self-deconstruction, I realise that it is raining and that I am effectively homeless. Getting out of the train station at Kandy I am greeted by a wall of pouring rain, with nowhere to go. "Where can I find a cheap hotel?" I ask a monk who steps out of the bus before me. "Sorry, I'm a monk. I don't stay in hotels," is his reply. Serves me right for assuming that everyone depends on the same creature comforts as I do. Eventually I am directed to the Olde Empire, a small two-storey wooden relic of a bygone colonial era. (The establishment bears an uncanny resemblance to our dear old Colesium Hotel in downtown Kuala Lumpur.) This has to be the place for me, I think, and I walk up to the kindly old man who mans the desk on the porch.

Buggered and plastered

That night I find myself lazing on the balcony of the Olde Empire, sweating profusely from the lack of a smoke, and desperately trying to concentrate on Radhakrishnan's book. It doesn't help that the only other resident in the hotel is sitting next to me, smoking like a chimney, and totally plastered too.

"This whole damned place is buggered, mate. I've been coming to this country for more than fifteen years now, and it's been going downhill ever since." John is an out-of-work Englishman who has seen better times and is the worse for wear himself. On the run from a nasty divorce, he is back in Sri Lanka, a country he adopted during his days as a student researcher long ago. "Why do you think things have deteriorated?" I ask him.

"It's not just the violence that's got totally out of control, mate. It's the religion too. Everyone has become more conservative, more intolerant. I mean, look at this place. I've been staying here for more than ten years, every time I get here. But now we can't even get beer at the bar downstairs! I have to buy it outside and sneak it in in some plastic bag! What am I? A thief?"

John offers me a swig of his local brew, which looks like it has been distilled in some bin in a backyard. I decline the offer but press him with more questions. Why does he keep coming back to Sri Lanka if he thinks things have become worse? Surely there are cheaper places to travel to, especially when you're on the dole. John gets all sentimental suddenly, and with the beer taking its toll he begins to speak. John says he wants to fly up north to Jaffna. Apparently, backpackers can hop on board some military flight for the right price. Jaffna? Now? When the ceasefire has broken down and the Tamil Tigers are on the march again?

I wonder what John really does for a living. Intelligence? And if so, for whom? Nobody back-packs to Jaffna while entire divisions of the Sri Lankan army are being sent up there for the big showdown. And, unemployed blokes from London don't go hitchhiking in rebel territory when buses are being blown up weekly. But I remind myself that I am on leave and that I have left my researcher's hat back in Berlin. I've met dozens of men like John in my travels: wild-eyed journalists on speed, whose eyes have seen too much; broken to pieces, and trying to put themselves back together at the journalists' club in Peshawar (a favourite haunt of journos and spies from all over the planet). I bid John good night and wish him well. The next morning he disappears and I know we will never meet again.

As I lie under the tattered mosquito net with the rusty fan creaking above me that night, I think of the country I have come to visit. Arab navigators who chanced upon the island called it *Serendib*, which is the root of the English word *serendipity*, meaning the discovery of something pleasant by accident. Sri Lanka is indeed pleasant, and has been billed as a tourist paradise populated by cheerful people who seem to get on with their lives regardless of bombs in the markets and, not to mention, the odd tsunami. For thousands of tourists who come here, it is the ideal tropical paradise, and one can see why. The landscape of the island is astounding: from the lush hills and mountains in the centre to the drier plains up north, from the crowded bustling metropolis of Colombo to the ever-so-enticing beaches that dot the Southern and Eastern coasts. It all seems too perfect to be true.

But there is always another side to the story. Sri Lanka's complex social and cultural history is one of overlapping territorialities where cultural and ethnic frontiers collide with religious and political ones. For more than a thousand years this island, which is one of the global centres of Buddhism, was also the stomping ground of Hindu armies that sought to extend Indian hegemony to the South. Sri Lanka's tortured landscape speaks of centuries of struggle, first against the environment, and then against external aggressors.

Kandy, where I am, was the last bastion of Sinhalese power before it fell into the hands of the invading Brits of the East India Company. The temple of the Buddha's tooth relic is symbolic to this struggle, for it marks the peak of Sinhalese-Buddhist resistance to foreign power and the committed desire to preserve the Buddhist identity of Sri Lanka at all costs. The ancient kings of Kandy made a good choice when they picked it as their last capital, knowing that the dense mountain forests would serve as an effective bulwark against all foes. The Portuguese tried to take the mountain kingdom several times, in 1594, 1611, 1629 and 1638, but to no avail. Then came the Dutch who were also beaten back in 1765. When the English adventurer Robert Knox was captured by the soldiers of Rajasinha II in 1660, it took him years to escape from Kandy and to return to England to tell his tale: the maze of thick jungles and mountains make movement almost impossible except for those who know the secret routes in and out of the Kandyan kingdom.

But Kandy's demise came about due to internal factors. In 1739 the last Sinhalese king of Kandy, Narendrasinha, died, bringing an end to the Sinhalese-Kandyan dynasty. After that, it was the age of the Nayakar kings of Indian origin, but who converted to Buddhism. Things, however, came to a head during the reign of the mad despot, Sri Wickrama Rajasinha, whose bloody exploits included the execution of seventy of his own chieftains and the murder of his son-in-law and rival Maha Nilame, along with his family. The Kandyans finally decided that a regime change was in order. The British marched into Kandy in 1815, took over the last independent capital of Sri Lanka and built the railway line, the very same one that had brought me up to this mountain retreat.

For centuries the temple of the Buddha's tooth stood firm, as a reminder of an age when Buddhism held sway over the island. Then in 1998 the Tamil Tigers decided to make a point by ramming a truck loaded with explosives right through its front gate, killing dozens and reducing the temple walls to ruins. Since then guard posts and machine-gun nests have festooned the outer perimeter of the temple, where occasionally one comes across sergeants who grope your balls when you seek entry.

Remembrance of things past

As I sit in the temple compound, I cannot help but reflect on the parallel lives of nations and individuals. If the individual 'Self' is nothing more than a fiction strung together by the vain heart-strings of one's ego, then wouldn't a national identity be likewise fictional? Around me are hundreds of old women clad in white saris who have come to pray, drawn to the temple. "This (is a) very holy place," the wizened old granny tells me as she flashes a toothless smile. "You go there, under the bodhi tree, and light a lamp for your loved ones," she suggests. I take her advice and light a number of coconut-oil lamps, one for my ex-wife, one for my ex-girlfriend, one for my mother, then my brother, then one for myself, so many flickering little flames in the fading light of dusk. How many souls have I saved, I wonder?

The thought comes back to me on the road to Anuradhapura, up north in the dry central plains of Sri Lanka. My driver Gamage is speeding along at 140 km an hour, sending up clouds of brown dust as we tear through the country roads. How many souls are being saved in Sri Lanka; how many other vagabond travellers like me are here, looking for some kind of answer to their own existential questions?

As we race through the bush, the countryside becomes browner, grittier and dustier. Lush green forest give way to sparsely wooded dry land. This is elephant country. The central plains of Sri Lanka was the scene of a great civilisation akin to the ancient Egyptians, one that was founded on irrigation and canal-building. For a thousand years this civilisation was kept alive by human technology, and Anuradhapura was the capital. Along the way we speed past jeeps and lorries carrying troops and armour of all types: jungle commandos, light infantry, mobile armour brigades, the lot. Their uniforms vary from khaki-green to black to blue jungle stripes. Their arms and armour are new and flashy, and at one point Gamage is forced to step on his brakes to avoid the barrel of a field cannon from smashing through the front window of our van. I've had a gun pointed in my face before, but never a cannon.

"What's going on, Gamage? Why all the soldiers?" I shout to my driver over the loud blaring Bollywood music on the radio. "Big fight in Jaffna, boss! Now there (is) big fighting in Trincomalee too! Going to be war again, bad for business. Gamage won't get customers, tourists don't come to Sri Lanka when Tamil Tigers go on offensive!"

Gamage laments the passing of the good old days when he could pick up the odd Japanese or German tourist who would hire his van for the week at extortionate prices, to be taken to places like Anuradhapura, Polonaruwa, Sigiriya – the familiar spots in the so-called Cultural Triangle of Sri Lanka. These days, all he can hope for is an underpaid academic like me who simply wants to meditate in temples and not spend money at the ayurvedic massage centres, thereby depriving him of the extra income.

I spend most of my two weeks travelling all across the northern central plains, with Kandy as my base-camp and the Olde Empire as my watering hole and hideout. Standing barefoot before the great Mahastupa of Anuradhapura, a majestic white-washed dome 187 metres in height and made up of more than a million hand-placed bricks, I marvel at the spiritual ambition of humans, as if by sheer will alone, one can find God and ascend heavenwards, step by step. Greater than the pyramids of Egypt, the white brick and stucco stupas of Anuradhapura floats skywards, rising from a carpet of green jungle surrounded by the huge man-made lake around the city. It is from here that hundreds of Buddhist monks made their pilgrimages and trips across Asia, bringing Buddhism to Burma, Thailand, Java and the Malay peninsula. In the boiling heat of summer I do not notice that the sweat that pours down my face is intermingled with tears of wonderment. How great it is, to be Asian. For a brief moment, I am outside myself and free.

Flight, again

My final days in Sri Lanka are spent on the coast, shuttling between Colombo and the somewhat overblown playground of playboy-expatriates that is the Mount Lavinia Hotel, a former residence of the British colonial governor and now all tarted up to celebrate – of all things – the great old days of the British Empire. I'm joined by my chum Henry, fellow antique-collector and lover of Asian art, whose great-grandfather Sir Robert Brownrigg was the British commander who returned the tooth of the Buddha to its rightful abode in the mountain temple of Kandy, much to the relief of the anxious Kandyans then. We potter about Colombo doing an inventory of churches Henry's great-grandfather built, while I do a study of Sinhalese temples and compare them to traditional Malay-Javanese mosques.

The night before I leave, I have dinner with my new friend Gowrie, who explains to me that Sri Lanka cannot be explained. "I don't know how to explain this place to someone like you," she says. "Sri Lanka is such a beautiful country, and yet I've seen some of the worst violence here as well. The politicisation of religion and the ongoing ethno-religious conflict is something that has been with us all our lives, and we don't know when it will end." A sombre reminder that all is not well in paradise, I think – though it is a familiar story that I've heard many times in other places I have visited, like Southern Thailand, Java, Bali, Pakistan and Afghanistan. Paradise needs its serpent, its poisoned apple, and its bittersweet aftertaste. I pause at that thought as I sip my tea, reminding myself that on the average one soldier or policeman has been killed every day since I've been here. (And God knows how many civilian casualties.) For every oil lamp lit under the Bodhi tree in Kandy, another life is snuffed out. Karmic balance perhaps, but the law of life and loss stands still here.

For solace I turn to Radhakrishnan once again on the balcony of my hotel, as I watch the sun set over the horizon. "Pain comes from the false sense of loss of Selfhood, and in our struggle to overcome the pain that is inherent in our human condition, a contemplation of the path of evil is necessary: 'Asubhabhavana': one steps out of oneself, looks back, understands how and why one is on the path that one finds oneself now, and tries one's best to break the karmic cycle of loss and suffering." I was not born a smoker, yet how did I become one? I was not born to suffer, yet why has my life taken this turn? As it is for individuals, so it is for nations: Sri Lanka is not a land of pain and violence, yet how did it come to this? When was the fatal step taken, that brought the nation to where it is today? Can I turn back? Can this bloodied land turn back?

For a fleeting instant I think I have the answer in the serene face of the sleeping Buddha at Polonaruwa, I think that this is the solution to all my problems: frozen forever in solid granite, it is an image of stillness, of calm, of gravity. Perhaps if my heart can be stilled for a moment, that same serenity will visit me. Perhaps if Sri Lanka could stop, arrest the passing of time, cease its bartering of blood, its pain will ease too.

As I sit before the sleeping Buddha, a family comes up behind me. The kids cavort like kids are wont to do, until their mother shushes them, warning them to keep still. I hear her say to the boys, "Keep still! Look at the uncle over there, see how he sits still like a real Buddha. Go sit next to him like that and be quiet!"

My identity is lost, robbed from me, and others take me for what they want me to be. All I am is stillness now. Despite the searing heat that beats down upon me, I feel at peace. But such peace seldom lasts. Time drags us on. Deadlines await at work, and peace treaties are waiting to be signed, only to be torn up and signed again.

I climb the steps and board my Condor flight to Berlin knowing that my return to work is not back-tracking. There is never a turning back: like sharks we move relentlessly forward, despite the best of our intentions. And wherever I go, and no matter how hard I try, I will never be free of this hateful thing I call my 'Self'. One can never take a holiday from oneself. That is the tragedy of individuals and nations.

Oil lamps at the foot of the great bodhi tree, at the temple of the tooth of the Buddha in Kandy

A monk in Anuradhapura

The great Mahastupa at Anuradhapura in Sri Lanka

Fire and Brimstone
(Jogja and Solo, Central Java, 2006)

The earth shakes as they ride in on horseback.
"*Ayuh Farish, jaga-jaga! Mereka datang dengan kuda kok!*" I barely have enough time to adjust my camera before the defenders of the faith come riding into view: clad in blue fatigues and army boots, they wave their swords as their banners flutter in the wind. Here are the honour guard of the Majlis Mujahidin Indonesia, weapons flashing; slogan-shouting hotheads thirsting for a brawl. My colleague Nur, a fellow academic-activist like me, manages to steady himself as the first horse bolts past him. They fly past so close I can smell the sweat of the beasts.

"*Dengan rasa bangga, kita sambut kedatangan pria-pria Mujahid kita, anggota Majlis Mujahidin Indonesia, anggota Fron Pembela Islam, anggota Fron Pemuda Islam Solo, anggota Hizb'ut Tahrir Indonesia ...*" the speakers blare in the scorching heat of Surakarta. It is as if the swollen arteries of the city have burst open, bleeding onto the streets the ranks of angry masses. Here comes the heaving tide of the new order: ranks of disciplined bodies, marching in unison, like multicoloured streams all merging into one great flood. The deluge has arrived; to wash away the corruption of the past, to build the world anew. Here are the arms and legs, the hands and feet that will do the rebuilding, as well as the kicking and trampling that is sure to follow. The young men are clad in bright hues of orange, red, blue, green. Only the Hizb'ut Tahrir stick obstinately to their chosen black.

The banners are likewise colourful: green for the PPP, yellow for the PKS, red for the MMI, blue for the FPI. A riot of colours encrypted with a riddle of abbreviations, names of religious parties and movements reduced to random alphabets decipherable only to those who are in the know. I spy a banner that stands out among the rest. Typically, it is another one of the Hizb'ut Tahrir's: a long, black shroud that bears the profession of faith in bright white Arabic letters, with two swords of suitably Oriental provenance criss-crossing across its middle, and beneath them the slogan: *University of Jeehad*. Damn! I want that for my office, I think.

The atmosphere turns electric as a four-wheel drive comes into view. Here, at the intersection at the heart of the city next to the grand Kraton of Solo, has been scheduled the first public appearance of Ustaz Abu Bakar Ba'ashir, founder and head of the Pesantren al-Mukmin of Ngruki, figurehead of the Majlis Mujahidin Indonesia, alleged mastermind of the Bali bombing, alleged spiritual leader of the Jama'ah Islamiyah. For an instant the discipline of the young men appears to falter: the smaller boys stand on their toes trying to get a better look at their idol. The horses foam at the mouth and neigh as their riders rein them back into line. The voice on the speakers quavers: *"Dan masa sudah tiba, kita sambut ketibaan bapa kita, ustaz kita, pemimpin kita, guru kita, Ustaz Abu Bakar Ba'ashiiiiiiiiir..."*

We are swept along by the wave of emotions. Inching forward to get closer to the man himself, Nur and I suddenly realise that we are amongst the red-shirted bodyguards of the Majlis Mujahidin, holding what looks like guns. *"Eh, Farish! Itu Kalashnikov bukan?"* Nur shouts at me from behind. *"Nggak*

apa Nur, hanya plastik – yang betul saya sudah pakei di Pakistan!"
I laugh back. The guns are made of plastic.

Then before we know it, there he is, the man himself. Towering before us as he stands on the stage is Ustaz Abu Bakar Ba'ashir, with black plastic Kalashnikovs held aloft beside him, like strange epaulettes. In the searing light he appears radiant, angry and beautiful. He launches into a bitter tirade against the injustices that the world has meted out upon the Muslims, and the crowd grows angrier with every word. The list of atrocities continues: Afghanistan, Bosnia, Kashmir, Iraq, Palestine, Chechnya, Mindanao, Aceh and Lebanon. At the mention of the last, the sheer timeliness of the reference triggers the reaction long-awaited. Out come the kerosene and the lighters, and the flags of Israel and America go up in smoke. The stomping of feet and the crushing of effigies follow. The guns wave, the speakers boom; fists are shaken, angry shouts puncture the air. Surakarta's legion of radical movements have come out to welcome their hero. Ustaz Abu Bakar Ba'ashir is home, the city is his again.

While changing the roll of film in my camera, my eye chances upon a lone policeman at the street corner, his uniform hidden behind a tabloid held close to his chest. He is minding his own business; this is no longer his beat, the day belongs to the *jihadis*.

"Porno-grafi dan Porno-aksi"

I am in Solo to do preliminary research for my next project: mapping out the political geography of politicised religion across Asia, from Uzbekistan to the Moluccas. Solo and Jogja seem the obvious starting points, for here can be found practically every major player in the great game: Majlis Mujahidin, Fron Pembela Islam, Hizb'ut Tahrir, the alumni of Ngruki, the good old boys of the Darul Islam, the lot.

What makes my work all the more urgent is the seismic shift that is taking place in Indonesian politics, in particular in the area of political Islam. With the election of Din Syamsudin as the new head of the Muhamadijah organisation, the centre ground as far as Indonesian public opinion on Islam is concerned, has moved decidedly to the right. All over the country a myriad of religious groups and NGOs are calling for the speedy implementation of Shariah law. In some places – such as the province of Nangroe Aceh Darulssalam – the Shariah process is already taking place. The good flock of Solo are not about to wait for the state to give them the green light to start their campaign to impose Shariah on their own terms. The Hizb'ut Tahrir has jumped the gun by launching their own moral policing under the somewhat sexy title: *'Aksi Kontra Porno-grafi dan Porno-aksi'*, while the Fron Pemuda Islam Solo has already taken the lead by 'sweeping' off Western tourists, whom they regard as a malignant influence on public morals, from their city.

"No, we never attack any of the foreign tourists, we just scare them, politely," Ustaz Khalid assures me during my interview at the mosque run by the Fron Pemuda Islam Solo. "We walk into the hotels, demand the register of guests staying there, note down the names of Westerners and then politely tell them they are not welcome. We tell them, they will be safer in their own countries – why come to a Muslim country and bring your bad habits? We don't want your beer and bikinis here. Stay in Europe or Australia, and there you can do all the sinful things you like. *Di sana bisa makan daging babi, bukan?*" he quips, smiling.

Solo has long since been a hotbed of sorts. Its citizens, though majority Muslims, also happen to be predominantly of the *abangan* variety, who don't take their religious duties and rituals all that seriously. From the early 20th century Solo has been one of the few cities in Indonesia where support for the secular left has been strong: At its peak it was one of the centres of the Partai Komunis Indonesia (PKI), at least before the PKI was smashed by rampaging mobs of religiously conservative youth gangs let loose by the army during the anti-Communist purge of 1965. Since then, it has been a bastion for Soekarnoists of the country and it is hardly surprising that the Democratic Party (PDI) of Megawati Soekarnoputri remains strong here.

The tension in the air is palpable by the time I get there. My next stop is the headquarters of the Hizb'ut Tahrir of Indonesia, a movement that was first launched in Palestine in 1953 but which now has spread its wings all the way from London to Sydney. Solo is a major centre for their activities, and their leader is keen to impress upon me the need for moral policing and their brand of tough love.

"Young people today have lost their way," Ustaz Yoyok grumbles as he nurses his swollen ankle that was injured during a recent fall. Limping on his crutches he straightens himself as he lectures me on the evils of democracy and secularism. "This is what happens when we opt for Western-style democracy and not an Islamic government. Look at the way politics is conducted in this country, with corruption and abuse of power everywhere. Every politician is immoral, decadent, corrupt; and their corruption is reflected in the popular culture of the masses. Young people have forgotten religion, forgotten how to pray; all they think about is *dangdut* concerts and sexy performers like Inul. That's why we have launched our anti-pornography and *porno-aksi* campaign."

"*Porno-aksi?*" I ask, amazed by the plasticity of Bahasa Indonesia and the ability of Indonesians to re-invent language on the go. "*Porno-aksi* means actions and behaviour that can be seen as pornographic, like the way *dangdut* singers wiggle their bottoms when they sing and dance. That has to be stopped. Firmly. Decisively." Certainly, in his present state the Ustaz is not about to demonstrate the wiggle in any way, though I understand how serious he is. But why this great need to arrest, to stop, wiggling bottoms? I recall my meeting with Taliban leaders in Northern Pakistan who bemoaned the fact that kites were flying in the skies of Kabul, as if weightlessness itself were a problem. To that end, they banned kite-flying on the grounds that it was un-Islamic, and the kites were finally grounded. This obsession with gravity leaves me gobsmacked.

"Everything has collapsed."

Why this need for the arrest? I find my answer on the back of Nur's motorbike as we tour the devastated areas in and around Jogjakarta, scene of the recent earthquake which had levelled to the ground tens of thousands of houses. At road-side stalls, cafes and bus-stops, the incredulity of the victims is still apparent. "We don't even trust the ground anymore," says the *bechak* driver who picks me up from my rest house. "Nothing is safe, nothing can be trusted. Even the earth will open up and swallow you. Indonesia's economy has collapsed, and so has our city." Across the street is a huge placard celebrating the country's independence day. The slogan beneath it reads, 'God have mercy on Jogja and Indonesia. May we rise again.'

If there is anything that is on the rise, it is the force of resurgent Islam. Scattered across and outside the city are numerous tent-camps set up by Islamist groups like the Majlis Mujahidin Indonesia (MMI), reminiscent of scenes I had witnessed in Kashmir where the most active relief operations were carried out by Islamist groups that had transformed themselves (albeit temporarily) into NGOs. The MMI were among the first on the scene after the tsunami that wiped out the coastal settlements of Aceh, and here again they are the first on the scene to provide comfort and succour for the traumatised citizens of Jogja. At the headquarters of the MMI in Kotagede we are shown hundreds of pre-fabricated houses made of bamboo, capable of housing no less than 3,000 families, all hand-made by MMI volunteers – all of them poor, ordinary Muslims keen to demonstrate their piety. The Western-educated liberals of Jakarta, who talk of pluralism and multiculturalism in Islam, are nowhere to be seen, of course.

"Of course, that is why the people now love us. At first when we began talking of Islam and Shariah, and called for an Islamic state, they were afraid. They thought we were like the Taliban, or like the Arabs of Saudi Arabia. But now they see that we care, that we have only their welfare in mind, and that we – not the politicians, not the liberal elite, not the military, not the Western donors – are their real brothers, their real friends. We gave them food and shelter. We rebuilt their mosques, we gave them our books and we taught them real Islam. Now, thank God, they are on our side and they see that we are the only friends they really have," Ustaz Shobbarin proclaims, sitting back in his chair and sipping his sweet Javanese coffee.

Our interview at the headquarters of the Majlis Mujahidin is interrupted by phone calls and the constant entry and exit of representatives of different relief teams from all over the province. But what distracts me the most is the television set in the corner, and on its screen is the face of a man who appears to be whimpering uncontrollably. Who is he, and why was he crying, I ask.

"Oh, him? He is a Christian spy who infiltrated our organisation. He was with us for a few months but we checked him out. It turns out that his real name was Boedi and he was not a Muslim, but a Christian! So we caught him, brought him here to our office and interrogated him. We even made a video out of it, and that's what you are watching now!" the Ustaz beams. I turn to the screen again and am struck by the expression of abject fear on the face of the man. Who he is and what he has done to get himself into such a mess no longer matters. I am fixated by his tears that seems to run forever. "Don't worry," the Ustaz chips in, "We didn't kill him, just scared him a bit. Then we passed him to our friends in the police. They will sort him out." Just how the alleged spy would be 'sorted out' by the police is a question I left unasked.

Then, without my asking, the Ustaz adds, "We have always had good relations with the police and the army. Why, even when we launch our *razzias* on night clubs and cafes we call them up first, to tell them we are going to smash the place up. Many of the police support us in this, but because they have to serve this secular un-Islamic government they cannot do anything. But they let us do our good work. It was the same in Aceh, where the army was our closest supporter. The Indonesian army is not popular in Aceh, as you know, because of their conflict with the Free Aceh Movement (GAM). So when the tsunami happened, who could they call on to move aid and supplies? Us, of course! That's why we were the first to get to the airport in Aceh. We built the first camps, we cleared the jungles, we buried the bodies. The army owe us a lot for that, and they know it."

But what of the perception of the Majlis Mujahidin abroad, I venture. "Who cares what the foreigners think?" the Ustaz shoots back. "This is our country and we will work with our supporters and sympathisers to get what we want. Sometimes we have to make some small concessions, like the time when Bill Clinton came to Aceh to visit the relief camps. The general called us up and said, 'Do you mind taking down your Majlis Mujahidin flags, especially the ones near the airport, while Clinton is around? You can put them up again after he leaves!'" the Ustaz says, laughing. His laughter is met by the laughter of others in the room. It's all one happy family here. The only one crying is the Christian 'spy' on the TV.

As I leave the office of the Majlis Mujahidin, Ustaz Shobbarin runs up to me, panting. "Wait, wait! You cannot leave us without a momento of your visit. Here, this is a little present for you – sorry, it's not much, but thanks for coming!" He gives me a Majlis Mujahidin T-shirt, the logo of which looks very similar to that of Hamas': two M-16s crossed beneath the image of the Masjid al-Aqsa in Jerusalem, crowned with a hand grenade.

The success of the religio-political groups in Indonesia is something that many casual observers of Indonesian politics prefer to ignore. Despite all evidence to the contrary, outsiders still think that the kind of Islam that dominates the country is of the 'friendly, exotic' type, like a kind of Carmen Miranda multi-culti garden variety Islam, with pineapples and bananas thrown in for the exotic touch. Fewer still will acknowledge the fact that in some parts of the archipelago a virulent turf war between Muslim and Christian groups is being waged in earnest by militias like the Laskar Jihad and Laskar Kristen. Making sense of this shift towards a more confrontational form of religiously inspired sectarianism will mean having to take its adherents and agents seriously.

One last meeting is in order, and for this I have to make my way to the Pesantren al-Mukmin of Ngruki, Solo, to meet the man described by the Western press as the 'monster' behind the Bali bombing: Ustaz Abu Bakar Ba'ashir.

Light and darkness

'Monsters', if we have to use such terms, are often misunderstood creatures, and Ustaz Abu Bakar Ba'ashir is certainly misunderstood by many. Dismissed as a marginal voice in the 1980s when he first appeared on the scene, his is now one of the most relevant and resonant voices in Indonesia. Don't rely on my opinion for that, just talk to the *bechak* drivers, the stall owners, the road sweepers of the city who look upon him as their hero. While Jakarta's liberal elite are wined and dined by their patrons in Washington and invited to pontificate at length about the liberal face of Islam, Ustaz Abu Bakar Ba'ashir plies us with insipid tea and stale biscuits in his humble, almost drab, green-carpeted living room. We haven't come for tea in any case. His ideas are what I am after.

"There is no democracy in Islam," he begins. "We do not want democracy in Indonesia, but Allah-cracy. Why should there be any more discussion about the technicalities of Shariah? The Shariah is complete – so just implement it!" In the course of the long interview, the Ustaz berates the weak and feeble governments of the Muslim world for their subservience to the United States, other Western governments and donor agencies. The man has balls, I think.

In between the calls for *jihad* and for Muslims to unite against the outside world, his own world-view becomes clearer. His is a monochromatic view of the universe predicated upon a simple, dialectical logic of 'us' against 'them'. There is no room for relativism or subjectivity in the midst of the chaos and uncertainty of the times. I begin to understand the formula that has made him and his ideas so attractive to so many: it is logical, coherent and consistent. Abu Bakar Ba'ashir may be a monster to some, but to millions of ordinary Indonesians whose lives have not improved since the economic crisis of

1997-98, he offers a message of hope. This is a world that can be built, though only through sacrifice and martyrdom. It is a world with bloody frontiers, but the frontiers are permanent and fixed. In a land rocked by earthquakes and overrun by tidal waves, such permanence has its charm.

The fear of radical Islam lies in its liminality, and the fact that it has always stood at the edge of the public sphere. Ustaz Abu Bakar Ba'ashir scares the liberals of Jakarta because he brings the liminal to the centre, and renders mainstream what they would prefer to keep at the margins. Here is a subaltern discourse making its presence felt in the main streets of Solo and Jogja. A Western diplomat once asked me if it would not be better to have left the man in jail, to rot forever. No, I answered. The problem is not Ba'ashir the man, for there now exist thousands of Ba'ashirs out there, some of whom I bumped into during the demonstration in Solo. Ba'ashir is now at the centre, and if the timid hearts of the liberals are trembling, they had better come up with their own discourse for salvation and hope pretty soon.

As we get up to leave, the Ustaz shakes my hand and grips it firmly. I am struck by his long, slender fingers. His eyes are bright, like a child's, and I sense that he can see my admiration for him – despite my fear of everything he represents. "Visit us the next time you are here. It is good that you will soon be teaching at the university in Jogja, that's close to Solo. *Tapi jaga Mas Farish, banyak dosyen yang murtad disana!*" He laughs, we laugh. Like it or not, I'm one of the family now. "Come and study here, I will teach you," he says, not letting go of my hand. My God, I think, after he scares the hell out of me, he comes with the promise of comfort, acceptance, homecoming. What a genius. I have seen the light, and I am blinded.

Homecoming

My nerves are chafed, my will is spent. On my final day I return to Jogja and seek out Ibu Yus. I met her a couple of years ago, during one of my field trips to Indonesia. A chain-smoking woman whose breath smells of sweet *kretek* cigarettes, she looks as good as she did the first time I saw her, if not sexier. I have always had a thing for older women who smoke, and she understands the yearnings of a younger man in search of a woman with a strong hand.

Ibu Yus' rickety shop had moved after the earthquake, and it takes me a couple of days to track her down. When I finally get there it is dark – as it always is at her place – and she is sitting by the door, her eyes shut, a slender column of blue smoke rising from her cigarette. Barely opening her eyes, she greets me with a fine, shadowy smile. She even remembers my name: *"Ayuh Mas Farish, kembali ke Jogja lagi? Ibu senang sekali ..."* I surrender myself to her tender mercy.

On my final night in Jogja she invites me to her gallery, which doubles as her home, for dinner. We eat quietly as she speaks about the changing times. "When I was young we never saw anything like this, Mas. My life is dedicated to the cloth trade, the batiks you admire so much, the *kebayas* you get for your girlfriend. When I was young that was all I wore. But now, these people – the religious ones you study – tell us that all this is *haram*. The young girls don't like batik anymore, they won't wear the *kebaya*. Where are we heading, Mas? You are the doctor, you are the historian. Tell me, where are we heading?"

I pause as the *kretek* cracks and fizzles at the corner of my mouth. "I don't know, Ibu. I don't know." Over coffee we discuss the prospects of my return to Asia, to Java – my real home. *"Bagus kalau begitu, Mas. Ibu rasa senang kalau Mas datang kembali kesini. Tinggal di rumah 'bu saja, nggak payah cari rumah di Klaten."*

It is past midnight when I bid farewell to Ibu Yus and kiss her hands. She makes me promise that I will come back, and settle down for good. My feet take me away from her doorstep, yet the sound of her voice lingers: *"Ini tanah airmu, Mas Farish. Jangan lupa, ini tanah airmu."* Yet my 'homeland', this shattered patch of earth, bound by little else save my willful imagination and the homesick longing for an asylum, is being overrun by *jihadis* on horseback. And one wonders how long it will take before the plastic Kalashnikovs are replaced by real ones. My feet touch the ground, but its solidity offers little comfort. I am coming home, but home has left me.

Ustaz Abu Bakar Ba'ashir takes to the stage after his release from prison

Santri: Another Look at the Pesantren al-Mukmin of Abu Bakar Ba'ashir
(Surakarta, May-June 2007)

"Well, it wasn't that easy at the beginning; and you know some of the other Ustazs were not too happy with it. But we made our decision and so yes, from the end of this year we will start teaching martial arts and self-defence to the girls of our *pesantren* as well." Ustaz Muhyuddin sits uncomfortably in his seat, adjusts his collar and fiddles with his pen as we discuss the reforms and innovations that have been introduced at the Pesantren al-Mukmin of Surakarta, and ponders the outcome of his decisions. Then he lowers his voice and adds, "But, you know, not all of us are sure about this idea. After all, what will happen if the girls get too tough and out of control later? They might end up beating their husbands!"

We chuckle as we contemplate the fate of the girls at the Pondok Pesantren al-Mukmin, and the lot of their future husbands. Next to me is the producer and the cameraman from a foreign TV channel. We wade through a pool of wires and cables, snaking all around us. I desperately need to smoke, but am stuck as the filming has just begun. For a second, I long to fly out the main gates of the Pesantren and sit down with a good *kretek* and a cup of tea – but I'm here for work, I remind myself, so I have to behave like a good *santri!* So, I am back at the Pesantren I've visited five times before, to do a documentary on the daily life of the students of al-Mukmin. This is a *pesantren* that has been in the limelight since 2002 and the bombings in Bali many years ago.

Of all the *pesantrens* and *madrasahs* of Indonesia, the Pondok Pesantren al-Mukmin of Surakarta remains the most well known and, for some, the most notorious. The reason for the Pesantren's reputation is obvious when we consider that one of its teachers is none other than Ustaz Abu Bakar Ba'ashir, founder of the Pesantren al-Mukmin and *Amir* (leader) of the fiery Majlis Mujahidin Indonesia (MMI). But I know that the Pondok Pesantren al-Mukmin is a complex institution, with quite a story behind its walls. I am here to do justice to that story, and tell it the best way I can.

The gaze of the outsider

Writing and researching the *madrasahs* and *pesantrens* of Asia has been my excuse for work for the past five years. In the course of my travels and research I have to say that I've been to, and lived in, some of the grandest institutions of Muslim learning on the planet. I recall my stay at the Dar'ul Uloom of Deoband and Nadwatul Uloom of Lucknow, grand *madrasahs* of old with more than their share of respectable patina to them.

However in the course of my research I've also visited some rather dodgy institutions. Once in Pakistan I had to interview some students while in the corner of the room played a videotape of the gruesome murder and decapitation of the American journalist Daniel Pearl. The boys I was speaking to were between seven to ten years of age, and were smiling and laughing – while others lay asleep. I tried to look away from the TV as long as I could, resisting the urge to puke.

The occupational hazards of writing on *madrasahs* are plentiful. Yet, despite the countless bouts of food poisoning, malaria, being eaten alive by lice and mosquitoes and other fuzzy critters that share your bed (or the floor), I remain drawn to the world of *madrasahs* and *pesantrens*. This other world of itinerant scholars and students, hidden and shut out from the rest of the world, retains for me an allure that straddles the frontier between the exotic and mundane; it stands as living proof that there is more than one world, and that here in the midst of the everyday are pockets of alterity and difference that few of us come face-to-face with.

Pesantren al-Mukmin stands out all the more so, because so much has been written about it, but mostly by those who have not made any effort to enter its doors. I asked the Ustaz if he was tired by the incessant stream of enquiries from researchers like me.

"Well, what can you expect?" Ustaz Muhyuddin replies. "As soon as the Bali bombings happened, all fingers were pointed at us and our association with Abu Bakar Ba'ashir. But what can we do? Ba'ashir was one of the founders of the Pesantren and he remains a fixture here. And he is popular with the students as well as the community. Do they expect us to kick him out just because the Western media claimed that he was responsible for the Bali bombings?"

Ba'ashir was, and is, indeed a permanent feature of the Pesantren. In the corner a notice board lists the names of teachers who will deliver the *khutbah* sermon for the weekly Friday afternoon prayers and Ba'ashir's name is at the top of the list. Yet, oddly enough, here in the heart of the Pesantren it seems perfectly natural: his name appears on the list alongside the names of other teachers I've never heard of. I wondered how the folk of the security and intelligence community would react if they realise how ordinary Ba'ashir is in his setting at the Pesantren, and indeed how ordinary the Pesantren is.

Ngruki revisited

Writing about the Pesantren al-Mukmin is rendered all the more tiresome and laborious because of the tide of nonsense that one has to face before getting anywhere near the truth. For a start, in many of the reports on al-Mukmin and Abu Bakar Ba'ashir, the Pesantren is described as a singular institution stuck somewhere out there in the Javanese hinterland: images of a rickety wooden and bamboo structure plonked next to banana and coconut trees come to mind. This is the leitmotif against which the image of the '*jihad* factory' producing an endless stream of mad murderous fanatics is set, though nothing could be further from the truth itself. My companions from the TV channel are surprised to find a huge *pesantren* complex with a large boys' dormitory, next to which are classrooms, a mosque, a canteen and computer labs where final year students are tested on their ability to build their own websites.

The Pondok Pesantren al-Mukmin is located in the middle of Desa Ngruki, in the Kebupaten Sukoharjo, in the centre of Surakarta, Central Java. Visitors to the Ngruki will note that it is a culturally and religiously plural area with as many mosques as there are churches. In the vicinity of the Pondok Pesantren are thirteen churches (both Catholic and Protestant) that are still in use by the local Christian community. During the peak of inter-religious conflict that swept across the outer island provinces of Indonesia in the early 2000s, none of the churches in Ngruki were attacked or threatened. This reflects Surakarta's plural society, which has always accommodated religious and cultural differences, and apart from the Christian minority there has always been a strong presence of Chinese, India and Arab merchants who also play a visible role in the city's *batik* and gold trade. Surakarta has also been the base for the Central Javanese *abangan* ('nominal' Muslim) culture and was historically one of the bases for the now-extinct Communist Party of Indonesia (PKI) that was banned after 1965. Today it is one of the most important support centres for the Partai Demokrasi Indonesia-Perjuangan (PDI), the party of Megawati Soekarnoputri, former president of Indonesia and daughter of the country's founder-leader, Soekarno.

Perhaps it is this curious combination of different and diverse elements that accounts for the vitality of this town which gives off the misleading impression of being laid-back and a rather sleepy hollow. After all, despite its multiculturalism, Surakarta is also the headquarters of many radical groups ranging from the Majlis Mujahidin Indonesia to the Fron Pemuda Islam Solo to the Jundullah (Army of God) movement. Surakarta – or Solo, as it's affectionately known to the locals – is also a place known for its eclectic tastes, which includes a penchant for *satay jamu* (dog satay), as I discovered thanks to a prank played on me by my university students a year ago.

The Pesantren al-Mukmin is just one of the many schools run by the Yayasan Ngruki that was set up in the late 1960s by a group of Muslim activists and scholars, among them Abu Bakar Ba'ashir and Abdullah Sungkar. The Ngruki foundation is first and foremost an educational institution set out to provide schooling for the orphans of the city. When the Pesantren was set up in 1972, it had no more than 30 students. Today the foundation runs not only this *pesantren* that has around 1,500 boys and girls, but also a string of schools ranging from kindergartens (with walls decorated with images of a rather colourful version of Spongebob, for some reason), primary and secondary schools, as well as the Ma'ahad Aly college. Apart from that they also run a small hospital, a maternity clinic, some phone centres, a mini-market and a mineral water shop.

At the mini-market run by the Ngruki Foundation I meet a local satay-seller who seems nonplussed by the idea of yet another academic coming to his little *desa* to do a report on the Pesantren. "I really don't see what the hullabaloo is about," Ichwan tells me as we chew on his satay (which he assures me is made from *bona fide* chicken and not cute puppies). "When the Americans and Australians complain about Ba'ashir and the Pesantren, why don't they send their people here to see what life is like in Ngruki itself? See that big drain that cuts through our *kampong*? Before the Pesantren was built it was basically everyone's dustbin and toilet! You could smell the stink right across town. But the Pesantren people cleaned it up. They provided watchmen and guard patrols at night. They built the roads, cleaned the alleys, sorted out the electricity supply and all the other things that nobody cared to do. That's why we are grateful to the Pesantren, even if Ba'ashir is there. Did the Americans do that? Did the Australians do that? Why doesn't John Howard come here and clean our drains for us?"

I will suggest that to the Prime Minister of Australia if ever I see him, I assure Ichwan. But what puzzles me is the reputation of Ngruki and the image of Ba'ashir himself in the eyes of his local community. The man has been vilified by all and sundry, yet here on his turf he is seen as a kindly old father-figure, so beloved by his motley crew of boys from the Majlis Mujahidin. What gives?

Pastoral care and faith politics

"The reason why the people of Desa Ngruki accept us and send their children to our *pesantren* is that they know that we are not what the media has made us out to be," Ustaz Nurhadi assures me as we stroll around the inner court of the largest dormitory of the *pesantren*. He is one of the more than three hundred teachers employed by the Ngruki Foundation and like the rest of his colleagues, he works here on a contract. In return for his teaching services he is given housing, rice and food subsidies, and insists that his salary is better than that of a teacher employed in the state schools of Indonesia. "That's why the Desa community is close to us, and we in turn are close to them. We never forget that this is our community and we need to care for it first. We were set up as a foundation to care for orphans and our agenda has always been education. Every boy and girl that ends up here is taken care of by us for six years, after which they return to their parents. Here we teach them everything, from Arabic and English (both of which are compulsory) to geography, mathematics, computing and sports. All these subjects are taught to the boys and girls equally – there is no favouritism and we make sure our girls are taught to the same level as the boys."

I pause for a second as Ustaz Nurhadi and Ustaz Fikri take me on a tour of the girls' wing of the *pesantren*, a gendered space totally cut off from the other half where the boys are. Comparing the two, the girls' wing is evidently cleaner, although the girls are just as noisy as their male counterparts. Peals of laughter emanate from the girls' rooms as some of them shout, "Hey, Mister, what's your name!" Along the neat pathways are speakers mounted on poles, where occasionally public announcements are made in English. "Rohaiza, please come to the reception room," the speakers blare over the crackle of white noise. "We are trying to teach the *santris* English, and that is why the public announcement are made in English," explains Ustaz Nurhadi.

I ask Ustaz Fikri if I can take a photograph of the girls' quarters, to which he replies, "Of course you can take photos. After all, CIA spy satellites have photographed us millions of times already!" The two Ustazs laugh, as I do, cognisant of the ridiculousness of the situation. This *pesantren* has been spied on, monitored and infiltrated more than all the other *madrasahs* and *pesantrens* of Indonesia put together. A group of female students scuttle past with brightly coloured bags that have *Hello Kitty* stickers on them. I wonder if any security expert out there has written a paper about the ideological links between *Hello Kitty* and resurgent political Islam, especially its more radical form?

As we head back to the main boys' dormitory, the final bell rings to mark the end of the day. It is time for prayers and, after that, the boys will be free to be boys and do what boys do: play football and basketball and generally loaf about till dinner is served. By now I have come to know some of them, and they refer to me as 'Ustaz Farish al-Almani', he who hails from that faraway land called Germany. Usually, it doesn't take us long before we start talking about football and girls.

'Forget Manchester, I prefer Milan.'

Wildan is adamant that he is right. The rest of his roommates vote for Chelsea, Manchester, and Liverpool, but to underscore his difference he opts for Milan as his favourite team. Our first meeting was a case of mistaken identities and erroneous assumptions. He thought I was too young to be a lecturer and I though he was too young to be among the seniors. Despite his small stature, Wildan is fifteen years of age, the eldest son in a family with two kids. His parents have sent him and his sister here to Ngruki all the way from Jakarta.

While filming the documentary on al-Mukmin, Wildan ends up being our model student for the day. We set about chatting while he is filmed doing everything that any other teenage kid does daily: eating, studying, playing, even waking up. Once again I find myself in the unenviable position of having to tell a story that would otherwise be so painfully dull, had it not been set in Ngruki. Wildan himself doesn't seem to see what the fuss is all about, and why he and his school mates have been singled out for media attention.

"My parents have sent me here because they cannot send me to the more expensive schools, but I really like it here. All my friends are here; we study, eat, play football and basketball after break, and we share everything." I join them as we eat from the same plastic plate – overflowing with rice to fill hungry teenagers' bellies – on the canteen floor. I tell them that I've done the same in all the *madrasahs* I've been to over the years, and how in India we polished off a huge pile of chapatis in less than five minutes. They in turn ask me questions about India, Pakistan and the other countries I have been to, and what life in Germany is like. "It's okay, the food is normally potatoes, and occasionally you get beaten up by skinheads in the park if you're not careful. The girls are pretty though …"

Here we enter forbidden territory and the boys begin to giggle as boys often do when the subject of the opposite sex is brought up. But the cameraman is filming us while we eat, so, for once, the boys behave themselves. I ask Wildan what it's like to be a student at al-Mukmin, and whether he is worried about his future and the reputation of the place. As if reading from a prepared script, he gives me the same reply I have heard so many times before. "Why should we be worried? Everyone here knows what goes on in the Pesantren, and we are not hiding anything. Why do they keep worrying about us? Why don't they just come here and see for themselves, and leave us alone?"

My liberal conscience is struck by the plaintive appeal of Wildan as we sit on the porch in front of his class, the camera rolling behind me, and Wildan's image is being captured for posterity. The scene is beautiful and even the fading sunlight is obliging, giving the shoot a decidedly soft 'instant coffee' ad effect. The academic in me is forced to wrestle with his conscience as he tries to get to the truth of the matter, in the same way that a journalist has to get the story right. But this is not the first time I have had to write against the grain of popular prejudice, if only to show that a *pesantren* that is home to Wildan, the fan of Milan, is not that den of radical obscurantism it has been made out to be. "We are not monsters, you know," Wildan adds, and he is, of course, right.

At the root of my dilemma is the convoluted and ambiguous image and identity of the Pesantren al-Mukmin. On the one hand, the Pesantren's organic links to its community is evident for all to see, but on the other hand this *pesantren* is also linked to some of its alumni who were said to be responsible for the attacks in Bali. Practically everyone has an opinion about the place, and often that opinion is divided. One cannot be neutral with regards to al-Mukmin and what it represents, yet is that not the first criteria for anyone who claims to be an academic? By this stage I find myself prepared to kill for a cigarette, and so I slip out to have a smoke.

While pacing the alleys and backstreets around the Pesantren I watch the tide of human traffic that ebbs and flows around the community, a tiny Indonesia in microcosm, shot in close-up. Girls in tight jeans, with their flowing jet-black hair uncovered, cycle past, while crudely painted signs on the walls remind them that they are in a '*jilbab* zone' and that they should have their heads covered. The *dangdut* music that wafts out of the sheltered roadside stalls is raunchy and suitably hot for the time of the day, and the singer on the radio blares, *'Abang, saya suka yang keras, yang keras!'* 'Brother, I like it hard, real hard.' This is the Indonesia I know, and which I regard as home – with all its pleasant contradictions and irony. So where does Abu Bakar Ba'ashir fit into all this, he of monochromatic vision and reputation? All that is left to complete the documentary is to meet the man himself and record the words of the one who has been summarily labelled a monster by the West.

The monster unplugged

Long before the interview with Ustaz Abu Bakar Ba'ashir is finalised, I warn my companions of what to expect. Four times have I met the man and without fail he has been consistent in his words and deeds. While in every way he represents values that are in direct contradiction to all that I hold dear, I have come to respect this man who can be accused of anything, save being a politician. Ba'ashir doesn't play politics – in fact, he thinks it is *haram* – and is not a diplomat either. Upon meeting him I present him with a photo that I took of him earlier (which was excluded from an exhibition I had organised in Europe on the grounds that it was a photograph of a terrorist). That's bound to amuse him, I think.

"So they call me a monster? Well, it means I must be doing something right!" Ba'ashir beams as I hand over the photograph. "That's what they are doing to me now. In the past they wanted to destroy me, wreck my reputation, demonise me. But when the Americans and their Zionist masters realised that they had failed, they opted for another tactic. Now they want to silence me completely, to pretend I don't exist."

Ba'ashir then goes on one of his long diatribes against the machinations of the dreaded West against Islam, a speech I've heard many times before. What I really want to know, however, is how he feels about people like me barging into his home time and again, this time with a camera crew in tow, and cluttering his space with wires, lamps and all sorts of techno gadgets. So I get to the point just when he begins a new speech on the neo-cons of Washington and their puppet rulers in the Muslim world. "Ustaz Abu, how do you feel when people like me call on you again and again for interviews like this? Aren't you fed up with the likes of me by now, and don't you find this media attention taxing?"

"Look, it's like this: they in the West have made up their minds about me, and it doesn't matter what you do or how hard you try, you won't be able to convince them otherwise. Even if you showed that there is nothing sinister going on in this *pesantren*, and you film the *santris* playing football, studying computers, learning English – they have made up their minds. So for me, it doesn't really matter. They call me a monster? That's good! It means that they still hate me, and if that be the case, then I am still on the right path. I do not hide the fact that I oppose their Western secular capitalist values and that is why they fear me so much. They are not afraid of violent Muslims, but they are afraid of thinking ones. That is why for them Ba'ashir is more dangerous than bombs and guns!"

On the one hand stands the mighty hegemon of the West, and on the other are the figures of Ba'ashir and his followers. In this zero-sum logic, objectivity and academic distance have long become redundant. Ba'ashir is fixed on his aim to spook the West as much as the Western media is fixated on demonising him. Yet in the midst of this, one wonders what lies ahead for the *santris* of al-Mukmin, including young Wildan and his dreams of watching Milan win the Italian Cup?

As the interview winds down I chat with Ustaz Abu about a number of things, technical and academic: what he thinks of Said Sabbiq's *Usul-ul Fiqh* as a text for Islamic jurisprudence; his view of the Tablighi Jama'at movement; whether the Dars-e Nizami curriculum of the Indian *madrasahs* are compatible with those in Southeast Asia, and the legal status of adopted children in Islam. Alert as ever, he pounced on the last question with relish, "Does that mean your divorce is over and done with? Are you going to adopt a child? If so, go ahead. Adoption is highly esteemed in Islam and our Prophet has set the example. Good for you to adopt a child, marry a Javanese girl and come home to where you belong."

That he can remember details of my personal life strikes a chord with me, and reminds me why this man is so popular with his students and the local community. The other Ustazs tell me that when Ba'ashir was finally released from prison he was welcomed back to Desa Ngruki by the entire community, and thousands of people lined the streets to sing his praises and kiss his hands. Above us the satellites of the world's intelligence services may be criss-crossing the heavens to get a better look at the man they call the monster. But here on the ground, Ustaz Abu Bakar Ba'ashir rules, still.

I leave the Pesantren after passing on to Wildan and his roommates a large bag of Mars bars and other things to ruin their appetite. The boys are playing football and basketball in the inner court. The al-Mukmin all-stars seem set on winning as many a tournament as they can in the future. Next time, I'll remember to get Wildan a Milan T-shirt.

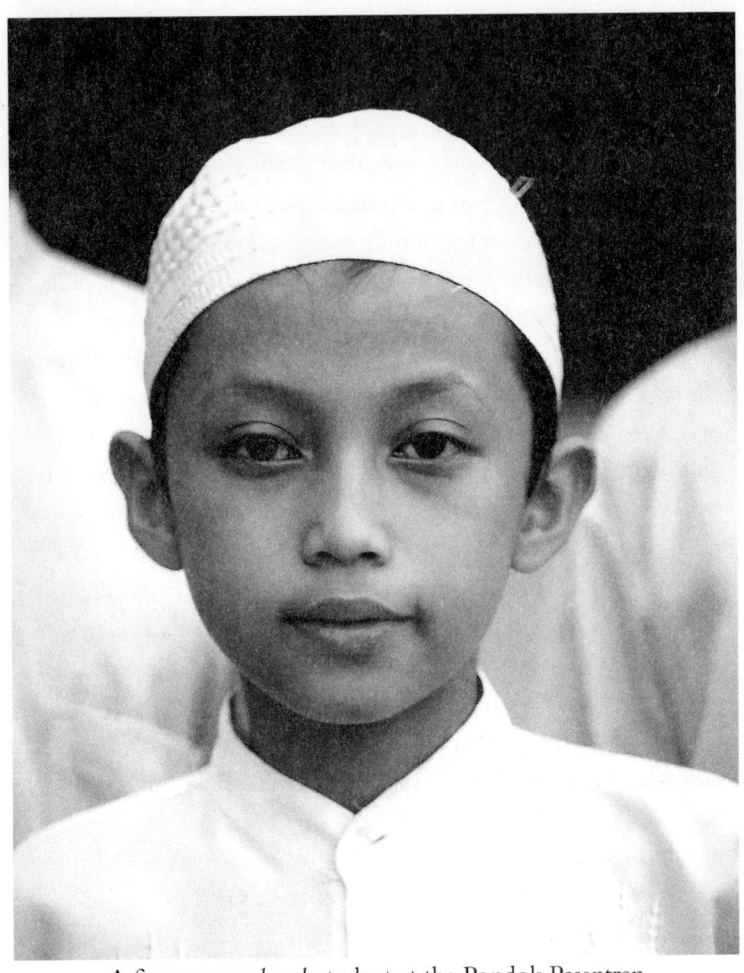

A first year *madrasah* student at the Pondok Pesantren al-Mukmin, Ngruki, Surakarta

The Merchant of Memories
(From the author's Jogjakarta notebook)

"Regard ...

Look at me.

Remember me for what I was; for this was my state then. This was how I dressed and posed for the camera. My smile, which is somewhat patinated now, was once a living, breathing smile. You may not know why I was smiling, but believe me, the reason for my happiness then was real, too.

I had hopes and dreams, as you do now. I lived a life not entirely different from yours; with moments of joy and distress, pain and pleasure attended me and memories trailed in my wake. I was a living being, an entire life that began with a moan and ended with a full-stop.

Now that I am lying in your hands, be tender with me. Regard me with care. It was a life, now passed. In your hands you hold my history. My entirety submits to your tender caress, so clasp me gently and do not let me go."

The photograph speaks to me as I run my fingers across its crenulated edges, the thin film of coffee-brown patina that it had acquired whispers its historical value. The rain pelts down mercilessly. I am dog-tired, worn to the bone and aching all over. Another field trip drawing to its close, my body is crying for sleep but my eyes refuse to obey. I puff on my *kretek* and force my eyes open in the gloom of the semi-darkness that washes over the balcony of my hotel room. I am home, in Java.

"*Masuk tak, Pak?*" Pak Sur says as he puffs on his own damp *kretek*.

"*Masuk, Pak. Ini bisa masuk. Bagus sekali. Warnanya mantap, cocok. Ada yang lain, Pak?*" I say.

And so our midnight bartering continues, in the rainy gloom of another night in my beloved Jogjakarta. One by one, I pore over the photos as they come into my hands, peering at them through my magnifying glass. Pak Sur has done well this time; a bumper crop of old photographs, some albumen tints, some early kodaks.

I have known Pak Sur for several years now, and he is one of my regular runners who ply the lanes and back roads of Central Java on my behalf, seeking out artefacts and antiquities. The forlorn son of Java returns, and seeks the help of his runner to recover the memory of times past. Like one of the replicants in the *Blade Runner*, I am seeking a past to call my own, some tentative link – no matter how fragile – to the home I lost long before I was even born.

Pak Sur travels around on his motorbike, regardless of the weather and the conditions of the roads. Often I lie awake at night wondering if he is all right, safe and well, on his excursions. I worry if he gets home safely, or if he finds a place to sleep on one of his longer journeys up north, like to the coastal cities of the Pesisir.

His large frame belies a body that has been wracked by work and age. He smokes heavily, as heavyly as I do, and his constant bouts of coughing, spewing forth thick wads of sticky sputum, remind me of my own fate in the years to come if I fail to curb the habit. I greet him at my balcony. He is drenched in the rain, covered in mud and shivering with a fever, but the father of three, who has sons to send to college, refuses to listen to reason and, like me, is hell-bent on a slow suicide with nicotine.

Once we drove up Mount Sumbing on his bike together to seek out a *keris* that had been secreted away by a crusty old man living in his humble hut in a tobacco field on the slopes of the mountain. We got there in the middle of the night, drank the obligatory half dozen cups of sweet tea, and then commenced to discuss the tricky subject that led me there in the first place. Our efforts were well rewarded: thanks to Pak Sur I found the *keris* that I now call my own, an 18th century Central Javanese blade with the fabled *blarak ngirid pamor* and a *dapor* in the mode of *Singha Barong*. '*Wong Jowo?*' the old codger asked of me. '*Wis pasti romo, kulo wong Jowo*' came my reply. I will never cease to be thankful to Pak Sur for that.

But if there is another thing that I have to be grateful to Pak Sur for, it is for getting me all those rare and old photographs that have gone into my personal collection over the years. With each passing year and with each visit I make, the tentacles of my memory dig deeper and deeper into the soil of Java. My roots strike down, ever downwards, searching for that historical life-blood of memories past that bind me to this land stronger than coils of steel.

I pause for a moment to give my eyes a rest. Too much to remember and too much to look at, I shut my eyes as Pak Sur and I take a long, languid drag on our murderous *kreteks*.

In the darkness my mind wanders back to that night in the auditorium of the School of Oriental and African Studies, almost two decades ago, while I was a student there. A fortunate chain of events – missing the bus back to my dingy flat that smelled of rotten cabbages, the pathetic absence of hard cash in my wallet that made a taxi ride an impossibility – meant that I had to linger a little longer before getting home. Scheduled that night was a performance of the SOAS gamelan orchestra, and I walked in to while away the time while nursing a tepid cup of English tea.

As the first notes of the gamelan sounded, a singular motion began deep in my chest. It paused for a moment, then stirred and announced itself in no uncertain terms. Slowly but surely, a forgotten memory that had been planted and left there eons ago was roused from its slumber. A dead memory was awakened by the sound that connected my present to the past. My eyes began to water, uncontrollably, for reasons that I could not comprehend. No voice, no touch, no kiss had hitherto moved me as much as the singular sound of the gamelan. The stories of my childhood, about a family's past, had been passed from great-grandmother to mother, mother to son, rang true for the first time. This sound, this music, this voice, was the voice of my ancestral land calling to me. Though I would tarry a little longer in Europe for a decade or so, on that night I planned my exit, and my homecoming was prepared.

In the years to come I would dress myself in the garb of the historian, with musk and dust as my perfume. I read philosophy and theory, but my passion lay elsewhere. The nightly visits to the libraries were like secret liaisons for me, a coveted hour alone with my beloved, my Java. In the quiet hours up on the third floor of the SOAS library I would keep my weekly appointment with her, kneeling before her as I slowly peeled open the pages of books about her. My fingers would glide slowly and gently above the pages of the books by Dutch Orientalists. My eyes would drink in the images: the maps, the lithographs, the woodcuts and the photos. I wanted her so badly that it hurt.

Today, the eyes of this historian have grown older and more tired. But that love, that first love, has never died. In courting my beloved, Pak Sur is my best man. He brings her to me in bundles of snapshots. Family photos of people I have never met, whose lives I cannot imagine. Their voices I have never heard, nor their laughter, nor their cries. But during these nightly visits of Pak Sur, I am comforted by the though that bit by bit, photo by photo, my love comes back to me.

I have often wondered how or why people would sell their family photos. At times, I have chanced upon entire albums that would otherwise have been lost or sold as scrap paper to the pavement paper-wallah. The replicant that I am yearns for memories of a life I never had. Yet, there are those who are quite content to sell away theirs for a bob or two.

On other occasions I doubt my own vampirish thirst for the memories of others; fearful that one day this obsession with history would reveal its true ghoulish aspect. Like a grave-robber I feed on the corpse of the past. Shiva Bhairava enthroned on a mound of skulls, lord of the grave, devourer of the dead. What have I become then? Devourer of memories, a cannibal of history?

The snakes within my conscience intertwine, wrapping themselves around my fingers as I hold one photo after another. No acquisition comes without paying the price. No sweet embrace of the beloved comes without the bitter aftertaste of guilt.

'Look at me,' the photo says. *'My entirety submits to your tender caresses, so clasp me gently and do not let me go.'*

I close my eyes, and think of home.

Javanese lass with bicycle

In the Land of the Living Shadows
(From the author's Jogjakarta notebook)

I savour the sweet accent of the *kretek* as it fizzes and pops in my mouth, lips curled around its moist phallic totem, inhaling the smoke of my adopted land and basking in the languid warmth of another humid night in Jogjakarta.

Pak Sulis and I lean back in our rattan chairs, and in the distance we hear the toot-toots of bikes and *bechaks* as the day comes to a close and night descends. Down the road from the Seno Budoyo, across the northern courtyard of the Jogja palace, a *tante* is grilling some *satay* for us. The singular light bulb that hangs from the ceiling of the *pendopo* sways a little, responding to the gentle push of a welcomed breeze that enters our shared space unannounced. We talk softly, and we talk of politics. Malaysian politics, to be exact.

"*Iyo, jelas sekali Mas Farish. Badawi orangnya halus, tapi 'gaimana mahu jadi pemimpin? Pemimpin mestinya ganteng, mantap. Halus dalam kraton bisa, tapi dalam dunia politik nggak cocok, nggak klop.*

"*Nanti orang bilang dia sama dengan Prabu Salya. Mahu jadi raja, tapi orangnya nggak mahu perang. Waduh, di Bharatayudha keretanya dipandu lemah sekali. Bila Rajuna nembak senjata cakranya, lewat ke sini, lewat ke sana. Matinya Karna kerana itu – Prabu Salya yang bikin repot semuanya. Takut menang, takut kalah: akhirnya tewas Adipati Karna dibunuh Adipati Rajuna.*

"Bila Karna sudah tewas, baru mahu menanggis. Tapi apa gunanya?

"Makanya orang yang mahu jadi raja, jadi pemimpin, harus ganteng juga: berani lawan, berani tewas. Hidup hanya sekali, tapi matinya mesti pas! Jangan mati begitu Mas, buruk jadi namamu, tak dikenali siapa pun. Bila saat mati tiba, terima dengan berani, bukan seperti Prabu Salya..."

The rise and fall of the former Prime Minister of Malaysia is dressed in suitably epic garb and viewed in the context of the great war between the Pandawas and Korawas. Pak Sulis's comparison strikes me as somewhat apt, knowing the context of Malaysia and the Mahabharata well. In the epic tale of the conflict between the warring cousins, Prabu Salya was the king whose role it was to drive the chariot of Karna, the forlorn Pandawa abandoned by his mother to the care of the opposing Korawas.

In the chariot duel between Arjuna and Karna, Prabu Salya was the one who drove Karna's vehicle while Arjuna enjoyed the double advantage of having Krishna – a god, no less – to serve as his charioteer. Prabu Salya's benevolent aspect and his divided loyalties between the Pandawas and Korawas drove him to distraction. Unwilling to witness the death of his beloved Arjuna, he was likewise unable to prevent the death of his equally beloved Karna. Thus it came to pass that the name of the hapless unfortunate King would go down in history as the ruler whose lack of will and purpose doomed him forever.

Again, I am bemused by the stories that Pak Sulis tells me. We have known each other for almost a decade, and my regular trips to Jogja, where I lecture monthly, are always rewarding thanks to the evening trysts we share together, in the company of *wayang* aficionados.

Pak Sulis is a *wayang* puppet maker, and in all of Jogja I know of none other who can match the work of his tiny little workshop. Save the tourist tat for the backpackers who pile into the city at the peak of summer. Nah, I ain't gonna waste my dosh on some hammered-out Arjuna or Sayudhana that was cut out in a week. I want the real stuff, and if you want the real stuff, then this is where you should head.

Over the past two years Pak Sulis and Pak Yudi have been kitting me out for my own private collection of characters. I promised them real gold leaf and so off to Europe I went, on my lecture tours, to look for the genuine article. If you want a private set for yourself that will last for posterity, then you ought to get an expert to make one for you with real *prodo* (gold leaf).

Our first character was Karna – my favourite tragic hero of the Mahabharata – and that earned me some brownie points from the man who knew his *wayangs* by heart. "Hahaha! You must be some kind of intellectual then, to want Karna first. At least you know what you want and what you are buying. Some of the people who come here just want the pretty characters without knowing that they are the losers and the jokers in the story!"

I have watched my beloved Jogja change over the past decade and I brace myself for the day when it will completely lose its lustre. Already the old coffee shops are slowly being replaced by upmarket coffee houses and bars, backpacker *losmens* and internet cafes. But here, at least in Pak Sulis's workshop behind the Seno Budoyo, time stalls, and the days pass slowly.

From early on my fascination for Pak Sulis lies in the fact that he is no tourist attraction. Sure, every night there is the same ritual of greeting the tourists arriving in buses who come to gawk in amazement at his *wayang* puppets; and I've heard the same litany of business-speak being repeated time and again. "It's always Arjuna that they want, the tourists. I tell them he is a hero and that he was the playboy of the Pandawas, and then next thing I know, another Arjuna is wrapped up in brown paper and they walk off happy. But why don't they ever ask for a Karna, a Suyodhana, an Indra, or a Srikandi? Even a Rawana would make me happy!"

I suppose what moves me the most is that the knowledge underlining his trade is the bittersweet taste of nostalgia, for a past that will likely be eclipsed forever. The *wayangs* are still popular, but pop and *sinetron* on TV have done their worst to slowly erode away any trace of common residual memory. "The gods of old are dying, Mas Farish." Gotterdammerung: the twilight is here and sooner than later the sun-chariot will depart and never return again.

Understanding is a constant effort for me, an on-going battle. My tired eyes have grown jaded, and the will to believe is thin. The Orientalists wrote of a people steeped in lore and culture, where every valley and hill resounded with the sweet humming of music and the mesmerizing tones of the gamelan. Java was a stage where the human pageant was enacted before your eyes. But we know that is not true, or at least no longer. Today, only a handful like Pak Sulis and Pak Yudi keep the traditions alive, and fewer still know them by heart. I am amazed by them because they are such a living depository of antiquarian knowledge; walking libraries, the pair of them.

And so our nights are spent talking about the world around us, seen through the prism of the *wayang* where shadows come to life and where the ephemeral and transient are more real than reality itself. In the land of the shadows, Pak Sulis is a god. The *dalangs* of the *wayang* depend on his hands to give life to the stories they tell. His blade and hammer cut the sheets of dried leather to form shapes that then are animated. The static visage of a Karna can be bent into angles undreamed of.

This time round I've come to pick up my Suyodhana, two months in the making. Pak Yudi beams as the Korawan prince is taken out of the cupboard. Pak Sulis examines me as I eye my coveted baddie. *"Gaimana, Mas Farish? Pas?"*

"Pas, Pak – pas sekali!"

We chat about the vicissitudes of Malaysian and Indonesian politics, leather gods in attendance and the shadows looming above and behind us. *"Kalau Perdana Menteri yang baru ini gaimana pula? Mirip Suyodhono, kok?"* *"Iyo Pak, tapi ada lemahnya juga – seperti Suyodhono – menanti Sang Bimo yang mencari peha kirinya!"*

We laugh as the night covers us, our private language spoken and understood by only a few. In this, my little asylum, I seek refuge in the dead and the familiar, in a past rapidly diminishing. Our world is shrinking, Pak Sulis, and the gods have left. And all that remains are us – puppeteers and politicians.

An *abdi dalem* (palace staff) working at the Kraton of Jogjakarta

Rat Pancake
Or, the lament for the bakso meatball that got away...
(From the author's Jogjakarta journal, March 2008)

The alleys of my beloved Jogjakarta are littered with the remnants of street vermin that have been run over by the incessant traffic of that bustling city. A testimony to the endurance of that species genus hyrax, are the number of flattened rats on the streets of Jogja. It is simply astounding. What with the broiling heat and sun that batters the city daily, the flattened rats are, in time, dried as well, lending the carcasses the curious resemblance of wayang kulit puppets that only require a stick to prop them up before they are put on display. Surely, one day someone will chance upon the idea of collecting these dried remains and selling them off (albeit dusted and polished) to tourists.

One night, after a particularly long day at the university followed by an even longer interview, I was crawling back to my hotel on Jalan Tirtodipuran, when I came across one of these flattened fuzzy fellows on the road, under the golden light of the street lamp. It seemed to be looking up at me, as if there was something it wished to say. So I lit up a kretek and listened to its story.

"Ah, so the good doctor returns. How goes it, home-seeking wanderer? Still in search of a homeland that you never left? Or has work gotten to you? And is that the reason you are delirious enough to think that I am talking to you?

"Please excuse my somewhat two-dimensional aspect for the moment. I am — or was — a rather more well-rounded rodent not too long ago. My former amplitude and depth may not be readily apparent to you now, weary-eyed as you are in your present state; but let me assure you that there was no more rounded a rat roaming these streets and alleys as yours truly at one time. My dimensions were ample and generous, and my, were ladies ever so inclined to exclaim as soon as I announced my presence.

"Unbeknownst to you, you were in my quiet regard as well. From the dark and cool confines of the bushes and dustbins I spied your lingering presence and I knew you well. Yes, whenever you came to Jogja and stayed at that hotel I was there, in perpetual silent attendance. On more than one occasion I have popped over to the balcony and into your hotel room to rummage through your bin, harbouring the vain hope that you may have left something for me to dine on. But alas, academic-wanderers such as yourself seem to live on a diet of kreteks and iced tea, so there was little for me.

"I recall the good old days when the tourists were plenty. And how generous they were. Ah, my heart pines for that happy day when that silly tourist — a vegetarian no less — emptied her bowl of bakso noodles down the drain in disgust, unaware of the simple fact that meatballs are, after all, made of meat. What a night that was! My sudden appearance by her sandaled feet sent her and her boyfriend helter-skelter, Canon and Leica in hand, generous tip scattered all over the cobblestones.

When I looked at the offering she was kind enough to leave me, I could not believe my luck: Four — count them, dear fellow, four — bakso meatballs in all their undigested glory; four succulent spheres of juicy meat, wrapped in ribbons of promises and lightly powdered with grains of sweet-smelling street-dust. Ah, the heavens smiled upon me, and what a feast it was.

"And I spied you too, oh beamish boy, as in uffish thought you stood by the tum-tum tree: tired, sweaty, worn out, dejected and lonely. I have followed you in your fantasies and wanderings as you sought that patch of earth to call your home. And while you walked through the market at the alun-alun while the Aidilfitri celebrations were in full swing, I was there too, munching contently on a bag of pop corn left behind by some kid who greeted my warm hello with a scream. Oh frabjous day! Kaloo-kajay! I chortled in joy.

"You see my friend, we are closer to each other than you may think: for we are both unseen. Forever wandering, looking for that place to call home, for that asylum – beyond the padded cell you have signed yourself into. And you and I are both misunderstood at times, as is the fate of all composite creatures whose porcupine-like demeanour manifests itself occasionally, spikes and pin-pricks being the only caresses we can muster. Like me, you are off-putting to most, and like me, you too make them run, cry, and whimper in terror.

"So think not of me in my present state, dear fellow. Your kretek is almost burned out, which means that our unlikely appointment is about to draw to a close. Head back to the hotel now and rest your head on the pillow. Think of me as you drift off to sleep and say your prayers so that the demons do not come again tonight. I will, as always, rustle in your bin for the odd scrap or two which I know won't be there. And remember your rodent friend who always kept you in mind, even during your long absences, and remember me in all my former rotundity and full-belliedness. Welcome home Suryaputra, Cahayadiningrat. You never left, but you just didn't know it."

And with that, I put out my kretek and went to back to my hotel room.

Antique shop in Jogjakarta

Saigon, The Devouring City
(Saigon, 2007)

Braised pig's brains in garlic may not be to everyone's taste, but there are, however, places in the world where the adventurous may take their taste-buds to places hitherto untravelled by many, and Vietnam is one of them. I've had prehistoric horseshoe crabs (or limules), that I am told is best washed down with snake and scorpion whisky, here before; and the cute little doggies with their curled fuzzy tails you find at the market of Hanoi are not sold as pets.

Puffing away on my cigarette at the balcony of the Hotel Majestic in Saigon's District One, I watch the ebb and flow of the Saigon river as it convulses, spewing forth its cargo of human flotsam and merchandise. As ships travel back and forth along this serpentine crook, and ferries dart across the river carrying humans sitting anxiously on their purring motorbikes, cyclo drivers whizzed past prowling for passengers, and trucks dragging huge containers ply the roads from dawn till dusk, and long after. Saigon. Ho Chi Minh City. The commercial centre of Vietnam is crammed with the young and the restless, in a city on speed. You need ear-plugs and cast-iron lungs to live here.

Coming from Berlin where I currently reside, I am struck by the similarities between the two cities: both have been terrain contested by opposing political forces; both have played their mediatic roles in the Cold War, being the ideological battlefields as the Eastern and Western blocs vied for global domination; both have become backdrops to spectacular scenes that remain etched forever in the collective political consciousness of an entire generation.

If Berlin is remembered for the wall that no longer exists and Checkpoint Charlie with its bunkers and barbed wire over which hundreds jumped and many lost theirs lives, then Saigon has been rendered immortal by the pens of authors and cameras of journalists. Here was where the Viet Cong lobbed their mortar shells across the river I am looking at in the fading glow of twilight, here was where American flags were burned by protestors and monks, where it was finally lowered and hurriedly packed up before being flown off in a helicopter, where the tanks of the North Vietnamese Army rammed through the gates of the Reunification Palace. Of all the cities in Southeast Asia, Saigon ranks right at the top as one of the most written about: over-determined and pregnant with symbolic meaning.

I am in Saigon in the company of Lois Lane, and the Majestic is our resting place. One needs a resting place in Saigon as the city does not spare its inhabitants, both locals and tourists. This is a city on the move, and one with an appetite. Saigon pulsates, convulses, devours; and it grows and morphs like some gigantic concrete organism that is slowly but ever so deliberately eating its way across the earth.

Like Berlin, which has been my home for the past five years, Saigon's architecture is a hotchpotch of clumsy and ill-planned affronts to good taste.

It seems to be the recurrent malady of all developing countries that growth is literally that: a sweaty, feverish primordial compulsion to propagate and multiply as fast as possible, heedless of the consequences. All over Vietnam and in cities like

Saigon in particular, one is struck by the absence of what might pass as building regulations. Owners demolish their tiniest and narrowest of shop houses overnight and then construct their own cash-sodden mega-follies as high as they possibly can, with a remarkable lack of concern for aesthetics, symmetry or even colour co-ordination. And so what used to be a row of cream and sienna-tinted tree-lined colonial-era shop houses is soon transformed into a row of narrow apartment blocks and shop lots, each of a distinct colour and architecture. A five-storey lemon-green apartment complex, five metres wide and fifty metres tall, is flanked by a seven-storey birthday cake of a business centre, painted in watermelon pink with gold flourishes and decked with neo-romanesque balconies, which in turn is flanked by an eight-storey block in sky blue with gilded rococo hints and a Japanese-styled penthouse as its crowning glory. The dream of every self-made Malaysian *Datuk* is here for all to see: money talks, and it also builds, and in Saigon it makes mountains out of molehills, with the cityscape reduced to mismatched patches of architectural expressionism that matches the greed and bad taste of the owners, and the conceit of the residents. These overcrowded residences have the appearance of cartoon inspired wheezing accordions, or a row of broken, uneven teeth that you see on the bad guys in C-grade movies. This city is too unbelievably surreal; and still it grows and grows.

Wandering through the streets and alleys of Saigon that are permanently choked with motorcycle traffic, we meander along until occasionally we stumble across what used to be a colonial monument or two. The *Hotel de Ville* that stands proudly in front of a square is flanked by the famous Rex Hotel, once the watering hole of American army officers and made famous in the film *Apocalypse Now*. Further along we dodge the speeding cyclos until we find the old Cathedral of Notre Dame, flanked by the somewhat inspiring (and nostalgia-inducing) Central

Post Office of Saigon, which remains as one of the few relics of the French colonial era. On the pillars that line its *façade* are etched the names of the great and the good of *La Belle France*: Descartes, Hugo, et al. The pantheon of *Paris-Ile-de-France* are all here, though the locals don't seem to care much for Descartes' philosophical meditations or his attempts to prove the infallibility of human reason. There is money to be made here, and the meditations can tarry for a while longer.

Parking myself outside the post office I look at the environs and watch the human drama unfolding in the big city. Tourist buses drop off groups of elderly middle-classed Francophone tourists at the Cathedral, where they are lectured on the achievements of the French in Asia during the 19th century. I don't tag along for the history lesson, but I assume that there would be little mention of the thousands of Vietnamese who died in the rubber estates of Indochina under French rule, or of the ignominious defeat of the their troops at Dien Bien Phu. Sugar-sweet tommyrot is all that is required to put a smile on the faces of the rich tourists, so academic objectivity and historical accuracy can go fly a kite. Remember: money is to be made, and nostalgia tourism pays just as well as any other form of trade these days.

Across the road, in the middle of the square, young newly-wed couples don their tuxedos and bridal gowns in the blistering heat to be photographed, quickly before the mascara begins to run. The couples take their turn, for each one seems bent on having a shot taken with the Cathedral in the background for some reason. Nobody seems keen to be photographed next to the post office with its statue of a Vietnamese couple standing close together in a suitably Soviet-realist manner. Marx and Mary (with 'Uncle' Ho Chi Minh in between), side by side in a city which has become the capitalist gateway for a (officially, at least) communist state. The deconstructionist in me revels at the joyful mess of colourful contradictions and juxtapositions.

Heartless and pulsating

Saigon is a city without a heart, yet it has a pulse.

That is literally true: looking for its core, we could not find one; for what used to be the centre, District One, has been sidestepped and marginalised as the city grows and expands in all directions. What drives this city day and night? The Saigon river runs its course through its centre and the main trunk road which serves as the primal vein for its human bloodline follows, running parallel to it. But the river does not stab at the city's heart, for it has none. So what is keeping it – Saigon – alive? All day long the traffic continues unabated, and not even for a minute does it pause for rest.

But by the second day, I detect the signs of routine: at 11.00 am just as I am having my first cigarette on the balcony, an elderly woman and a young boy shuffle laboriously past, pushing what appears to be a tiny bicycle with an enormous trolley in front, overloaded with goods of some kind. Every day, they pass me by at the same appointed hour, going along on their own lonely errand. The faces grow familiar, and a pattern begins to settle in.

From the vantage point of the Majestic's rooftop I see the city laid out before me and, unlike the other cities of Asia, Saigon has at least been spared defacement by skyscrapers. Instead, the city spreads itself horizontally, as if it fell out of the sky and then splattered itself in all directions, turning fields of grass into yards of concrete. In the unending battle between green and grey, grey seems to be winning. Why are these people here? Why have they come to the city? What drives them on, to toil and trade till ungodly hours, only to start the day again after a few hours of respite?

"We come back, we always come back," Lucien the temple-keeper insists. Lucien Tranh Ngoc is all of seventy-five years of age and is the keeper of the Cantonese Ming family temple in Cholon, down in the old part of Chinatown in Western Saigon. On a tour of the temples, churches and mosques of the city, we bump into him and it proves to be serendipitous. In his short-sleeved shirt and short pants and slippers, he cuts an unlikely figure for the role of the guardian of all that is hallowed and revered, but that remains his lot, nonetheless. In this pulsing city where memory is short, Lucien is the custodian of history itself.

Lucien is happy to show us around the place and takes pride in the fact that his family has been in Vietnam for eighteen generations now. "We are descendants of the Ming dynasty and our ancestors came from Canton. But we all grew up here and we became Vietnamese, and we lived through all the historic eras of Vietnam. We served under the Viet rulers, the Chinese, then the French, and the Americans. I studied in France, you know? In Lyon and then Grenoble. Why, I was even a member of the French Indochinese army and I carried the flag of France at the head of my battalion! We fought with the French, and, later, against them; but I am proud that we remain Vietnamese," he adds.

We converse in a clumsy creole French, and Lucien waxes about the glory days of the Empire and the *mission civilisatrice* of the colonial masters. "Hehehe ... I was in France as a young boy and I travelled across Europe. I even had a French girlfriend, but then my grandfather asked me to come back to Vietnam and take part in the building of the country. Now, most of my family members have left and I am one of the few who remain. I have two passports, you know? I'm Vietnamese but also French. *Je suis Francais quand meme!*" he chuckles as he shows me the family treasure cabinet, with hats and uniforms going back to the last years of the Ming dynasty. There are mandarin robes, hats, letters and flags – like the prerequisites for some elaborate costume drama waiting to be filmed and passed off as yet another multi-culti gem of Asian cinema.

But Lucien doesn't need to star in some soap opera; he is the drama itself. He has lived through all the turbulent years that witnessed the rise and fall of the Ngo Dihn Diem dictatorship – undoubtedly one of the most detested rulers in Asia – that was propped up by the Americans who regarded Diem as 'a son of a bitch, but at least our son of a bitch'. He witnessed the pitiful exit of the French and the coming of the Yanks when Saigon was turned into an overheated, and over-sexed fleshpot for GIs on leave. He was here when the city was bombed every night by the Viet Cong camped on the other side of the river. He was around when Ngo Dihn Diem and his brother were forced to flee the Presidential palace in the dead of night by crawling through an underground tunnel all the way to Cha Tam Church down the road, where they were shot and stabbed to death the following day by their own troops. And he was here when the tanks of the North Vietnamese Army rolled into town with red flags a-fluttering and portraits of Uncle Ho held aloft.

"Back then when they – *les Nordiste*s – won, everyone panicked. All the Europeans and Americans left, and the other immigrants, the Chinese and Indians, were terrified. We all thought the Viet Cong would round us up and send us to the death camps. This quarter, Cholon, where the Chinese lived, was almost empty. *Maintenant il y a que les nordistes ici!* Everyone packed their things and got the hell out of here as quickly as they could. They took to the boats and went out to sea. Many of them died, most of them never came back. But I stayed. I watched the Communists take over, I lived under Communist rule, and now I am still here. The country is still communist but we have a capitalist economy! Hahaha! Now even the white people are back, and Saigon is full of

French tourists and French residents who have opened up French restaurants. *Donc, voilà: Plus ça change, plus c'est la même chose.* It's like the old days again!" Lucien's boyish laugh slips through his yellowed teeth and dimpled smile. The good old days are back again. Break out the bubbly, *quand meme*!

"But why are you still here, Lucien? What keeps you here in Saigon?" was the question I needed to ask. "Me? I'm too old to go anywhere now. I love my Saigon. I know, I know, the streets are full of traffic and the pollution gets worse and worse," he laments as he puffs on his Saigon cigarette. "But this is where I have lived most my life and this is where our family shrine is. This is our family shrine. Our family. Our past. Our history. This is where I belong."

Lucien's attachment to his shrine strikes me as poignant. Around us, hidden behind wafting clouds of incense and altar smoke, sit solemn figures of his ancestors. On the central altar is the figure of the clan's founder, flank by other illustrious notables whose deeds are remembered by Lucien who once carried the French Tricolour at the head of his battalion, but whose legendary exploits have all been forgotten by the younger generation who race headlong to their own appointed destiny in that hybrid communist-capitalist Utopia. In the middle of the shrine sit three cobweb-covered chairs made of ebony laced with intricate arabesques in tortoise-shell. "These chairs are special: nobody can sit on them because they are for the founders of the Ming dynasty. That big one in the middle, that's for the Ming emperor himself," Lucien says. Not that the emperor is about to make a sudden appearance, I thought – even postmodern Saigon has its limits.

Lucien offers us a cup of coffee and a smoke before we go. As we leave, he calls out to us, "Remember to come back. Old Lucien may not be here when you return, but remember to come back. They all come back. We all do. We all come back." I will probably never see him again, but promise to return nevertheless.

Hell and torment

"They got the hell out of here." Lucien's words linger in my mind as I reflect on the frenetic pace of this city. Rushing, running, speeding along – hell-bent on getting somewhere, but where or why? And what fuels this race?

For a communist country the Vietnamese seem to believe a lot, still. If their insatiable appetite for all things weird and exotic serves to sustain their bodies, their faith in the future seems to sustain their ambitions. One is struck by how young the country feels, and the smell of teen spirit hangs heavy in the air. The lingering image of Saigon one takes back is that of blurred faces racing past on motorbikes. A nation and a city kept afloat by faith in the free market and the promise of free enterprise, but at what cost?

Back in the days of the Cold War the cold warriors lamented the spread of Godless communism across Asia, and Vietnam was cast in an appropriately devilish light as the source of the contagion. The faithless proles had taken to the jungles with the dreaded Viet Cong in their black pyjamas and farmer's hats lurking behind every bush with a Kalashnikov in hand, grenades in their pockets, ready to shoot in the name of the Communist International. When Saigon fell to the NVA in 1975 it seemed as if all hell would break loose, and the red devil himself would come home to roost. Thousands of Europeans, Chinese and Indian migrants fled, certain that their bastions of capitalism and freedom of religion would be razed to the ground.

Three decades later one finds the capitalist pulse beating strongest here, and even Uncle Ho has been packaged as a tourist attraction and a commodity. Plaster busts of Ho Chi Minh are sold by street kids to backpackers for a dollar, as are old Viet Cong posters celebrating 'our glorious three thousand feats of arms against the Western Imperialists'. Everything has a price, anything can be commodified here. Hell, even communism can be packaged and sold.

What is more, God seems to have made a comeback of sorts, though in a very post-modern ecumenical way. Contrary to the fears of many, the Communists did not destroy the cathedrals, temples and mosques of the city. Instead, many were turned into schools and kindergartens, as under the communist regime education and healthcare became priorities. I look for the old Jamia mosque of District One that was built by the Indian Muslim merchants who came from Punjab in the 1920s, only to find that, though the building still stands, it has been converted into a motorcycle park. The Muslims have left, leaving only a handful behind. In the mosque I find a framed photograph of a tree in Australia with a trunk that is bent over sideways. The caption beneath the faded photo reads, 'See proof of God in tree: tree bending to pray in direction of Mecca.'

The temples are far more interesting places to visit, not only for their architectural attractions but also because they seem to be the only places in town where one is spared the din of traffic and the pollution. Hopping from one temple to another across District One to Cholon, the temples blur into one long, uninterrupted succession of devotional vignettes. The crowd gathered has come to pray. We end up at the Temple of the Jade Emperor in the northern Da Cao district, and the place mercifully lends itself to some tasteful postcard shots.

Taking a break from the obligations of the researcher-tourist, I give my camera a rest and sit to watch the spectacle of throngs of devotees coming to pray for everything under the sun: a marriage partner, a child, a promotion, a spanking new motorcycle. In the hushed silence of the red-lined walls and corridors of the rain-soaked temple, the faithful pray in earnest. In the inner sanctum I walk into the 'Hall of Ten Hells' where the walls are lined with carved wooden depictions of the torments in hell, where an unfortunate guest is given his or her just deserts. Neither Marx nor Jesus – and not even Uncle Ho – can save you here, for this is the domain of Thanh Hoang, the King of Hell himself, and he doesn't look like someone who can be bought.

The panels tell the story of human folly, reminiscent of the depictions of the seven cardinal sins and the retribution that follows. Looking closely at them in the dim candlelight I see the guilty being led to the supreme judge of heaven, having their case read aloud and the sentence meted out by nasty-looking pot-bellied devils and demons. The greedy, the lazy, the faithless, the conceited, are all here; and their punishments are depicted in spine-chilling detail: one of them is chopped into pieces and cooked in a pot; another is sawn in half; a sorry-looking chap is impaled on a stake, while another bloke is being eaten alive by dogs and pigs; and I wonder if that will be my fate.

Everywhere around me I see faces with hope and desire painted on them, as if acts of prayer had to be acted out with some theatrical effect, in case the gods are not fully convinced of your sincerity. Plaintive expressions of longing are intermingled with outward demonstrations of piety often acted out by the desperate tugging on bell-ropes, the scraping of foreheads on floor-stones and the excited shuffling of joss sticks. Yet the contradictions are obvious, and almost embarrassingly so: the hurried denizens of the sleepless city pray in earnest for the miraculous transformation from rags to riches, while the carvings in the Hall of Ten Hells reminds them where greed will lead them to. Outside the motorbikes and cyclos race pass, here inside the temple the guilty and condemned remain in a hell that is static and unmoving.

Saigon is perhaps a mirror of the real Vietnam of today, and as a mirror it reflects better than Hanoi, for it does not distort or hide the truth. In this city one finds the country with warts and all, and upon closer inspection the body politics is not that unappealing. The extended topography of the city embodies the ever-expanding catalogue of experiences of being a Vietnamese today: the battle-hardened Viet Cong and NVA veterans have aged and traded in their Kalashnikovs for Nissans and Toyotas. The younger generation on the other hand probably think that 'Sputnik' is a club, and seem more interested in Nike and Zara. No doubt, in time they will be able to afford the real ones, too. Uncle Ho's benign smile shines through and illuminates the confines of the Grand Post Office where his portrait hangs above the stamp counters, but few recall his speeches or his poems.

On my last night in Saigon I park my arse at a strategic spot by the roadside to get one last parting shot of the city in motion, but the motorbikes are too fast for me to focus and the opportunity is lost. This city will not stop for anyone. On the way back to the airport our taxi races past new apartment blocks and shopping centres under construction. Somewhere in the midst of this sprawling city the old woman and the young boy are pushing their cart burdened with goods. Out there in Cholon, the venerable Lucien sits in his temple guarding history and memory while singing paeans to the glories of old.

I never found the city's heart, but I can feel its pulse.

Pulse, pulse.

Pulse.

Qur'an and Cricket

Newlyweds in downtown Ho Chi Minh City

In the Shadow of Ataturk
(Turkey, 2007)

She sleeps. And in her restless sleep she cradles close to her bosom fourteen million souls.

Odalisque-like, she lies stretched across the mighty Bosphorus; ancient mother, whose tresses have been touched by many a great man before. Emperors and kings have vied for her attention. Her walls were clawed and sullied, yet with each passing tide that came and went her dignity was restored to her. Sultan Mehmet Fatih conquered her last, and did it with a stratagem that baffled his Byzantine adversaries: maybe swine cannot fly, but he managed to transport his warships overland, over the hills, to surprise his enemy. The subsequent siege that led to the capitulation of the Byzantines spelled the death of that Empire, and confirmed her status as the gem of the Mediterranean, the Jewel of Europe: Istanbul's doors were opened to Sultan Mehmet Fatih, the Conqueror.

I adore this city. Four times have I visited it, and with each visit my fondness for this metropole grows. Istanbul sprawls across a wide expanse of hills, and in her dark and narrow lanes one finds a world in convulsion. She is the world itself, and in her one finds people of every nation: Turks, Asians, Europeans, Africans, Caucasians, Russians; all crisscrossing and bustling past one another, driven by hurried ambition – only to be halted by the scent of coffee or the mesmerizing trails of blue-grey smoke from the *shisha* around the corner. The city of tulips and conspiracies, the one that is immortalised in Orhan Pamuk's *My Name Is Red*. And justifiably so.

I've had quite my share of Turkish conspiracies: during one of my earlier visits I took part in a conference on political Islam; only to be reminded by unreconstructed Kemalists in grey suits that there were some things I could not mention in positive terms: the Ottoman past, the legacy of the Sultans, the role of Islam in politics. Needless to say, only the highest of praises were to be bestowed upon Mustafa Kemal, the great Turk and father of the modern republic. Might as well stare at the ceiling and wait for coffee to be served, I thought to myself then.

This beleaguered city was, and remains, a site of contestation: the symbols of the Republic are up for grabs, and everywhere one looks the emblems of the nation – the colour red and the star and crescent – are being fought over in earnest. I have seen the stringiest of micro-bikinis adorned with the star and crescent, strategically located to entice just the right amount of patriotic fervour by the natural inclinations of the male libido.

On the other side of the ideological fence the headscarves have grown in number, as have the furore and indignation of the secularists who are no less fanatical than their shrouded counterparts. Istanbul, and Turkey by extension, is kept on its toes by the question that has yet to be answered: what will be the future of this nation? Will Turkey witness the resurrection of the Caliphate, or will she take the plunge and finally hop over into the European fold? A difficult question to answer for a country literally divided by two continents.

Before this, my visits have been of a more academic nature: museum-hopping and antique-collecting taking up much of my time. This time round I have come to visit the local Turkish Islamist non-governmental organisations, and they prove to be just as organised and determined as their antagonists.

In the course of the week I trudge along to visit the Islamists' offices and political centres. Our hosts welcome us in the ceremonial fashion loathed by the secular Kemalists, for whom the very utterance '*Assalamualaikum*' spells the death-knell of their secular vision of Turkey. While the secularists bemoan the passing of Ataturk's legacy and wait on their knees as Turkey plies for entry into the EU, the Islamists seem no less adamant in their quest for a Turkey that is at once Muslim and Turkish, Oriental and European at the same time.

"Why should Turkey not be allowed into Europe?" asks Mustafa, whose Saddam-like fuzzy moustache goes rather well with his cultivated pot-belly. "What are these Europeans afraid of? That we Turks will lay siege to Vienna once more?" Mustafa's roaring laughter rips across the huge warehouse of the Islamist relief NGO I have come to visit, and echoes down the hall. Around me I see stacks and stacks of clothes of all types and sizes, destined to be tagged, packed, and then shipped out to the needy all over the Muslim world. He explains that theirs is the only NGO that sends new clothes (as opposed to tatty old rejects) out to families in distress in Africa, South Asia and Europe. I recall my trip to the earthquake-devastated region of Kashmir, and how well organised and welcoming the Turkish Islamist NGOs were, and how dedicated their staff appeared in comparison to all the others.

"Look at what we are doing here: we are sending out brand new clothes to people who need them. We provide education, healthcare, security, logistics, everything in fact. Where is the crime in this? Is it because we are Muslims that we are not welcomed by the government? Is it because Turkey is Muslim that we are not welcomed in Europe? And they call themselves liberals and democrats. Bah!!"

Mustafa has a point, of course, and anyone can see that. As is the case in many other parts of the Muslim world where the failure of the state has opened the way for religiously-inspired movements like his to come to the fore, offering basic services that should be handled by the government. Mustafa's frustration is apparent, as is his commitment to Islam. Yet this is Turkey, and ironically one cannot be too Muslim here these days.

Following the tour of his office and the warehouse, Mustafa takes us to the mosque for prayers. In the dim light the faithful stand before the presence of God and offer their humble salutations. Children run about and pull each others' hair; some laugh, others cry. Their fathers remain silent and upright in religious contemplation, their mothers sit at the back and gossip. This is living Islam, and it has been like this for centuries. How can Turkey deny what it is?

Looking at the domed ceiling of the Suleimaniya mosque I marvel at the ingenuity of Ottoman architecture: in the past the interior of the mosque used to be lit by huge braziers and wicker lamps. The damp, oily black smoke would rise to the ceiling, to be collected as it cooled in hidden ducts that were built within the dome itself. Slowly the liquid smoke would filter down and be accumulated in tiny pots, to be sifted, mixed with oil and gum, and made into ink. That ink would then be used to write the *Qur'ans*. An economy of resources at work: light to smoke, smoke to ink, ink to books, books that were read in the same light that would produce the ink. The hermetically sealed world of the Ottomans was a riddle that kept its answer to itself. But this world no longer exists and, in its absence, its admirers pray for its return while its detractors will do anything, and everything, to prevent it.

Courts and courtesans

My Turkish hosts are keen to impress upon me the greatness of things past, and so invariably I find myself wandering around the courtyards of the Topkapi Sarayi, the fabled palace-complex of the Ottoman Sultans.

This is not the first time I am visiting the palace, but the place never ceases to amaze and dumfound me. The view from the private garden of the Sultan is breathtaking, and from the verandah of the final, innermost courtyard one beholds the Bosphorus and the city stretched out before one's eyes. In the distance I can clearly see the Kemal Ataturk bridge that spans the wide expanse between Europe and Asia, and even here, in the inner sanctum of the Ottomans, Ataturk's shadow looms large. Walking past the *Sultanlale* tulips now in full bloom, I cannot help but indulge in a private fantasy, to see the place devoid of tourists – save myself, of course. I wonder how the Sultans would have felt about their private gardens becoming the stomping ground of crowds of American, European and Japanese backpackers? But my guide Mehmet, is fidgeting next to me and I sense that he is about to launch into one of his speeches again.

"Look at that!" Mehmet exclaims. "How beautiful it is, how grand, how great. We were great once! We were the centre of the world, the conquerors of Europe," he extols. "Not that you Asians were not great too, of course," Mehmet quickly corrects himself. "You must have done some great things as well, built mosques, written some books, and the like. But look at that – we were really, really great; we were the greatest!"

I politely assure Mehmet that Malaysians have never produced anything as great – or as expensive – as the grand palaces of the Ottomans. All we seem to be capable of building are roads and highways that break up and swallow cars, and which miraculously sprout toll-booths when you are not looking.

As Mehmet savours the afterglow of his self-induced orgasm, I reflect upon the logic of displacement and association, something I've grown used to by now. In practically every Muslim country I've visited, nostalgia and authenticity cast their spells. From Morocco to Pakistan to Indonesia, ordinary Muslims — be they taxi drivers, school teachers, clerks or lumpen activists — seem ever so inclined to return to the past in order to escape, albeit momentarily, the squalid realities of the present. The imperial architects who built these grand palaces and mosques probably had in mind precisely that effect, knowing that their works would pass down forever into posterity, long after their bones crumbled to dust.

Yet Mehmet, like so many others whom I've met in my travels, fails to recognise the obvious. The greatness that he so dearly relishes and covets was never for the likes of him. The Topkapi Sarayi whose gates have been flung open to let in the unwashed masses — including the odd academic — was never meant for the public. It was strictly for the eyes of the Sultan and his harem only. Had Mehmet lived in the time of the Ottoman Sultans, I wonder if he would have loved them as much as he does now? It would have been impossible for him to even step into the palace.

While Mehmet revels in the splendours of the Ottomans, he turns decidedly coy when I press him for details. Realising that I may have done my reading, I think he begins to suspect that I may know more about the place than he does. As the tourists perambulate along well-trodden paths, I snatch a quiet moment to reflect on the bloody history of the palace.

Topkapi Sarayi remains a model of classical Ottoman architecture at its best. Its green paths, gardens and courtyards are decidedly Oriental in the way that they connect spaces while keeping them apart. The shrubs and bushes, the patches of tulips and the water-ways, have not been placed there for mere decoration; they marked the constantly-policed frontiers of class, status and power that kept the Sultan at the top of the violent social and political hierarchy that the Ottomans so jealously guarded. Although modest in size and strangely humble by its lack of height, it has never failed to amaze visitors. Despite its relatively diminutiveness, this was the centre of an empire that stretched from Morocco to the Arabian *hijaz*, from northern Sudan all the way to the Caucasus.

With so much power – sacred, profane and symbolic – invested in such a small patch of earth, it is no surprise that life in the palace, and its harem in particular, was stifling. The suffocating confines of the chambers echo many acts of suffocation, strangulation, poisonings, stabbings, beheadings and other assorted forms of bloodlust within its walls. Hurrem Sultana, the favourite wife of Sultan Suleiman the Magnificent, conducted all her grisly campaigns against her rivals and enemies from the plush comfort of the harem, her thirst for blood only sated when there were no more foes left to kill. Her successors – the Sultanas Safiye, Kosem, Turhan, Gulnus, Ruhsah, Mihrisah et al. – were likewise adept at the homicidal practices in the Sublime Porte. Needless to say, Mehmet the reconstructed Islamist was not inclined to wax lyrical about the murderous exploits of the beloved ladies of his court.

The Islamists in my company don't take too kindly to my own impromptu lecture on Ottoman history, for in their eyes the Ottomans were among the last and greatest of the Muslim powers who were authentically Islamic. How, I ask, can they explain away the fact that the greatest Ottoman Sultan – Suleiman the Magnificent – came to power only after his father Selim the Grim murdered all his brothers and cousins – the youngest then being five years of age – by having them garrotted with violin strings? After my lecture, they leave the plush surroundings of the Topkapi with lingering doubts in mind. I, for my part, have never been all that enchanted with the palace: the smell of blood still hangs in the air.

Nostalgia, again

It is impossible to escape the lure of nostalgia in this city. Notwithstanding the trappings of modernity that litters the urban landscape of Istanbul, the place is decidedly ancient. Anyone with even a smattering of history would realise that while walking on the cobblestones of the city, one is stepping on the same stones that were once trod on by Crusaders, Mamelukes and Janisaries.

At dusk I find myself navigating the circuitous back lanes and alleyways in the vicinity of the Beyezid mosque. Eager to stay as far away as possible from the yobs and touts of the grand bazaar, I trace my steps along familiar walkways I have come to know by heart. Here, in the narrow lanes, is where you find the good stuff: real Ottoman antiques, carpets and *kilims*, brass *hookas*, *meershaum* pipes, the lot.

I'm looking for the shop of an old acquaintance of mine, Halim Cam, who happens to be a runner and dealer of fine cloths and tapestries. But the urban geography of Istanbul is about as still as the Bosphorus that slices through it: what used to be a market street selling table cloths is now a row of shops selling rather tacky underwear and suspiciously-cheap suits. I spy a shop selling tight-fitting men's boxer shorts, with cheeky slogans branded on the butt. One says 'Follow Me'. Another pleads 'Spank Me'. I choose one of the latter as a memento, and harbour the playful wish that it would come in handy one day.

Then I fall upon an even narrower alley. This leads to Halim's place, one that is grotty and baleful, as it has always been. I enter his Aladdin's cave and finding him smoking a Samson cigarette. He offers me one immediately with the customary smile he wears. "Welcome back, Dr Noor! How long will you stay this time?"

The good thing about being a dedicated collector of antiques is that it also serves me well as a researcher. Dealers and runners know as much about the murky underworld of finance and politics as any good political analyst, and they often keep their ears close to the ground. I've taken Halim seriously from the first time I met him, and he's never failed me once. I ask him what he has for me and he takes down a gorgeous rose-pink *uchetek* – a three-fold skirt *kaftan* – that was worn by the noble ladies of court in the Ottoman era. "Look at the sleeves and you will be surprised!" Halim beams. He is right: upon inspection, the sleeves are indeed spectacular, opened at the cuffs to hang languidly down, they are decorated with open-work stitching with complex intertwining motifs of tulips. We both come to the same conclusion and agree that the piece in question is mid to late 19th century, probably Sultan Abdul Aziz period, and Halim is more than pleased to sell it to me.

"It's so nice to sell my things to people who understand and appreciate them. Istanbul is so vulgar these days; so many Russians and Americans – all money but no taste! I can sell them anything and they will buy it!"

Halim is apparently in need of an audience and I have time to kill. I settle on his divan and sip his tea as he vents his spleen.

"Ustad, do you think Turkey should join Europe? Look at Istanbul today. Already the Russians are buying property all over the coast and along the Black Sea. But cost of living is rising, and don't even ask about the price of petrol! My brother had to sell his car, so expensive it was to run it! And the black economy is still so strong, so big. They tell us the economy is doing well, that our clothes are being sold in Europe, that our currency is stronger now than before. But where is all that money? Do you see it?"

I ask Halim if he paid taxes himself. He grins mischievously and replies without batting an eyelid, "Of course not! If I declared all my earnings I would be finished! Hahaha! Do you think all those dealers in the bazaar declare their earnings? If they make a hundred thousand Lira they will only declare ten! And so will I; we need to eat and live, you know."

Who buys all this stuff, I ask him. "Mostly foreign collectors and dealers like you," Halim shyly admits. "But nowadays, there are Turkish collectors too. One of them just bought the entire set of velvet-embroidered Qur'an covers. He must be rich: they cost twelve thousand dollars, the lot. But the younger Turks, they don't care about the past and they don't buy any of these things, like that *uchetek* you bought – that could be worn by a bride at a wedding. These days, Turkish girls prefer to buy designer clothes made in Italy or France!"

Halim laments the passing of time and the decline of taste, in just as much the same way that the Islamists do. Yet his grief stems as much from the loss of revenue as from the erasure of history. Even nostalgia can be measured with dollars and cents or, in this case, liras.

Twilight of empire

On my final night in Istanbul I decide to return to an old haunt of mine, despite the fact that I'm almost broke and know that I can't afford more than a glass of drink. Crossing the straits I direct the taxi to the Ciragan Palace Hotel, which gets its name from the somewhat garish Ciragan Palace next door.

The Ciragan Palace, like her equally impressive sister the Beylerbeyi Palace, are stark reminders of the collapse of Ottoman power. At the time of the collapse, sultans Abdul Aziz, Abdul Mecid and Abdul Hamid II were husks of men whose power was more symbolic than real. Indebted to foreign banks and lending houses, they spent their wealth ostentatiously. They tried to emulate the monarchs and royals of Western Europe, in a vain attempt to qualify as modern rulers in a modern age. There was, however, one crucial difference between the Ottoman Sultans of the late 19th century and their Western peers: while the Kings of Europe presided over empires that were growing, Turkey was by then considered the sick man of Europe whose empire was shrinking. Unfortunately, as Turkey's imperial territory shrank, her palaces grew. The marbled and tiled confines of the Topkapi Sarayi were no longer deemed appropriate, nor to the liking of 'enlightened' monarchs bent on modernisation and progress. Both the Ciragan and Beylerbeyi palaces are an awkward, if not downright clumsy, ensemble of tastes and styles: Gothic arches stand next to Corinthian pillars, with overhanging mock rococo flourishes and pseudo-Oriental Arabo-Turkish embellishments. The Sultans who commissioned these architectural outrages were themselves an unstable lot of *bon vivants* and ne'er-do-wells: Sultan Murad V managed to warm his throne for a mere ninety days before he was kicked out, to spend the rest of his life as a token ruler in his gilded cage.

That night I found myself sipping my drink with the Bosphorus in front of me and Murad V's playground to my right. A century after the last Ottoman Sultan was taken to exile on board the *HMS Malaya*, a Malaysian academic dines on fish next to the palace of the king.

Staring across the straits at the European side of Istanbul, I wonder where this country is heading. Deeply Turkish, Muslim, Asiatic and European, all at the same time, Turkey is a country of bold stripes painted in solid hues, but a multi-culti paradise it ain't. Raising embarrassing questions can earn you a bullet in the head here. While the Islamists wax eloquent about the Ottoman past, their secular opponents try their best to drag out as many skeletons from the Ottomans' closet, and as often, as they can. Neither side will even begin to address the Armenian legacy, and the Kurdish question remains unasked. Confident, assertive yet in denial, this nation with its selective memory and episodes of forgetfulness fascinates me still. I pocket the last handful of liras, but not before flipping one into the Bosphorus for good luck.

A Dialogue in Hell
(Amsterdam, 2007)

"He was shot right there, just outside the town hall, as he was coming out. Then somehow he managed to stumble across the road, till he ended up here where he collapsed. The man who shot him followed, stood over him, and then took out his gun and shot him again. Theo cried out, 'Look, don't do this! We can talk about this! We can talk about this!' But he didn't stop. He shot him again, then stabbed him and cut his throat. Everyone around was shocked, but nobody could do anything. It was too late. In a matter of minutes , Theo was dead and the assassin's letter was stuck to his chest, pierced by the knife that stabbed him in the heart."

Martein recounts the morning when he was woken up by the sound of people crying outside his flat. As he emerged into the street outside, he saw a neighbour walking hurriedly past, her face bathed in tears. "Oh my God, oh my God, they have killed him! They have killed him! Right there in the street!" he heard her muttering.

"Who? Who has been killed? What has happened?" he asked. "Theo! Theo Van Gogh! They murdered him right there in the street and his body is lying there right now!" Martein recounts.

"I could not believe it. I ran, ran all the way. The spot where he was killed is just around the corner of my house, no more than two hundred metres away. As I turned the corner I saw him in the distance, and the closer I got the weaker my legs felt. I needed to see for myself but my feet couldn't carry me. It's odd how memory plays tricks on you. I could have sworn that he was lying there with his head in my direction. But in all the photos I saw in the newspapers later that day he seemed to be lying the other way round. But there he was, Theo Van Gogh, whom we all knew. And he was lying dead in a pool of his own blood, and the police were questioning those who witnessed the incident …"

9.00 am
Linnaeusstraat,
Amsterdam

The time, co-ordinates and circumstances of the murder of Theo Van Gogh are well known by now. Shot and then stabbed several times by a young Muslim by the name of Muhammad Buyeri, the controversial Dutch director whose ancestor was one of the most famous painters of Holland, was killed in broad daylight in a busy street in the middle of Amsterdam.

I stand on the exact spot where Theo's body lay, where his assassin fired the fatal shot and plunged his knife into the body of his victim. At my feet are the bullet holes that have since attained a patina of their own, covered by the dust, exposed to the smoke of traffic, levelled by the trampling of feet and baked by the summer sun. "You are standing on the spot where my friend was killed," Martein says to me. Were it not for Martein's impromptu tour, I would probably have walked over the spot without knowing.

"You know what? The craziest thing about the whole story is that Theo chose to live here, in this part of Amsterdam where all the Moroccans and Turks live," Martein reflects. Behind him is a Turkish bar, a typical coffee-house that doubles as bar and rendezvous point for older Turks who while away their time playing cards or backgammon. "Despite what his killer thought, Theo was deeply sympathetic towards the Moroccans and Turks; he supported many of their young directors and artistes; he constantly promoted their work, and he was profoundly anti-racist. His murderer called him a Muslim-hater because of the documentary he did on the abuse of Muslim women, but he forgot that Theo was also the biggest critic of the extreme-right in Holland. He hated the racist right, and saved most of his venom and anger for the conservative right-wingers whom he regarded as fascists. The tragedy of his killing was that many who didn't know him thought that he was killed for being a racist. That's really, really sad. It makes me want to scream when I think about it."

The silent scream

From Martein's flat, with its infernal rickety Dutch staircase that strains your legs and your butt every time you go up, we walk to the park nearby where he shows me the monument erected in honour of Theo Van Gogh. It is called *The Scream*, and stands as a poignant reminder of the passing of one of Holland's most famous sons. A series of steel silhouettes show a face in profile, overlapping one another with the mouth slowly opening until it finally bursts forth in a silent scream for the loss of free speech, or freedom itself. The plaque nearby merely names the artist who designed it. There is no mention of Theo, nor the circumstances of his murder.

"They took so long to decide what form the monument should take, and in the end they could not even mention the fact that Theo was murdered by one of his own countrymen. The politically-correct lobby were afraid of reprisals; some thought that it might offend the Muslims; others thought that it may be used by the extreme right to garner more support for their anti-immigration policy. Either way, it's Theo who was killed and we cannot even remember him properly," Martein says.

The silent scream of the monument is heard across the park and resonates through the quarter where Theo lived. Around me I see families at play in the park, couples cuddling and kissing, women sunbathing – despite the plummeting temperature – and gay couples walking hand-in-hand. "This is all about to go, you know. This country is now divided between the *burqas* and the bimbos. We don't talk to one another anymore. This is not the Holland I grew up in." Martein's mourning for a Holland he has lost matches my own. This is not the Holland I knew either.

I am in Amsterdam at the invitation of the Dutch Labour Party, the PVDA. Many years ago, as a visiting lecturer in Leiden, I had my taste of another Holland where one could indeed call the place the land of libertarianism at its purest.

My memories are of a country where the sauna was my second home, and my daily routine involved the constant to-ing and fro-ing from the university to the clubs. Absinthe was in at the time.

I remember admiring the Dutch for their openness and capacity to give and receive insults playfully and in equal measure. This was a nation constantly pushing the limit, with one leg precariously hung over the horizon of possibility. At times it even seemed as if the land was blissfully free of the constrains of that most repressive of all regimes: good taste. On a televised debate between a gay activist and a conservative Christian politician, the former replied to the latter's condemnation of sodomy by suggesting that he would understand homosexuality better if he had at least enjoyed a mouthful of sperm once in his life. Pass me the joint, man.

Things have changed since. With Washington's unilateral War on Terror, hysteria is spreading across Europe in the wake of the killing of the enigmatic Dutch politician Pym Fortyn, the bombings in Madrid and London, and then the brutal slaying of Theo Van Gogh. New internal frontiers have sprung up. From Amsterdam to Berlin, and from to Paris to London, Europeans are now looking over their shoulders, fearful of the rise of political Islam in their midst. Exhortations for dialogue have fallen on deaf ears, and the continent no longer speaks with a single voice – if ever it had one. When news of Van Gogh's killing made the rounds I was already in Germany, and efforts to restore calm and reason were too little, too late.

'We've lost all sense of nuance and relativity here, bro! Everyone is forced to take sides; and the debates have become non-debates. The more traditional conservative Muslims don't endorse any form of religious violence, but they are too timid to speak up. Then there are those Muslims who have left their religion, and who now want to identify themselves as ex-Muslims and who claim that Islam is a fascist religion. Then to complicate things further we have the extreme-right who have been courting the ex-Muslims, and calling on Muslims to leave Islam or leave Europe. One politician has even called for a total ban of the Qur'an, comparing it to Hitler's *Mein Kampf*, and saying that Islam is a religion of violence that calls on its followers to kill all non-Muslims. There is just no middle-ground anymore. If we don't inject some sense and reason into this debate, soon this multi-culti paradise of ours is going to hell. That's why we want you to come and speak here." Eddy's email to me sounded like a panic call from the headquarters of Lefty Libertines International, so I immediately replied in the affirmative. Eddy Terstall is a Dutch film director who is also a member of the Dutch Labour Party. Over the year, our correspondence has been about the state of affairs in Holland, comparing the situation here to that in the rest of Europe where the rise of the right has not gone unnoticed either. Ironically, Islam – or rather the fear of Islam and Muslims – is the constitutive other to the extreme-right's renaissance. And as all good progressive pinkos know, when minorities are singled out and diagnosed as a nation's problem, witch-hunts and pogroms are not far away.

What freaked me out even more was, during my preparation for my trip to Amsterdam, a city I must have visited dozens of times and even lived in before, I was asked if I needed bodyguards and if the police should be put on standby. Bodyguards? For me? In Amsterdam? And what if I want to go to the sauna? Would they follow me there too, with their automatic revolvers?

Cockrings and chapels

Now the good thing about political scientists is that you can parachute any one of us to any location, give us the week's newspapers, sit us down with a cup of coffee, wind us up and we would go: we can pontificate at length about the world's troubles to no end, offering analyses aplenty and sometimes suggest a solution or two as well.

I've done speedy political overviews many times in my life, but mostly in exotic faraway places where I don't speak the language and where Kalashnikovs are part of the local scenery, and home décor. This is a rather unusual jaunt for me as I am expected to offer my understanding of the Dutch situation within eight-and-forty hours, and prattle on about it in public.

So having parked myself in the central square of Amsterdam with my coffee close at hand, I survey the irregular contours of the troubled landscape around me: a gaudy church with a funky dome to my left, gay club called Cockring to my right, Bob Marley Ganja Emporium directly in front, run-down suburban mosque where the gusts of Anatolia and the Rif are blowing behind me. Somewhere out of sight are my bodyguards. Conclusion: rise of right-wing majoritarian communitarian politics aided and abetted by external international variable factors – War on Terror, Bush's unrequited and unspoken reverse male-bonding pining for Osama, etcetera – and internal variable factors – Starbucks and McDonald's now being staple of European pop culture, not Goethe, Kant, Rousseau, etcetera – point to one thing: Holland's multicultural project has collapsed and the chickens have come home to roost. There is no longer a singular Holland to speak of or write home about. The country is now a plethora of nations whose borders crisscross, inter-penetrate (though that does sound rather Dutch) and defy each other. Holland, like the rest of Western Europe, has become parochialised by the end of the Empire, provincialised by the rise of America, and is now contested by the many nations that inhabit its territories.

Eddy and I grab a drink as he sums up the mottled canvas of his beloved nation for me, "The problem is that the Dutch Labour Party is not really one party. We are an assembly of trade unions, media groups, student movements, minority movements and a smattering of the traditional ideological Left from the past. Now the problem is that, in Holland today, the Labour Party is still seen by many as the party of the workers and migrants, and it is true that if the Moroccans and Turks were to vote for anyone, it would be for the PVDA. In the meantime, the extreme-right is playing up the fears of the public, and pointing to things like the murder of Van Gogh and the hate speeches coming from the suburban mosques. Why don't the liberal and progressive Muslims speak out? Can't they see that their religion is being hijacked by a minority of extremists in their own community?"

Good question, I note. But the same applies for the Muslims in countries like Malaysia. Why don't the progressives, the liberals, the moderates speak out? Why is the cry of the moderate always a silent one? Why can't liberalism find its voice? Or are we forever condemned to suffer the silent agony of the good but powerless, whose ethics remain abstract and whose sense of justice offers little response to baseball bats and steel clubs of the skinheads and fascists?

In the course of my stay I meet with a number of Dutch Muslims who had in the past taken the risk of speaking out against the Pharisees in their midst. Eddy introduces me to Ahmed Aboutaleb, State Secretary for Social Affairs and perhaps the most prominent Muslim in Holland today. Ahmed Aboutaleb is an imposing man both in bulk and presence. A former cop who fought hard to clean the suburbs of vice and crime, he is known to all as a no-nonsense sort of guy. Following the killing of Theo Van Gogh he was one of those who immediately led a public vigil and demonstration calling for peace and good relations between the communities, but not without reminding the Muslims of Holland that they lived in a country where there was more freedom of speech than in any other Muslim country in the world, and that if it was an Islamic state that they wanted, they could bugger off back to where they came from.

"But our young Muslims are getting more and more restless today, and despite everything the Moroccans and Turks remain among the poorest of our citizens, and they live in dilapidated areas where unemployment and crime levels are intolerably high. Liberals like you can talk about freedom of speech and democratic participation, but what solution can you give to a kid who cannot even get a job at a fast-food joint because he does not have basic schooling? That's our worry here, and that's why the conservative Mullahs in the suburban mosques have got a following," he says.

I see the State Secretary's point and can only agree on the apparent futility of the efforts to improve race relations in the country. If the Turks and Moroccans of Holland – like in the rest of Europe – do not take part in the cultural mainstream of the West, it is not because they avoid the opera due to a loathing of Wagner, but because they cannot afford the tickets. Class, rather than religion, is the real issue; but it also is a problem that nobody really wants to discuss. Instead, a Freudian dissimulation occurs: Muslims of Europe are pathologised and accused of all that has gone wrong with Europe's experiment with integration and tolerance. "But tell me," Secretary Aboutaleb says, "how many of those secular Europeans are as tolerant as they claim to be? How many of them really tolerate gays? How many of them really tolerate alternative lifestyles? And can they really understand that a Muslim in Europe can and wants to be both European *and* Muslim at the same time?"

The hell of everyday life

And so my public talk comes to pass, and I bla-bla for a couple of hours or so. The public attending are all from the clan of the converted; well-meaning, sincere, honest, frank and committed to the ideals of pluralism, democracy and free speech, as I am. It is always nice to be in the company of one's family: the Left.

But over the days I am in Amsterdam, I am struck by the disappearance of the country I once knew and even loved. So on a pitiable note of despair, I begin by saying that we are all in hell. Not going to hell, but already there: in the hell of everyday life.

Hell occurs as a leitmotif in all religions. Perhaps it stems from our collective fear of the unknown and the probability of an ultimate reckoning for our misdeeds on this earth. But in almost all of the iconographic and pictorial accounts of hell, one common image stands dominant: humanity is in pain, and each of us is confined to our private suffering. In the images of hell we see, every one of us is locked in an eternal torment that is solitary. Hell is the pain of individual anguish, of the cry that goes unheard – for no-one listens to your plea for help in there. It is the hell of an individualism so selfish that society itself is absent. Hell is the loss of human bonding, of the impossibility of communication. And hell is where we are today; in Holland, in Europe, across the world. We no longer communicate. We speak past each other and address only the instrumental fictions and the stereotypes we have created to scare ourselves and anaesthetise our reason. Hell is a world gone mad where we do not understand our neighbours; where politicians can declare crusades and holy wars against an idea; where a man can be murdered in the street because he is not understood.

The way out of hell is love. Love is the recognition of the Other; the acknowledgement that the person before us is a fellow human being whose life is an abundant store of emotions, feelings, memories of hope and loss, tears, smiles, laughter. Love is the prerequisite of communication, even when that communication is difficult and one is not always understood. But love dictates that we need to understand, or at least make the effort to understand; and not to demonise, to scapegoat, to sully, to abuse. Love is the thing that stops the finger as it presses on the trigger; it is the thing that stills the hand before it reaches for the knife.

In the discussions that follow, I am struck by the feeling of love I see and feel around me. Despite the headlines and the bellicose threats of the fascists and communitarians, there are still those who want to understand, to help and to sympathise with their fellow countrymen. Here I am, a Malaysian, in the company of Dutch leftists, and we are united by a common desire to see a world that is open, tolerant, plural and diverse. Perhaps Eddy and Martein were too pessimistic in their rush to write the funeral epitaph for Holland?

Babel in red light

On my last night in Amsterdam I am free to roam around at my leisure. I meet up with an old friend of mine, Lina, who is a scholar like me and who, for some reason, has taken it upon herself to fly to Afghanistan to solve the world's problems there. We talk about the state of things in Holland and the rest of Europe, about a world teetering on the brink of insanity, about piecemeal efforts to reach out and save our fellow human beings. Lina is about to fly to Afghanistan to help with some development projects, and I caution her that the first thing she would have to learn is how to pay a bribe to get the phones working and the mail delivered.

Being of mixed Arab-Dutch parentage, Lina is, like me, one of those who straddle several frontiers at the same time. Edward Said once wrote something to the effect that being hybrid is a cool thing in this postmodern world. Tell that to the kids who get abused by their friends for being a mixed-race mongrel, dear Professor, and perhaps you would re-appraise the value of hybridity again.

As we walk through the alleys and lanes of Amsterdam I comment on the apparent ease with which the Dutch present themselves to the public eye. Homes are open to the glare of passers-by and through the living room windows we see couples and families dining together, watching TV, sleeping and even playing in bed while life walks by less than a metre away. Nowhere is this more apparent than in the red-light district of Amsterdam where the prostitutes stand before the windows of their parlours, dressed in gaily coloured thongs and bikinis that glow in the ultraviolet light, like living butterflies dancing beneath the red lamps above. Lina and I decide to talk to one of them to see if the denizens of the Amsterdam underground scene (which is not all that subterranean as some might think) concur with the view that the country is pulling itself apart.

I have to admit that I am strangely drawn to the girls who wears glasses; the combination of lingerie and spectacles working wonders for the academically-attuned libido of *moi meme*. But sadly the cute bespectacled ones at the windows decline to be interviewed. Finally Lina and I chance upon a tall blonde whose knee-high boots proved to be every bit as enticing, and we knock on her door and ask her if she minds us doing an interview on the spot.

"What, you don't want sex? I think you want a threesome!" Nisha teases us on the threshold of her space. After forking out a sum that would have bought us an hour's worth of debauchery, Nisha leads us into her room that is minimalist in its decoration and clinical in taste. The bed is lined with a plastic sheet under the mattress and along the head are jars of assorted condoms in many colours, numerous types of gel and lubricants, and the odd dildo or two. On one side is an elongated mirror where presumably one could enjoy a narcissist view of oneself at play. Nisha is mildly amused by our request, though this being Holland we are all cool about it and there is no problem with two academics interviewing a half-naked hooker on her bed.

As Nisha recounts the story of her life – how she was lured into prostitution at the age of 18, how she grew to like her independence after a while, and how she was saving enough money to open a restaurant one day – I take a step back from myself and observe all of us acting out this strange ritual of research bordering on titillation. Even here, in the tiny world of Nisha where many men have come, there are some rules and norms that are sacrosanct. Is it not odd, I ask, to be so open to the public and yet keep your distance at the same time?

"Listen baby, I tell you the first rule of being a hooker, okay? No kissing. The guys can come here, play with me, do what they like, but no kissing. I tell them 'this is just sex, ok? Not love'. And kissing is only for my boyfriend, because he is the one I love. The rest are just customers. They can ask whatever they want but I decide if I want to do it with them. Sometimes there are the weird ones who want to lick my boots; sometimes they want me to spank their asses until they are blue. I get all the types here, normal ones, weird ones; but I am my own boss. I do only what I want."

I assure Nisha that wanting to be spanked is not that abnormal and that it can be fun, to which she laughs and asks if she should do it now. No, no, this is research dear, and we are scientists as you can see by the way we are dressed so badly. But I want another kind of penetration altogether, to get into her world and to see what it feels like to see the whole of Amsterdam walk past, night after night. "Are you worried about the rise of conservative politics in the country? I mean, there are religious people – both Christian and Muslim – who now say that this area should be closed down and that women like you are a menace to society."

"C'mon baby, this is the oldest job in the world and these people are all hypocrites! They talk like that, but they also come to see me when they feel horny, so what's the big deal?

Why the morality? Like these Jehovah's Witnesses who come here all the time to convert us. Why don't they see we are human beings, and we don't need them to save us? Why can't they respect us?"

Respect. Tolerance. Recognition. Reciprocity. The touchstones of the secular democratic creed that sound like the lyrics of a suburban rap song. Nisha wants her respect and to be treated like a human being who happens to sell her body every night, but whose lips are reserved for the love of her life. The minorities want their respect and to be treated like citizens who nonetheless want to cling to a faith that seems alien and foreign to many. The right-wing conservatives want their respect and wish to maintain a country that is mono-cultural and essentialist, fearful of the loss of their own identity. The progressives want their respect and to create a world where one can disagree with another without fearing a shot in the head. Their worlds have always rested side-by-side, but was there ever any real communication, and have they ever understood one another? Can any country, and Holland here is no exception, ever hope to develop a national narrative that somehow captures the diversity of stories and narratives that run through its urban arteries? Where is the heart of Holland? Here in the red-light district, resting on Nisha's bed? Or in the mosques and churches where God's name is used in vain? Or in the Parliament where the politicians argue with on another?

I am back where I started, unable to account for how such a diverse country could have taken this slide to communitarianism and sectarianism. I ask Nisha if she is worried about the future, or if she thinks that Holland will always remain the same, if she believes there is a God who is witnessing all this.

"God? I don't know if I believe in religion but I do believe there is something out there; something good and something kind. You know, whatever you see or read in the press today doesn't really matter. Yeah, the politicians talk about hating this, or hating that. And the religious people are the first to condemn everyone who don't agree with them. But I remember when I was a child my mother took me to church and the priest told us this story. He said once long ago there was a place where the people all spoke one language, but they were too arrogant. They wanted to reach God so they built this big tower. This tower was so big that finally it reached the sky. Can you imagine that? But God was angry with them, and so he cursed these people. Their tower collapsed, and they could not speak properly anymore. They began to speak in different languages and they no longer understood each other. I don't really believe the story, but it is funny, don't you think? Maybe that is why we don't speak to each other anymore. We have become arrogant. Everyone thinks he is right. Everyone wants to be like God. But me, I am only human."

Babel. We no longer speak. We are undone, by our own profound arrogance and pride. I have found Babel in the redlight district of Amsterdam, and am dumbstruck by the poetry of Nisha the hooker.

As the interview comes to an end, Nisha plays with us right up to the last minute. Just as we are about to leave she exclaims, "Now when you walk out everyone in the street will think we had a threesome! Hahaha." To rub it in, as we say goodbye Nisha calls out to us in public, "Bye, bye, babies! That was great! We do it again soon, okay?"

She laughs. We laugh.

In the midst of the absurdity of it all, I feel that prejudice and racism can, after all, be overcome with humour and tenderness, a recognition of the common humanity we all share. Between the fascists and the fundamentalists, I know who comes closest to me, whom I can call a comrade and a friend, the Magdalene of Amsterdam, whose world is still big enough for others.

Silence

(Western Egypt: The Great Libyan Desert,
Dec 2007 - Jan 2008)

Will some woman in this desert land;
Make me feel like a real man?
Take this rock n' roll refugee;
Oooh, Babe set me free.

Pink Floyd,
The Wall

Flight is easy but escape never.

Being of a somewhat sentimental (albeit corny) bent, I had decided to give myself a little treat in preparation for my departure from Europe — where I had lived, studied and taught for the past twenty-one years — and return to Southeast Asia. Poetic flourishes look good on a map and it was a rather whimsical gesture from the start: To break my journey home with a short five-week stop in North Africa and to explore the Libyan desert before heading eastwards to warmer climes was just what my good head doctor prescribed as I handed over my last cheque to him.

It was also meant to be one of those selfish moments in my adult life where a month would be devoted to myself, and when I would be able to do some personal accounting before moving on, physically, psychologically and emotionally. And of course December is the month where the yearly ritual of I-will-try-to-stop-smoking-but-oh-no-I-wont is played out on a tiresomely regular basis. A clearing of the decks was in order, but I hadn't realised what was in store for me amidst the shifting sands...

It is 3.00 am in the morning and my teeth are chattering uncontrollably. It's not just the cold though: I am hanging onto the hand-rails outside the driver's cabin of a bulldozer as it plods along noisily at a laborious pace down the gravel path to where I'm headed for the night; a tiny outcrop of mud-brick houses nestled around a spring flanked by palm trees (but I can't see it because it's pitch black), in the sleepy settlement of al-Farafra, the westernmost outpost along the oasis track that fringes the barren wastes of the Great Libyan Desert. The driver of the bulldozer yells at me above the din of the engine, "There, you see? Oasis town! There you sleep tonight, okay?"

I nod. I'm too tired to say much or argue. It has taken me eleven hours to get here and I have crossed much of central and western Egypt. Here, at the furthermost point of the desert track, is where I have come to spend a week alone in silence and meditation. Though at the moment there isn't all that much silence, and meditating on top of a bulldozer isn't exactly what my funky head doctor had in mind when he said that I should take a break from myself and escape into the unknown for a month or so. For now, all I want is to sleep and to forget. Forget, mostly.

I am in Egypt as part of my DIY therapy to clear my head of a clutter of bad and painful memories.

Seven years in Germany and four years of living a single life in Berlin leads you down alleys and recesses in your head that should have been posted with warning signs. Over the past few years I have been spending most of my time researching the wonderful world of political religion and meeting all sorts of quirky, loveable characters whose heads are more screwed up than mine, and have had the privilege of looking at life from up close with the gilding off.

Sorting through my mental diary I come across many memories of my travels that have left too lasting an impression on me, though I wish they hadn't: I recall sitting in a religious school watching little boys watch a video of a man having his throat slit and then his body cut to pieces with a meat cleaver. I recall walking through the ruins of schools in the hill towns of Kashmir after the earthquake and finding children's toys tucked in the rubble; an exercise book with a sentence half complete; a little girl's shoe with laces undone. I recall interviewing a *jihadi* leader in a darkened basement who, with tears in his eyes, related his grief and regret at not being able to join the young boys he had sent across the border to kill *kafirs* and to die a martyr along with them.

My little jaunt in Egypt is meant to be a break from all this, a sort of mental colonic irrigation intended to detoxify my head and bleed out the poisonous memories. I tried to lose myself in Cairo, though that only happened literally, as I lost my way time and again and ended up thoroughly brow-beaten and demoralised. My dear friends Andree, Uli and Philip – long time chums from Berlin and also denizens of the great Egyptian megapolis – then persuaded me to take more radical measures to clear my head: run to the desert and hope that Saint Anthony will rescue you with a few tips on meditation.

And so, a few days before the coming of the new year, I caught the bus out of Cairo and headed West, as far out into the desert as I could go.

Catching up with Saint Anthony

Now leaving Cairo is not that easy a task. As it is winter and the sun begins to set by 5.00 pm, and it is already dark by the time the bus makes it to the outskirts of the megapolis, with the sticky traffic slowing us down. The roads are packed, and depending on one's luck one could end up in a spanking new bus or something that is positively prehistoric. As fate would have it, the bus I find myself in must have been dragged out of the great flood of the Biblical era, and is stuffed like a can of sardines. Next to me is a rather large imam who keeps me awake throughout the ride by chomping on his skewered meat and bread, and then wiping his greasy hands on his gallabiya. Just when an out-of date-movie is about to be played on the TV with the volume at full blast, he started praying for us all, his supplication to God along the lines of, "Oh merciful God, please let us get there in one piece and let us not fall down a gully or be crushed by an oil tanker on the road." No prayers are offered for the luggage, which probably accounts for why some pieces go missing along the way, presumably swallowed by the hungry sands of the desert.

I am determined that my destination will be al-Farafra, the westernmost oasis along the oases circuit that links Bahariyya, al-Farafra and Dakhla along what used to be one of the basins of a, now dead and dry, Nile tributary. The Great Libyan Desert has its own stories and, by Gum, what stories they are too. One episode is worth recounting here, just to add a little depth to my little tale and for some atmospheric effect: when the Italians invaded Libya in the 1930s, Mussolini was keen to cut as big a slice of the desert as possible for his quaint little Fascist empire. The Italian troops marched out into the desert on the backs of camels, donkeys, trucks, tanks and armoured cars. One by one the outpost villages that speckle the Great Libyan Desert fell under their heels and were forced to capitulate.

The news of the advancing Italians spread faster than the Italians themselves did, and many of the Libyan desert dwellers were uncertain of what to do. As the Italians got closer to one of the easternmost villages, the inhabitants decided to simply cut and run, taking everything with them – save water. Six hundred of them walked out of the desert and marched East, in the direction of Egypt. For weeks and weeks they walked in the searing heat of the desert and one by one the weaker ones fell; only to be picked up by the rest who could still stay on their feet. The band of villagers marched until they could not walk any further, and then sent out their fittest members – again with no water – to walk on ahead to seek help. Eventually some of them were met by members of the British and Egyptian army posted at the oasis settlements, and rescue parties were despatched post-haste to round up the survivors. All in all, more than three hundred of these Libyans made it and were eventually settled in settlements like al-Farafra. To this day, this remains one of the greatest, if not the greatest, feat of desert travel ever attempted by amateurs, and it ranks as one of the greatest desert treks ever accomplished by anyone. Tough blokes, these Libyans. It is good to know I am soon to be amongst them.

When I get off the bus at the roadside stop in al-Farafra – literally a one-road town – the policeman who greets me has a look on his face that says, "Another dumb foreigner about to get himself lost in the desert." Thankfully, he is kind enough to persuade another passing bulldozer (though what on earth the bulldozer is doing on the road in the wee hours of the morning is anyone's guess) to give me a ride, and so off I go. Half an hour later I reach my rest hut, and the cooks who are asleep when I knock on their door have a look that suggests something like, "Another dumb foreigner who gets here at 4.00 am to wake us up, and doesn't know we have to work all day tomorrow." The young men, descendants of Libyan migrants who made that great trek across the desert decades ago, promptly lay down a mattress on the kitchen floor and bids me to sleep next to them while one of them makes me tea. But, before the tea is ready, I am already asleep. And, the dreams began.

In my dream I am walking on the seabed naked, and for reasons not entirely known to me, I seem to have developed a new pair of lungs that allow me to breathe sea water. I walk on the soft sand of the seabed and in the near distance I spy some shapes. They appear to be long, sleek, and silent, and I walk closer to them, though not without a sense of foreboding. By the time I get close enough to realise what they are, it is already too late. I find myself standing on the ocean floor, surrounded by a school of sleeping sharks. They could wake up at any moment, and I would be done for. I look to my side and stare at the dead eye of a shark in slumber. Its pupil dilates, the shark awakens. At the moment it turns to devour me, I wake up. It is dawn, and Mahmud Effendi the caretaker smiles at me and asks, "Coffee, or tea?"

The Great Sand Sea

"So you want to go out to the Great Sand Sea, do you?" Hamada asks me as we sip thick sweet tea at the teahouse on the only road that cuts through al-Farafra.

The al-Farafra teahouse is quite the place to be in town, as it also happens to be the only place in town. The original lime-green walls are well patinated with years of hookah-smoking. Local boys and old men while away their time sitting in the shade of the teahouse watching life go by, and make comments on the latest makes of Pajeros and Range Rovers that dart past carrying tourists and researchers into the desert. Occasionally something new pops up, like a jeep with a computerised global positioning system, and the crusty old codgers climb down from their chairs and walk out to inspect it, commenting on the latest developments in communications and transport technology invented by the Japanese or Americans, but always ending up with the same conclusion, "Still can't beat a good mule that can find its own way back to the village in a sand storm."

The teahouse is also the place where you hire a jeep or land cruiser to take you out into the desert, and where you can meet the drivers (called navigators) and their sand-gliding crafts. I am talking to Hamada and we discuss the dates, duration, time constraints and petrol requirements for my little expedition. Hamada knows that all the cards are in his hand as he is the one with the keys to the Range Rover and he knows the desert better than I do. I play coy, plead poverty and an academic's salary to keep the price as low as possible. We finally agree on a week's worth of travel that would include a second driver (his brother Muhammad), enough fuel to get us to Chad or Libya if I want to go there, and the most basic meals of chicken, chicken and more chicken with some bread thrown in. To economise further we decide that toilet paper is for wimps, and that we will stick to sand and coconut husks. The deal is stuck and I go off to buy some cigarettes, only to discover that the only brand on offer is from a company that went bankrupt five years ago.

By the end of the day al-Farafra is buzzing with activity: on that same day several other desert safaris are getting ready to leave and they all seem to be made up of Western Europeans with their families. Jeeps, Pajeros and Range Rovers are packed to the roof with tents, jerrycans of water, firewood, barbeque kits, carpets, candles, musical instruments, even fireworks.

"Why the fireworks, Hamada?" I ask the driver – oh, sorry, navigator, I mean. "Aaah, these are the tour operators from Bahariyya. They bring all this nonsense for the tourists who don't like the silence in the desert, just to provide entertainment after dinner. Tourists like music. They go crazy in the desert when they can't hear anything at night. Damned amateurs! Ptuuiii …" (Hamada shoots forth a wad of sputum in disgust.)

"Well, I am already crazy in my head and that's why I don't want any music, so let's get as far away as possible to enjoy the silence, okay?" I reply. Hamada concurs, "Good man, that's more like it. That's how desert people live. We listen to the silence, and if you keep quiet you will hear the desert speak to you." Hamada is showing disconcerting signs of Oriental wisdom for a man only 24 years of age, and I realise I am old enough to be his father. We climb into his dirty, unwashed Rover and send a cloud of dust up as we speed past the shiny red and blue Pajeros that have just been washed in the morning. Hamada and his brother chuckle to themselves, and the operators from Bahariyya raise their fists in anger in our wake. Libyan desert, here we come!

The Great Sand Sea is aptly called that: by noon Hamada is ploughing the sand with me riding shotgun next to the driver (sorry, navigator), with Muhammad yelling in delight in the backseat. The lightness of our Range Rover (for we are packing just a tent, some firewood, water and some chicken) sends the vehicle hurling upwards every time we clear a sand dune, and the undulation of the sand does give the impression of a craft sailing across the waves. "It's like water, don't you feel it?" Hamada shouts above the roar of the engine. "You always drive straight up the dune, never along the spine, in case we tip and fall over. There is only one car in our safari, so we cannot make any mistake. Nobody is going to rescue us here! Hahahahaaaa!" Hamada's demonic laughter is somewhat unnerving, as is Muhammad's glee.

Sand dunes grow along their horns and move at a snail's pace, covering a kilometre or so per year. Eventually the horns connect, and this forms the crests that Hamada is driving over, rising higher and higher as we claw our way into the desert. We clear dunes with crests that are 20 metres high, then 30, then 40, and then 50. By then, even Hamada has lost his nerve and he decides to slow down. Muhammad's glee has also subsided and I realise that we are now getting deep into the desert, and this is when one should keep silent and remain attentive.

As we drive Hamada and Muhammad recount their experiences and tales of the desert. I am given the essential tips: in case of a sandstorm, park your jeep or car with the back to the wind, for the sand is so strong that the front windows will be sandblasted milky grey otherwise, and you won't be able to see anything through it afterwards. Never drive alone if you want to go all the way to Libya, as in the heart of the desert there are many sand pits behind the dunes that can swallow a bus and all its passengers whole, in one sandy gulp. Never, ever, park your jeep sideways along the ridge of a sand dune in case the sand shifts and the jeep sinks sideways.

"Occasionally, there are those crazy Americans who think they are Rambo. They come here, rent a jeep, and go out driving alone. They always say the same thing: I'm an American and we have deserts in our country too, so I know what I'm doing. Next thing you know they get lost, like the idiot we rescued last week. He drove around in circles until his petrol ran out, then abandoned his jeep (stupid thing to do, apparently) and we found him half-dead from walking without water in the desert for three days. When we rescued him, he was half-mad and crying like a baby. Hahahahaaaaaa!" Hamada and Muhammad cheer me up with yet more delightful tales of tourist escapades in the great desert that once swallowed the entire Persian army.

By dusk we find ourselves at the edge of the Great Sand Sea and, by God, I witness the majestic, awe-inspiring beauty of the desert at sunset. The sky above is bereft of clouds and, as the first pin-pricks of stars made their appearance near the horizon, the dark Prussian blue of the Egyptian sky mellows to a tawny maroon-burgundy that is soon stained blood red, and then crimson, and then burning orange. The glowing orb of the sun descends slow and heavy, stands poised on the edge of the desert for a moment, before bowing out for the night. A gentle wind begins, and Hamada and Mumammad make themselves busy preparing our roofless tent. Muhammad chops up the chicken and boils some beans. Hamada rolls out the prayer mat to thank Allah for a day of smooth sailing across the desert sea. I ask if I can do anything to help. "Just smoke your cigarette and enjoy the sunset, Effendi. We see this sight everyday, you don't. So, sit back and enjoy." And I do.

Silence

The next three days are spent exploring the Libyan desert and paying our respects to the Great Sand Sea. We begin on a westward journey, then shift south by the middle of the second day, and then turn east and north-east by the third, to pay a visit to the Sahara el-Beida, the Great White Desert. Now allow me to gloat for a minute and tell you that unless and until you have seen the Sahara el-Beida up close, you can't really say you have seen the world in all its phenomenal beauty. Nothing can really prepare you for it, for there is really nothing else like it in the world, period. As we make our way north-east Hamada points out the fringes of the Sahara el-Beida to me. "You see those white stones in the distance? What do you think they are?"

The Sahara el-Beida is actually a gigantic limestone plateau with enormous limestone outcrops that have been blasted and hewn by the wind for thousands of years. Today they stand as extraordinary outcrops of chalky white rocks that stick out of the flat limestone floor, like great white pillars of mysterious, outlandish, extra-terrestrial countenance. The landscape is positively lunar, or even martian for all I know, and all one can say is that this is not something one would expect to find on earth. The limestone basin, however, does terrible damage to the underbelly of Hamada's Rover and he winces every time we hear the dreaded sound of a limestone ripping and scratching the length of his vehicle. The Rover rocks from side to side, and our little sand boat is tossed and turned with every single move we make.

After a day of tortuous driving avoiding the nastier looking terrain, we finally decide to stop in the shade of a large outcrop that bears a striking resemblance to a sitting camel. Once again we strike camp, and I am left to walk about with my camera to get shots of this surreal landscape. "Don't get lost, okay?" Hamada shouts as I wander off. "Sure, I won't." I shout back, and just as soon I feel a pang of regret for sounding so confident.

I wander amidst the outcrops trying to make sense of this landscape that looks like one of God's jokes. Nobody lives in the Sahara el-Beida as the climate and environment is too inhospitable: there is no soil to cultivate, no water to dig for, nothing to build with. It's as if the entire desert is saying to humankind, "Go migrate to some other place. This place is not for you, okay?"

Predictably, I get lost after an hour of wandering. Finding myself smack in the middle of four outcrops, all of which bear a curious similarity to the fabled Sphinx, I wonder if this is Nature's way of playing tricks on me and knocking me off my pedestal a peg or two. Unable to orientate myself, I don't even know where Hamada and our Rover is parked, and I begin to panic. Dusk begins, and I realise that in less than an hour the temperature will plummet by 30 degrees while I am out here barefoot, in a T-shirt and linen pants. I fear the prospect of ending up as yet another tale that Hamada will recount to his next traveller-passenger, the one about the dumb Malaysian academic who got himself lost in the Sahara el-Beida and how all that they found of him was his camera and his packet of stale cigarettes. Just when I am about to start screaming for help, Muhammad yells at me from half a kilometre away. "Hey, Farish Effendi, over here!"

As I make my way back to the camp where the fire is already lit and yet another chicken meal is being cooked, Hamada laughs and asks me, "Didn't you hear us cooking over here? What did I tell you? Keep silent and you will hear the desert talking to you. The desert will tell you what to do." As I have yet to learn to speak desert, I put my misfortune down to my lack of knowledge of the local idiom. For now, however, I am happy that I can get to enjoy Muhammad's salty overcooked chicken stew for another night. I soon realise that it's 31st December and in 6 hours time the year 2007 will draw to a close.

Greeting Saint Anthony

The fireworks begin and Hamada and Muhammad are annoyed that their plans have been ruined. Their aim is to take me to the middle of the Sahara el-Beida so that we could enjoy new year's night in the peace and quiet of the desert under the stars. Instead, there are fireworks in the distance, accompanied by the sound of drumming and — wait for it — music of the latest party hits of 2007.

"Sheesh ... it's those flunky amateurs from Bahariyya again; them and their stupid tourists! Bloody amateurs!" Hamada and Muhammad are undoubtedly annoyed by the noise being made by our neighbours, whose music is as loud as their manners; save for the fact that they are two kilometres away and that all we can see are the dimmed headlights of their Pajeros and Land Cruisers. Yet this is one of the amazing things about the desert: that its silence is so profound that one can actually listen to a conversion taking place two kilometres away. I could clearly make out French and German words and sentences being uttered by other tourist groups camped in the distance. Being monolingual, neither Hamada or Muhammad are interested to know what the tourists are saying, even though I am ready to translate it for them. "They've spoiled our mood, these tourists. Let's pray they all fall asleep as soon as possible," grumbles Muhammad. And sure enough, they do.

By 11.00 pm, with less than an hour to go before the arrival of the new year, the desert is silent again. Our camp fire is dying slowly and it is bitterly cold; even colder than the winter I spent in Budapest when my lips cracked in the wind and blood stained the suit I was wearing, just before my lecture at the university there. The winter nights in the Sahara el-Beida are truly unforgiving and merciless, as Uli had warned me before I left Cairo: "Make sure you bring several blankets to the White Desert. I've slept in deserts all over Africa and Asia, but nothing and nowhere is it as cold as the Sahara el-Beida." With four blankets on top of my pants, shirt, jacket and boots, I am still freezing and shivering uncontrollably. Even Hamada and Muhammad are freezing out of their wits, though for some reason they choose to remain barefoot. As our teeth chatter as we smoke our last packet of cigarettes in the gloomy silence, Muhammad turns to his side and his ears perk up. "Listen," he says to Hamada. "That's Ibrahim, isn't it?"

"Ibrahim?" cries out Hamada. "*Aiwaa* (yes)," comes the reply. The muffled footsteps grow louder with each step until out of the inky darkness comes Ibrahim, another driver (sorry, navigator) from al-Farafra whose own safari is two kilometres away. His tall lanky frame is silhouetted against the fire and I marvel at the fact that in the freezing darkness Ibrahim had walked two kilometres in the night, barefoot, with only a cotton galabiyya and a scarf around his head. "Got a light?" he asks. Ibrahim, Hamada, Muhammad and I puff away as the final embers of our campfire die out and we are left sitting on the black, cold floor of the desert under a dark blue sky that is lit by a million stars. Our cigarette ends burn crimson red, like warning lights on ships passing by in the night. I look up at the stars and count one, two, three, four and then five shooting stars crisscrossing the heavens. Ibrahim asks Hamada and Muhammad about me, and they answer, "He is Ustaz Farish al-Almani, from Germany. He came to find quiet in the desert." "Good place to be quiet," Ibrahim opines. Then, we shut up as the clock strikes twelve.

Lying on the cold desert floor with four blankets on top of me, I am immobile, tired and sleepy. My eyes struggle to stay open but lose the battle, and soon enough sleep overwhelms me. As I drop off I hear Ibrahim, Hamada and Muhammad talking to each other in hushed tones. And then the dreams come again.

In my dream I am walking naked in the jungle and it is dark. The trees are so dense that their roots and vines are like limbs that tug at me and pull me down. My feet are lost in the murky, sweaty undergrowth and the air is heavy. My lungs are tired and I cannot breathe, I have lost my way and I sense the coming of darkness. Suddenly, and for no reason, I am not able to move. And at that point I realise that the vines and branches around me are alive and moving. They are not branches after all, but strong, sinewy snakes that slither and glide around me effortlessly while I am paralysed with fear and fatigue. I feel the slimy, muscular body of a serpent as it wraps around my neck, suffocating me. I look up, and see the face of the skinhead who strangled me from behind as I sat on a bench in the middle of the park in Berlin. I see the hatred in his eyes, and I do not understand. Why is this young man trying to strangle me to death?

I try to wake up but I cannot. The blankets on me are too heavy and they weigh me down, and I cannot breathe. I try to call out to Hamada and Muhammad but I cannot see them. In my stupor I am drowning in fear. Strangulation, drowning, being buried alive: my demons are all here and they smile at me in the desert. Every memory I have been trying to run away from returns. I stare heavenwards, into infinity, into an ocean of stars that stretch on forever. I am back on my mother's lap, sitting on the swing under the tree in our garden in Ampang, gazing into space and staring straight into the face of God. God, I beg you, please let me forget. But my past is here, fangs bared and its crusty nails buried in my throat and around my neck. "We will never leave you. You will never forget us," they say. So this is my lot. Even in the middle of the desert, my past will not leave me. Even in the darkness, my shadows will not leave me. Maybe that is the lesson I've come to learn, after all.

Dawn and homecoming

I wake up late, and it is the 1st of January, 2008. Hamada and Muhammad are working on the Rover's engine as we make ready our flight from the desert and our return to al-Farafra. Coffee is on the boil and the syrupy aroma is a pleasant way to greet the new year. With a touch of embarrassment I ask Hamada and Muhammad if I made too much noise the night before. "What noise? You slept like a baby. It was Muhammad here who was snorting and snoring all night!" Hamada beams.

By evening we reach the oases track and are on the desert highway to the settlements. We race past shepherds and peasants who cut lonely figures on the desert tracks on their tractors and mules. Hamada revs the motor and flashes the headlights again and again. "Why do you keep flashing the lights, Hamada?" I ask. "It's for the donkeys and mules. They keep coming to the road and sometimes one of them gets run over."

By the time we reach the main road to al-Farafra, Hamada's Rover is wheezing and groaning, as if it is about to give up. Then, in the eerie darkness on the desert highway we see many headlights and realise that an accident has taken place: sure enough, a donkey cart has been hit head-on by a speeding jeep, and the donkey is lying in blood by the road in the dust. Hamada stops the Rover and we join the crowd of locals who have rushed to help. By the side of the road I see two boys who look dazed and stunned, with one of them bleeding from his head, a crude bandage made from someone's shirt sleeve his only comfort.

The eternal itinerant observer, I stand by and watch the scene of this tiny isolated desert oasis community coming together, the elder men console the boys who are crying over their donkey. The dwellers of the oasis love their donkeys more than all the Pajeros and Range Rovers, for the donkey is a loyal friend who can save your life when you are most in need. They pat the donkey, stroke its injured head, recite prayers, and console it by saying, "Salaam, salaam, old friend. It is okay, it is okay." Then, the donkey snorts and brays, and it is miraculously up on its feet again! The men and boys clap and cheer, smiles return, and the dazed donkey backtracks, recovers its feet, hisses and farts loudly.

"You see?" Hamada smiles to me in the dim light by the road. "You always need to keep your wits about you in the desert, in case it is about to warn you. Keep your ears open, Farish Effendi, okay?"

Two days later I am back at the al-Farafra teahouse waiting to catch a ride from any van or truck that will take me back to Cairo. My companions for this trip are five young boys who are about to leave the oasis town for a new life in the great city that will devour them whole and spit them back, broken and twisted. As I look at them I am struck by their youthful vigour, their handsome looks, their boundless optimism and the honey-brown eyes. I don't have the heart to tell them of what life will be like for them in Cairo, in that infernal city of millions. Perhaps, in the end we all have to battle our own demons in our own time, on our own terms. I have come to the desert to fight mine, but instead found them waiting for me. The battle, as the story goes, continues. This will be a good year.

Hamada and Muhammad contemplate the Libyan desert

A limestone outcrop in the middle of the white desert, Egypt

Another Country, Another Election
(Kelantan and Trengganu, March 2008)

"Kelante doh come lote, ngak uboh buat apo?"

The sweet vernacular of the Kelantanese dialect tastes better when served in its local setting; the rolling consonants and the melodious vowels spill forth like thick syrup and I lap it up gleefully. I am trying on a plain white cotton *baju melayu* as part of my effort to blend in and stop looking like some *orghe lue*, sticking out like a sore thumb in the crowd, though even here, at the stall in front of the grand Muhammadi mosque in Kota Bharu, my *peranakan* ancestry trips me up yet again.

The clear-skinned young man with the goatee and *kepiah*, *tasbih* beads rolling in the palm of his hands, looks me up and adjusts the collar of my shirt. He leans forward and flits the quiet enquiry: *"Eh, abe ni orghe putih ko Bengali?" "Ambo ni campo semuo beloko, deh. Orghe putih pun ado, Bengali pun ado,"* I reply.

Welcome to Kelante, deh. This is a different country, folks.

Our Confederates up north

I have been in Kelantan throughout most of this election period to cover the campaigns of the Pan-Malaysian Islamic Party

(PAS) and their nemesis, UMNO. Riding shotgun is Danny, armed with three cameras, all ready to catch the action as it happens. Between the two of us we smoke enough cigarettes to cause severe environmental damage to a small country; and the days are long and hard with whistle-stops all across Kelantan and Trengganu.

The mood in Kelantan, however, catches us off guard and, with the expected fiery skirmishes and battle of words not materialising, it was decidedly cool. Where is the fireworks, the fire and brimstone? Between rainy days when the rain pours down in buckets, and the sunny days when the sun roasts our brains as we walk, little seems to be happening on the ground.

The UMNO *ceramahs* we attend are by far the most lacklustre: at one meeting that is held in the outskirts of Kota Bharu, the captive audience of around five hundred civil servants has the distinct look of punters who have been roped in to fill the seats in a Kenny G concert, mouths agape in mid-snore and gummy blood-shot eyes desperately trying to remain open. Even the cops who are stationed nearby seem indifferent to the sonorous rambling that emanates from the diminutive figure of the YB in the distance, pink batik shirt and slick oily hair shining in the blistering sun.

We check with the bookies and the odds are fifty-fifty. It is too early to tell, and the information we receive is conflicting and confusing. No, I am not about to make any money calling in this one, I think.

The UMNO delegates we meet, however, seem more upbeat about their prospects. Walking into the UMNO campaign offices, the party machinery seems to be in full throttle. Says one of the Pemuda UMNO members I meet, "This time, we are sure to win. We know it. Victory is certain, and we have all the big guns coming to town soon. Badawi, Najib,

Khairy are all going to be here and it's just a matter of time before we take them with one big sweep, just you wait and see." Brave words indeed, think I. But if they are so confident, why are the bookies hedging their bets? And why is the mood so muted and sedate? This is not the Kelantan I know. Heck, if anything, the Kelantanese are perhaps the proudest of Malays, and no Kelantanese worth his salt would sit by and let a boast like that pass.

I've always been asked about the Kelantanese and why they are so damned infuriatingly stubborn and different. I know of foreign diplomats who return to their villas in Kuala Lumpur after a visit to the state, stunned and dumfounded, and file their reports blank. Bangsar urbanites seem to think that you need a passport to get past Tok Bali and drive up north. Western-educated cosmopolitans look upon them as a glitch in the system, like they have some anomaly in the programming. I, for one, think of them fondly as our very own Confederates flying the flag of Mississippi in the face of the Union's guns. How I love our Kelantanese cousins – they would be as stubborn and unpredictable as us Penangites were it not for their King, and that is another conundrum.

Desperately searching for that Kelantanese spirit – that defiant sneer and confident smirk I have come to know so well by now – Danny and I saunter forth to attend the PAS *ceramahs* and rallies in Kota Bharu (KB) and beyond. And sure enough, soon after *magrib* prayers on a balmy Monday evening, we hear the rebel yell.

The rebel yell of the Kelantanese

"We – we Kelantanese – are the only ones left. We are the only state left standing before the might of UMNO and the

Federal government. All the other states have fallen to them. Trengganu, Kedah, Perak, Perlis, Selangor, Johor: they have all fallen, save us. Are we going to let them walk into our Kelantan and take over our government, the government of our beloved Tok Guru Nik Aziz? Are we going to let those in Kuala Lumpur take over Kelantan? Are we going to surrender our state to UMNO?" Cikgu Rahim – Parliamentary candidate for Kota Bharu – riles the crowd at the Dataran Stadium Sultan Muhammad IV in KB.

The crowd grows agitated, and shouts of defiance pierce the night sky. "Noooo! Never!" cry the boys with the Pemuda PAS T-shirts, caps and bandanas. Here is local Kelantanese politics at its parochial best, the plaintive strains of the subaltern and downtrodden bristling like spikes on a beleaguered porcupine pinned under the claws of a predator; terrified yet resisting, outnumbered yet unwilling to yield to the claws of the invader.

The appeal to the solemn pride of the Kelantanese, whose self-worth stems from little save the knowledge that they are Kelantanese and therefore different and unique, is something that I have not seen or felt anywhere else in Malaysia. This is a state which is a nation on its own; it even has its own geography. With its historical lens pointed towards the glory days of the Greater Patani-Kelantan kingdom of the past, the Kelantanese refer to Patani as their western neighbour and themselves as the easterners. Throw the maps away and sell your compass on eBay: here, even geography has been reinvented to serve the interests of the locals.

While the election campaigns in the west coast are replete with lofty ideals of democracy, human rights, accountability and transparency, here what matters most is who-is-who. Keep the People's Declaration and the debate on freedom of belief to the greener suburbs of Bangsar and Damansara. Here, we want to know if you are a local boy or not, and what you can and will do for the mother-country, Kelantan.

The rules of electioneering in Kelantan have always been unique to the state. Glitzy power-point presentations hold no sway, the English press is nowhere to be seen, or read. Here, it is grassroots politics at the level of the local, idiomatic and vernacular; and by God, you better learn how to play by the rules pretty quick. If UMNO's big guns are on their way, in helicopters and convoys of Pajero, the Kelantanese have their own howitzers of equal calibre. As Cikgu Rahim winds down his speech, the time comes for the biggest of the big guns to boom. The crowd falls silent, and the PAS leaders stand on stage to welcome the biggest giant-slayer of them all, Tok Guru Nik Aziz Nik Mat.

As Tok Guru speaks I inch my way forward to catch a glimpse of him on the tiny screen of the camera of the policeman who is video-recording the entire event. Not that the cop is trying to blend into the crowd, for he wears a sleeveless jacket that has the word 'POLIS' clearly marked in bold capitals on his back. How many members of the security forces are here, I wonder?

Tok Guru Nik Aziz looks a little grey and fuzzy on the screen, his voice trembling a little and his speech is interrupted by small dry coughs that pop out of his throat like little gremlins. Not having seen him for more than two years, I am struck by how frail he looks and how small he has become. Danny and I turn to each other with the same thought: "Damn, Nik Aziz has shrunk!"

But here, on his home turf, amidst his community, his nation, his Kelantan, the *serban* of Nik Aziz alone is worth one hundred thousand field workers and activists. As long as this man is alive, there is no way that Kelantan will fall to any party save PAS, I think. It is this unqualifiable variable, this curious and singular concoction of piety and humility, determination and earnestness, unshakable conviction and assured knowledge of his blood and kin, that makes Nik Aziz one of the most intriguing and powerful leaders Malaysia has ever seen. The magic can work elsewhere too, and I recall that even in the plush confines of Nikko Hotel, the same Nik Aziz was able to attract a dining room full of supporters and sponsors to hear him speak for fifteen minutes. But it is in Kelantan, his home state, that this descendant of the Kings of Langkasuka is in his element. It is here that the bloodlines of rulers and scholars come to meet and work the magic that is absent elsewhere. Here, Nik Aziz is not merely a politician, but also the *Tok Guru*, teacher and *Murshid'ul Am*: the spiritual guide of one and all. All the Pajeros and helicopters of UMNO cannot touch him here.

Fighting Islam with Islam

As he speaks, Tok Guru Nik Aziz showers the crowd with his pious wishes for a Kelantan that would remain forever under the leadership and guidance of the Ulama. No exhortations to human rights or democracy are offered, no promises of pluralism or the respect for diversity. Not that any of these sweet promises are expected, for nobody has come to hear Nik Aziz speak Bangsarese. The rules of political correctness do not hold, and the discursive economy that is spun is a neatly encrypted economy with rules of its own: this is Islam-speak ala' *Kelante'* and there is no need to be apologetic for being pious. In fact, that's how one gets elected in these parts and Nik Aziz knows that for a fact.

It strikes me that despite the strides that have been made on the west coast, this is another country, and in this other country, another election is being fought. The sniping posts are familiar to me as I have seen it at work in 1999 too. Up for grabs are a host of claims ranging from who is the most pious (and visibly so) to who is the most Kelantanese of them all. And all you interfering busybodies from KL can go back to where you come from: have your elections there if you want to, but here in Kelantan we are having our own elections on our own terms.

And the terms have always been the same: Islam and localism, localism and Islam. From Gua Musang to Kota Bharu, from Bacok to Kuala Trengganu; the placards, billboards and banners that stand at the crossroads of highways and intersections, engaged in a perpetual duel of tongues, come alive only when your car is close enough for you to read them. UMNO is also playing the holier-than-thou card. Its billboards in Trengganu proudly boast that over the past two years sixty-two mosques were built all over the state. (A feat that made it to the *Malaysian Book of Records,* the billboard reminds us.) Right across the street the PAS billboard replies by listing the manifold sins and contradictions of UMNO's Islam Hadari project by pointing to the instances of youth violence, juvenile crime and, of course, the deplorable scourge of smoking that is apparently rampant among kids in Kelantan and Trengganu. Danny and I puff on our satanic *rokoks* and whip out our cameras to record this war of slogans.

UMNO's campaign up north is, for all intents and purposes, another campaign compared to the one going on in the west coast. With no pesky liberal cosmopolitan to hold them back, UMNO is firing all its Islamic guns. The billboards boast of UMNO's success in defending and upholding the image and status of Islam and Muslims, of carpeting the landscape of Trengganu with million-ringgit mosques, and of teaching thousands of Trengganu kids how to memorize the Qur'an by the age of seven. The peak of these achievements is the Islamic Civilisation Park that the state government has built on the outskirts of Kuala Trengganu. So, that's where we head next.

Crystal Mosques and merry-go-rounds

Just as you enter the walled enclave of the Islamic Civilisation Park there stands an enormous billboard that celebrates the rule of UMNO and honours the Sultan of Trengganu. But even here the good 'ol boys of PAS are not about to relent: affixed beneath the billboard is a banner that reads, "250 Million Ringgit for a Mosque Built for Tourists. What for? This is Islam Hadari!"

Driving into the park is a surreal experience as we cannot help but compare it to the opening scene of Jurassic Park. But right after we drive beneath the welcoming arches, there stands a monument that leaves even this jaded cynic speechless. As Bangladeshi workers clear the rubble and dust the road, before us stands a replica of none other than the Dome of the Rock in Jerusalem. The Dome of the Rock? In Kuala Trengganu? The Islamic Civilisation Park has, as one of its many attractions, a collection of miniature mosques from all over the world for visitors to look at and photograph. There is the Hagia Sofia of Istanbul, the Badshahi mosque of the Indian subcontinent, a minaret from the Timurid era of Central Asia, and even the mosque of Patani (that was built from funds donated by the Thai government shortly after the Thai army massacred the leaders of the Patani liberation movement.)

Danny and I walk through the theme park and notice kids at play on the merry-go-round and slides. The eclectic mix is disconcerting to say the least, though I notice that plastic palm trees have also been propped up here and there, perhaps to balance out the coconut trees in the distance and to add that much-needed 'Arab' feel. A large banner over the entrance to the playground-mini-mosque complex thanks the government for bringing Islamic civilisation to Trengganu. (Odd that such a note of thanks has to be registered, considering that Islam has been in Trengganu since the 13th century and that the Trengganuans seemed pretty civilised to me, even before the invention of Islam Hadari.) Danny and I are unsure whether we ought to play a round of mini-golf or run for cover in case a T-rex comes crashing through the tulgey wood and devour us.

Dazed and confused we make our way to the famous Crystal Mosque that is said to be the highlight of the park. Walking around its floating enclosure I talk to some Kelantanese women who are being bussed to Kelantan to vote. What do they think of the Crystal Mosque, I ask. "It's pretty, a bit like a toy," says one. "More like a paperweight," opines her friend next to her. "Is it really made of crystal?" they ask themselves; and I venture to suggest that it is actually made of glass sheets. Before saying goodbye one of them asks the question, "Is it finished yet?"

Preaching democracy in Kampung Slow

By the second week the political temperature is slowly rising. At last. UMNO's leaders fly in, day in, day out; and the media onslaught on the opposition begins in earnest. The leaders and members of PAS are beginning to show perceptible signs of strain and worry. The bookies still have it at fifty-fifty, though the odds are slowly shifting in UMNO's favour. When will the tipping point be reached? And where are the abstract notions of democracy, equality and reform that PAS is preaching to its new converts on the west coast,

I wonder? Fearful that this might prove to be a repeat of the 1999 campaign where Islam is the only thing on the menu, I head out of Kota Bharu to hook up with one of the few PAS progressives I know, Dr Hatta Ramli. Hatta had been given the tough seat of Kuala Krai to contest, but finding him is not easy as he is on the road doing his house-to-house rounds to win over the doubtful ones. I point the car west and hit the gas.

That is, until I come to Kampung Slow.

Kampung Slow is so slow that even the *biawaks* cross the road slowly. I hook up with Hatta and company as he visits a former PAS supporter who has jumped ship to UMNO, and who may well be on the verge of jumping ship again. Hatta and his wife, along with his team – doctors, every one of them – administer basic medical care while he preaches the gospel of the new PAS. The elderly man who welcomes us to his home has had a stroke, and Hatta reminds him to watch his diet and stop eating red meat. *"Pakchik merokok tak?"* Hatta asks, and I swear I catch a glimpse of his third eye at the back of his head, winking at me. "Try to stop smoking *pakchik*, it's bad for your heart. I know you will listen to my advise, unlike some *degil* people I know who want to smoke themselves to death," he adds, his third eye winking in my direction again.

At times Hatta uses me to break the ice in the company of new faces. We enter the *surau* near Kampung Slow and Hatta greets the common folk of *Ulu Kelante* and introduces me to them in turn. "This is Dr Farish Noor, remember? The one who writes on *kerises* and was accused of blasphemy not too long ago." "Ah, yes, Dr Farish, we were protesting against you before!" the crowd laughs.

There in the dusky confines of the rickety *surau* with only one fluorescent lamp shedding light on us all, Hatta pleads to the humble folk and extols the virtues of his Islamic party. "Remember that we in PAS are here for you. We are here when you need us, and we will always be here for you. I know that many of you are poor, that some of you are sick and old. But remember that in a just society, every one of us should be able to have basic healthcare, for that is our right. That is why we need to vote into power a just government, a caring government, a government that cares for us in this world and the next. That is what we wish to do in PAS. What we wish to give you is a *negara kebajikan* – a welfare state – so that nobody will be left out, regardless of race or religion."

The toothless grandfathers and grandmothers cuddle their grandchildren close to their bosoms, and their tiny eyes glint in the fading light. Here in a forlorn *surau* with cobwebs on the ceiling, Dr Hatta dons his white short-sleeved shirt, wears his stethoscope and preaches the new vision of a welfare state on behalf of PAS. Who says there cannot be a new Malaysia? I'd vote for him if only he will stop complaining about my smoking.

A new Malaysia

The day finally arrives when the masses go out to vote. Right up to the last minute the bookies hedge their bets, and we are all on tenterhooks. Danny and I drive up and down Kelantan and Trengganu to make sense of what is about to happen and we observe the action close-up at the *pondok panas* and polling stations. At one UMNO *pondok,* smack in the middle of downtown KB, the pretty lasses of Puteri UMNO, bedecked in pink and smiles, hold up cardboard signs promising million-dollar mosques to the people of Kelantan should they vote

UMNO into power. But having viewed the Crystal Mosque up close in Trengganu, I wonder if the people of Kelantan want or need one? And why is UMNO still promising Islam as the panacea for all that ails the people of Kelantan, when it is painfully clear that the terms of the campaign has shifted?

By nightfall Danny and I are pooped, but our work is far from over. We park ourselves at the Mutiara café right next to the PAS headquarters in Kota Bharu, as the crowd gathers to listen to the results being announced. One by one the early counts come in, and the crowd increases. The mood is electric. One feels the short hairs on the back on one's neck standing on end. Minute by minute, the calls begin to come in. By 9.00 pm it is clear that the bookies are wrong. One by one the State Assembly seats of Kelantan fall to PAS, and it is a crushing defeat that they mete out on UMNO. The crowd explodes with joy, and the victory cry sounds: *"Takbir!"* cries one of them, and the others reply, *"Allahuakbar! Allahuakbar! Allahuakbar!"*

The foreign stringers are there too, and no-one can make sense of what is happening. "My God, my God," cries a journalist from Singapore, "They are winning! They are winning! The states are falling one by one!" But I'm holding back still, and Danny and I are typing out our despatches at double-speed, fuelled by coffee and cigarettes. Suddenly, in the midst of the noise and flurry, the opening comes, and the moment of truth is reached.

The large screen that projects the live report by TV3 announces that Lim Kit Siang, leader of the Democratic Action Party, has won. For half a second there is absolute silence. Then the rebel yell is raised, *"Takbir! Allahuakbar! Allahuakbar! Allahuakbar!"* They scream with joy as the victories of Lim Kit Siang, Karpal Singh and Lim Guan Eng are announced. Danny and I sit back and bask in that historical moment. Who would have thought that here, in the heart of Kota Bharu, a thousand PAS supporters would be cheering on their allies, the DAP?

"Who would have thought that we would live to see this, man?" I scream to Danny above the tidal wave of noise and emotion. My eyes have seen the Mahastupas of Anuradhapura, the hills and vales of the Kashmir valley, the serpentine course of the great Amazon, the colossi of Ramses II at Abu Simbel, the Sahara al-Beida of the Libyan desert. I have seen the last columns of the Taliban march in their final retreat from Afghanistan, I have supped at the same table with the hash-dealers of the Tribal Areas of the North-West Frontier Province. But never did I think I would live to see the day when the victory of Lim Kit Siang would be met with the cry, "God is Great, God is Great, God is Great." Once again, the Kelantanese have surprised us all.

Homeward bound

The psychological hangover from the night's excitement has drained both Danny and me, though we promise ourselves one last serving of the *telur setengah masak* at the famous White House café in Kelantan. "How on earth do they do it?" Danny asks as we wolf down the famous half-boiled egg that only they at the White House can serve up. "I mean, for heaven's sake, it's just a half-boiled egg. How come it's so different?" That's something for Hishamuddin Rais to answer, I think. We are happy enough to have been there, seen that, done that.

I meet up with Hatta just before driving home and remind him, "Now that you've won, make sure you set up that free clinic you promised your constituents. Otherwise, we in civil society will *hentam* you!" Hatta, for once, stops pestering me to stop smoking.

We take to the road via Gua Musang and drive all the way back to Kuala Lumpur, getting home around midnight. Kelantan seemed so far away by the time the familiar landscape of Klang Valley comes into view. I realise that all along the way we have driven through states now in the hands of what used to be called the Opposition, though no longer. My eyes look forward, but my mind turns back to the events the night before, when a thousand Islamists cheered the victory of their secular-leftist comrades. That frontier may have been breached once and for all, I think. This is a new country. May it live and prosper.

Land of Bleeding Smiles
(Patani, 2005)

As I cross the border between Malaysia and Thailand, a huge poster stands before me. It bears the image of a smiling woman and the slogan reads: 'Welcome to Thailand, Land of Smiles'.

I've crossed the Thai-Malaysian border many times before, doing research on social and religious movements. It had never seemed to me as a crossing into the unfamiliar. The sights, sounds and smells are the same: from the songbirds in their colourful bamboo cages to the sickly-sweet smell of the *durian* fruit, a heady odour described by my ex-wife as a combination of petrol and a rancid dustbin stewing in the heat.

Both Southern Thailand and Northern Malaysia were once a single Malay-Muslim kingdom that was split apart by the Anglo-Siamese treaty of 1909. The British colonial government claimed Kelantan while Patani was unceremoniously left to the Thais. But the people of Patani now feel that they've been given a raw deal: most of them are Malay-Muslims and they're now reduced to being a four per cent minority in predominantly Buddhist Thailand. Many Kelantanese still hop across the border to shop at the local markets in Patani, though these days it can be quite dangerous.

On the day I cross the border into Thailand through the seedy town of Golok, a man is shot in the back of his head and left dead, face-down in the mud, in front of the market. This is not an isolated case of violence: for a year now Southern Thailand has been a hotbed for sporadic shootings and bombings. In this year alone more than five hundred people have been killed by both militant groups and the Thai security forces. Everywhere I go I see police and army roadblocks, manned by young soldiers whose fingers rest nervously on the triggers of their guns.

I try to talk to one of the soldiers when I am in the town of Narathiwat, but as soon as I approach him he waves his gun at me and says, "Go away, go away, don't stand there." The poor fellow is clearly nervous of me on my motorbike, as many of the shootings that have taken place have been drive-by killings with the assassins riding motorcycles. The soldier looks like he is in his late teens – without his uniform, he could pass off as one of my students. His fear, though, is real enough, for the situation in Patani is rapidly deteriorating.

A few weeks earlier a demonstration in the small town of Tak Bai turned ugly when the police tried to disperse the demonstrators. The crowd had gathered in support of some local Muslim leaders who had been arrested on the grounds that they may have some links with the mysterious militant groups operating in the region. In the chaos that followed, hundreds were arrested. Thai journalists reported what happened next: ordered to strip and lie on the ground, the protesters were then made to crawl on their bellies to the waiting trucks. Then, packed in like livestock, they were piled on top of one another and then driven off to a detention centre five hours away. In the course of the journey nearly eighty of the protesters suffocated to death, or were crushed in the trucks.

The slogan 'Welcome to Thailand, Land of Smiles' sounds somewhat hollow.

"Things are going crazy here, man! I'm getting out!"

My friend Don, a Thai journalist, runs up to me at our meeting point, at some hole-in-the-wall drinking place squeezed in between a couple of gaudily-painted massage parlours. Don is a veteran in that area, one of the very few journalists whose list of contacts seems to extend forever and ever, and who knows the region like the back of his hand. He pops out of a pick-up truck and the heat gets to him immediately. By the time he enters the protective shade of the tea stall he is already sweating profusely, like the rest of us.

As we sit and sip some tea, Don sums up the situation for me: "Things are going crazy here, man!" he says. "Everyone is paranoid, and nobody trusts anybody anymore. The army and police are over-reacting and the militants are exploiting this fear. What happened in Tak Bai is just what the militants want: it gives them the justification for their own killings and it allows them to tell their followers that the government is anti-Muslim. It's no longer safe for outsiders," he concludes. "I'm getting out!" It is cold comfort for me, as I've just arrived.

As we smoke, a row of green-painted pick-ups race past, bearing men in uniform with badges and insignia of various colours: jungle police, crack military commandos, counter-insurgency units, paramilitary, paratrooper brigade. It seems as if the brass tacks of the Fourth Army have pulled out all the stops, and the whole Thai army is here.

Thailand's slide into inter-religious conflict seems to be part and parcel of the country's slide towards a more authoritarian form of politics. When Prime Minister Thaksin Shinawatra came to power in 2001, he and the leaders of his *Thai Rak Thai* party claimed that they would restore law and order. Their first campaign was against the drug cartels and criminal networks in the country. As the campaign wore on, the body count rose. Local estimates put the figure of people killed at around two thousand – many of whom were killed by the security forces in shoot-outs. While it is true that the country is saddled with a chronic drugs problem, local human rights activists have condemned the violent methods that have been used, arguing that many of the alleged criminals were not given the right to a fair trial.

Following the Bali bombing in 2002, Thaksin was one of the first leaders of the region to embrace President Bush's 'global campaign against terror', with the security forces of Thailand going on a hunt for alleged Islamic militants in the South. Throughout this bloody campaign, the international community remained curiously silent. The governments of Indonesia, Philippines, Singapore and Malaysia were likewise engaged in their own anti-terror campaigns. And the American government – once the most ardent promoter of human rights in Asia – was slow to react.

The situation on the ground, however, is always more complicated than the politicians tell us. I have come to know Patani-Kelantan quite well, due to my research work. Patani and Kelantan have failed to benefit from the economic development of Thailand and Malaysia, and have remained among the poorest and most backward parts of the region. In the markets of Southern Thailand one comes across goods that are typical of any poor rural community: fruit and vegetables, fish and meat, farmers' tools and local handicrafts. Occasionally, one sees an Osama ben Laden T-shirt on sale.

At the local market I decide to interview the young man who is selling them.

"How's business?" I ask him. "Oh, it's doing well" comes the reply. "Who buys these T-shirts?" is my next question. He replies "Everyone. Lots of kids like them. We also sell them to dealers who come from Malaysia, Indonesia, Philippines. Foreign backpackers, too. They buy them by the hundreds and then sell them back home."

I ask the young man: "So do *you* support Osama too? I mean, would *you* be happy if people like them came here, and turned Thailand into a country like Afghanistan under the Taliban?"

He gives me a broad grin and said: "Oh no, no, noooo! I'm Buddhist and I have a girlfriend, man! I enjoy the motorbike races on the weekends and going out to have drinks with my friends, racing on the highways, playing computer games, and all that."

"So why *do* you sell these T-shirts then?" I ask. He replies: "It's simple. We are fed up with what our government in Bangkok is doing to us. I mean, look at how poor we are. Life for us here has been hard for years; we've had to cope with criminal gangs, smugglers, drug-pushers, and now, the army and cops. But Bangkok is more interested in supporting the Americans, and the Americans hate Osama. So we wear the Osama T-shirt to say: we don't care about your policy with the United States. We have our own identity and we want you to respect it."

I then notice that among the Osama ben Laden T-shirts is one with Che Guevara. I glance at the boy's shiny motorbike parked nearby: it is bright green and there is a sticker on it that says, 'No Fear'.

Fear and Loathing

No fear. An odd sentiment to express, particularly in a form that confounds the fundamental rules of grammar and syntax. Bravado reduced to expletives and expressed in bursts of gunfire sprayed from guns mounted on racing motorbikes. Speed kills here, and the situation seems to be spiralling out of control, blurring faster than any analyst can make sense of it.

In search of some kind of focus, some nodal point to keep my rambling story together, I turn to my local contacts. "Go to the mosque," he tells me. "There you will find some of the locals who may be able to tell you what is going on." With my Minolta in hand I head for the Markaz Tabligh of Golok, only to be told that there are two of them, each in a different direction.

At the Markaz Besar Tabligh I find myself in familiar company: the *markaz* is a combination of mosque, community centre, hostel, school and boarding house, all in one. As soon as I walk past its gates I see the familiar sight of young Tablighi boys all dressed in white, with neat little turbans wound round their heads. Books in hand, they all seem to be heading in the same direction: the main hall of the mosque where a *hafiz* class is going on. I listen to the familiar drone of a hundred voices reading the Qur'an in unison, young boys learning to memorise the Qur'an by heart by the age of ten. I greet the young bearded *ustaz* at the door and he beckons me to come in from the heat. "Welcome, brother. You are always welcome here."

I tell the *ustaz* that my destination is the Grand Markaz in Jala, and that my bike and its driver are waiting outside. "No, no, no, don't go there today. We just had word that the Thai police are about to raid the place, and they are rounding up all foreigners. You don't look like you come from these parts; in fact, you can pass for a Pakistani here. Once you're caught by them, God knows what might happen to you. Remember Tak Bai?" Yes, I do. It burns in my mind, in fact.

Unable to proceed any further I end up spending the night at the Markaz. Once again I'm back among the Tablighi Jama'at. I am home.

Forbidden to smoke, my nerves are on the edge and by nightfall I have gone cranky. The boys of the Markaz take a liking to me and I spend the night entertaining their predictably juvenile questions. There are twelve of them who are from Indonesia. I ask them which *markaz* they come from, and they mention the Markaz Kebun Jeruk in Jakarta, where I studied once. Most of them are in their late teens, and the slogan 'No Fear' does not apply to them. They are scared out of their wits, and rightly so. "Some of our passports are in Jala and some of us have come here to do the visa-hop to the Malaysian side and back. But now we are told that all our friends in Jala have been arrested and taken away. We cannot go back to Jala, and we cannot stay here either. What do we do, brother?"

I look at their faces and see the fear that is all too evident; young Tablighis lost in Patani without a passport, members of the world's biggest Islamic missionary movement – the Tablighi Jama'at – that emerged in India in the early 20th century and whose paths I have followed and tracked for several years as part of my research on transnational religious networks across Asia. How many times have I met such young men: poor, lonely, guided only by faith and the conviction that they are carrying out God's work on earth by spreading His message. Patani has become a major centre and the Grand Markaz in Jala is the biggest centre of Tabligh activity in Southeast Asia. Neo-Salafiyya purists at heart, the Tablighis are recognisable by their apparent Indian dress and manners, trademark of a movement that developed in Northern India. Indonesians or not, the Tablighis are commonly referred to as 'those Indians'.

Powerless to help, I can only tell them to keep a low profile until the heat blows over. But we all know that Patani is no longer safe for the Tablighis, and that moves are being made to arrest and deport them *en masse*. Their sullen looks betray their loss of confidence and the fear that gnaws at them. All over Patani paranoia and tension are on the rise. I write in my notebook the horror stories that they recount to me, in the dim light of the solitary florescent lamp that hisses in the corner. The rumour mill has gone into overdrive: in one village where the local *imam* organised villagers to clear their mosque compound with farming tools, the police, seeing the villagers walking to the mosque with machetes and axes in hand, opened fire, killing half of them. Blood for blood, and eye for an eye: the next day a Buddhist monk was shot in the face as he walked around the same village, begging bowl in hand.

"We feel cheated by the politicians, and the young are fighting back."

At dawn we wake up for morning prayer. I savour the last hour of coolness before the temperature begins to rise and my sweat pores begin to do their day's work. The boys I spoke to the night before have disappeared, and I do not ask for them. The young *Ustaz* who greeted me the previous day comes up to say goodbye. Trying to get to the bottom of things I ask his opinion of what is going on, and how could things here have degenerated so badly.

"For years we were neglected and left behind," he says. "The government invested millions of dollars into Patani, but where has the money gone? Are the people any better off? Do we look rich to you? We feel we've been cheated by the politicians, and now the younger generation is getting angry and fighting back. We can't control them any longer." Well, if the religious leaders aren't controlling the angry young men, then who is?

I ask the teacher about the renewed violence in the region and he says, "We don't know who is behind it; this is something new for all of us. In the past our struggle was political, but now it's becoming a religious issue. What do you expect? For so long the authorities turned a blind eye to all the smuggling that took place here, and now the whole area is full of guns and weapons. The militants who are doing the killing are a small minority, but all of us Muslims are being blamed. Nobody cares about us anymore. We feel that we are being victimised, like Muslims all over the world, like in Afghanistan and Iraq."

I notice the teacher's clenched fists, as he talks about the abuse of prisoners at Abu Ghraib prison and Guantanamo Bay. His final statement is telling: what began as a local problem has now become an international one, hence the popularity of Osama for a people who have never heard of him before, and the relevance of events thousands of miles away in Iraq.

At another school I pick up a text entitled *'Jihad in Patani'*, that spoke of a global campaign against Muslims. The mysterious author of the text compared Patani to Afghanistan and Iraq, and called for Muslims to unite against the United States of America. In all my years visiting and researching in Patani, I have never read anything like it. I leave Patani worried, not knowing what will happen to the people there. From the presence of the army to the tone of the people I have interviewed, the tension is palpable. This is not the Patani I once knew.

Comparing the markets of Patani and Kelantan with the sprawling, hyper-modern, air-conditioned malls of Bangkok and Kuala Lumpur is like comparing two different countries in two different parts of the world. In the capitals of Thailand and Malaysia one can find the latest hi-tech gizmos and fashion items for those whose wallets are fat enough to afford them. But such wealth is a million miles away from the lives of the folk in Patani. Now, it doesn't take a political scientist to tell you what all of this will lead to. It's common sense to think that if and when a community feels itself neglected, it will end up becoming more defensive, even hostile to the outside world. During my trip to Patani I have the distinct feeling that the mood have changed in the region: The people are as poor as before, but also more angry about their state, and what is happening in the world around them.

On my return trip to Malaysia, I notice a number of tourist posters too. Like the Thai ads, there are plenty of smiling faces, and the slogan reads, *'Welcome to Malaysia, Land of Harmony'*. My Malaysian contact sneers at me and says, "It's easy to live in harmony when we're all equally poor." All over Southeast Asia, the governments of the region are obsessed with the threat of Islamic terror. But these same governments cannot see the obvious link between poverty and public anger.

Back in my office in Berlin and sitting in front of my computer, my mind goes back to the young, smiling boy selling his Osama T-shirts; racing on the highways with his girlfriend. What would it take for him to cross that final, invisible line, and take Osama into his heart? What would drive anyone to express his frustration and anger through violence?

One of the reasons for the renewed fighting is the violence of the Thai security forces, which has often led to the loss of innocent lives. The other factor is the arrival of a new wave of militancy that is clearly alien to the region, and more violent in nature. But perhaps the root cause of all these problems, and the reason why Patani is now ripe for the recruitment of angry young men, is the underlying poverty and the neglect it has suffered over the years. As long as these problems are not addressed openly and honestly, suspicion will remain, and most likely continue to fester.

Already a spate of killings have claimed the lives of other innocents: a few days after the deaths of the eighty Muslim protesters at Tak Bai, a school teacher was murdered by militants claiming it was an act of revenge. So far, those killed include the poor and the ordinary: policemen, shopkeepers, farmers and fishermen. The body count continues to rise. And the smiling girl on the poster no longer convinces.

That Quaint Little War Up North
(Patani, Jala, Narathiwat; Southern Thailand, May 2008)

A sullen brooding Shah Rukh Khan saunters into the grand entrance hall, sideburns ablaze on his smouldering, sweaty face; pants so tight that one is tempted to call for an ambulance; piercing angry eyes staring at the moustachioed villain squarely in the face. His gait is feline, animal-like, his fists are clenched tight as his butt cheeks, and his shirt is opened mid-way down his chest. The baddie stares down at him from gilded rails of the spiral staircase, a nasty-looking scar defacing what would otherwise be a virile, albeit repugnant countenance that makes you wonder what happened to the last woman he slept with. The music crackles, then builds up to a crescendo, in anticipation of what the hero is about to say. The drum beat ceases, all is silence, and Shah Rukh Khan says: *"Ambo date' ke sini kerano nak kecek tengte' hok ogrhe kampong ambo ..."*

Welcome to Patani, where even Shah Rukh Khan speaks in Patani-Kelantanese.

"Hero dio ni, meme' hero kecek mace' tu deh!" the crowd surmises. I am watching a dubbed version of what appears to be a rather old DVD of a Shah Rukh Khan flick, played on a small TV hooked to a DVD player on top of a van stacked with scores of pirated DVD movies. Around me a small but attentive crowd of punters gather to take in the action, before all

hell breaks loose and Shah Rukh Khan gives the bad guy and his cronies a jolly good dressing down. Even the chandelier comes off the ceiling and after the bad guy's palatial mansion is reduced to a pile of ruins, it is only the good guy who remains standing, smack in the centre, unfazed and untouched by the mayhem.

Approving this latest dish of blood and gore, the crowd pushes forward to purchase their own copies of the DVD. It's roaring business at the roadside kampong market in Mayo, Patani; and again I stick out like a sore thumb despite my pathetic attempt to blend in by wearing a sarong and *kepiah*. Everywhere I turn I see the kampong folk staring at me, asking themselves, 'Who on earth is this fellow?'

Not too far away, my friend and contact Ustaz Meng is chatting with his kampong friends, and I can hear him telling them not to be too worried about this new character in their midst. "Yes, he looks Arab but is from Germany, and he now works in Indonesia, but he lives in Singapore, and he has a flat in KL," Ustaz Meng assures them, only to add to the confusion. It doesn't take long for the confusion to sediment, and by the second day I am referred to as the 'Ustaz Arab'. Great, I thought: right at a time when foreigners are being picked up by the cops all over southern Thailand, that's just what I need; to be called 'Ustaz Arab'.

I am in Patani again as part of my fieldwork on itinerant religious movements and the habits and customs of my dear chums of the Tablighi Jama'at, the world's biggest Muslim missionary movement, and a phenomenon all unto itself. For the past eight years I have been studying the world of modern religious praxis, travelling with itinerant Hindu pilgrims and Buddhist monks, living in madrasahs, monasteries and mosques; climbing up and down hills and mountains in search of temples and religious schools from Sri Lanka to the Moluccas. But of all the groups I studied — and believe me, I've studied a lot of them, as my bad back will testify — the Tablighi Jama'at remain the most fascinating for me.

The Tabligh began in the early 20th century in India and was at the outset a reaction on the part of conservative Indian Muslims against the spread of Christianity in India by Anglican and Catholic missionaries. Later, it also developed as a reaction against the rise of born-again Hindu revivalists in India who formed organisations like the Arya Samaj. From the outset it has retained its strong India-centric worldview and appearance, which continues to dictate the form and content of its practices, down to the sartorial norms of its members. Hence the fact that many of the Tablighis I've met have the tendency to wear the *shalwar khameez* of India rather than the *gallabiyas* of the Arabs, and no stay with the Tablighis is complete without the requisite diet of chapattis, chapattis and more chapattis.

Now, not many know that the Tablighis have settled all across Southeast Asia since the 1970s and the biggest centre of the Tablighis in the region is the Markaz Besar Tabligh based at the Masjid al-Nur in Jala, Southern Thailand. During its heyday, the Markaz Besar would host congregations that numbered in the tens of thousands for the annual *ijtima*, or great gathering, of the Tablighis from all over the archipelago.

This is meant to be just another routine research trip to the southern provinces of Thailand that I have been visiting regularly for the past decade, and my final destination this time is meant to be the Markaz Besar where I am certain to be fed chapattis again. But things do not go as planned, as contingencies do have the tendency to sneak up on you, and even the best made field trip plans are rent asunder. As it turns out, I have accidentally walked into a rather quaint little insurgency.

Barbed wire and Humvees

The cop takes a look at my passport, then stares at my face, and seems to wonder, How come he has a beard now but none in the photo? He then looks back at the passport, and back at me, and his attention turns to the passport yet again. "You what?" he asks.

"Me, what?" I reply.

"You, what? What, you?" he asks again.

"Me, what? Me, tourist. Academic. Teacher. Professor. Come to take pictures." I reply.

"What pictures? What, you what?" he shoots back.

This is the first of my four encounters with the friendly representatives of the Thai security forces who man the roadblocks from Tak Bai all the way to the town of Patani. There are, in fact, twenty-four such roadblocks on the way to Patani and thirty-four in all. As it is becoming clear that the interview is getting nowhere, I pull out a book that I have written on woodcarving and architecture of Patani, Kelantan and Trengganu to show that I am not some backpacker who is simply heading for the first beach in search of a local takeaway ganja depot. (Not that the southern beaches have any tourists left in the first place, for most of these destinations have already been bombed or burned down by the insurgents.)

By the time I get to Patani town it is almost dark and I say goodbye to my mates from Kelantan who had driven me here. Now where on earth is my contact, and how am I going to get to the countryside, and then on to Jala, without a ride?

Out of nowhere Ustaz Meng pops up in his pick-up truck. (By then I realise that practically everyone is driving pick-ups here.) The place has the feel of a hill-billy settlement and I am half-expecting to see moose antlers and the flag of St. Andrew's cross on the bonnets of the jeeps and trucks. "Hello there!" he beams at me. "Welcome to Patani! Was it difficult getting in? No trouble with the army or the police, I hope."

Just as I am about to answer the question, Ustaz Meng and the other customers of the tea house go silent. The smiles disappear and backs are straightened as they sit on the rickety bamboo chairs. I turn to catch a glimpse of what they are all looking at, my eyes following the direction of their collective gaze. The next thing I know, I am staring down the barrel of a submachine gun mounted on the turret of an armoured Humvee right next to me.

The Humvee rolls past ever so slowly, like some prehistoric beast clad in armour, with narrow slits for eyes. Its headlights are covered with wire mesh and the hood is slung low, giving the impression of a gigantic shelled crab resting on heavy, armoured legs that are stunted and squat. On the roof is a gun emplacement where a submachine gun is mounted, its barrel pointed right at my face, and then Ustaz Meng's, and then at the other customers of the tea shop, one by one. Behind the gun is the dwarf figure of a young soldier whose age is impossible to divine as he seems to have sunken into his uniform, burdened as he was by his oversized bullet-proof jacket, helmet and dark reflective glasses. The soldier aims the gun straight at our faces, as if he is acquainting the weapon with each and everyone of us. "Gun, this is Farish. Farish, this is my gun. Do you like it?"

The moment seems to go on forever but, ultimately, even armoured Humvees have to mosey off elsewhere to intimidate other people. Thankful that we were not the only ones whose luck it was to greet soldier-boy's machine gun at close range, we breathe a sigh of relief as the Humvee plods along down the road, its gun pointing at the cat on the dustbin next.

"You see what it's like for us over here?" Ustaz Meng turns to me with visible disgust on his face. "That's what it's like for us now. You can't even sit at the tea shop and sip your coffee or tea in peace without someone pointing a gun at your face. Do you ever experience these things in KL?" he asks. Well no, actually, I am forced to admit. Though the last time I was nodding off at a café, a handbag was stolen right in front of me.

"What is going on here, Meng?" I ask. "Twenty-four roadblocks on the road to Patani, police checks, and now this." "That's not all," the Ustaz points out. "On the village roads, it's worse. They've put up anti-vehicle barricades since the car-bombing that knocked out the car park and lobby of the C S Patani Hotel. They've got roving patrols on motorbikes. And the village defence forces are the worst – those guys shoot at you without even warning you first. You'll see when we get to the kampongs," he assures me.

"Don't we need to get a move on then? It's getting dark and I was told that there are curfews here. And the roadblocks will get worse at night, won't they?"

"Nah, don't worry. We have time. Have another tea and you'll see later. It's fine at night. The soldiers and cops will go back to the barracks. They know better than to man the village outposts after the sun has gone down. They're no longer in charge then." Ustaz Meng replies with a smile on his face. "If they are not in charge, who is?" I ask. "Why, they are, of course – the guerrillas."

"Waktu Geriya"

Over the next few days Ustaz Meng and I travel around the southern provinces at night with no problem whatsoever. Occasionally we reach a small town or village where the street lights are on and a roadblock has been set up nearby. Meng teaches me the basic rules of how to approach a roadblock at night without having the magazine of a submachine gun emptied in your face, and your pick-up reduced to cottage cheese. "Turn off your headlights as soon as you come near the street lights. Roll down the windows and keep your free hand out, so that they can see you are not packing anything nasty. Turn on the lamp in the passenger cabin so they can see your face. Smile. And keep smiling. And the cops and soldiers don't speak *Jawi*, the language of the Patani Malay-Muslims, so you better learn some basic Thai."

Once past the roadblocks we race into the darkness, and occasionally pass other roadblocks that are deep in the wilderness, along the rural village roads. We drive past sandbag emplacements near bridges, fortified bunkers near power stations and radio transmitters. All of them are empty, without a soldier in sight.

"See? I told you the roadblock posts will be empty at night! That's the rule here. In the daytime the Thai soldiers run the place. But at night they all run back to their barracks or stay in the well-lit towns and cities. They know better than to patrol the villages at night. And who would want to sit at a roadblock in the middle of the jungle in the dark, where they can get shot at from any angle? They're not stupid, you know. They know that after sunset, after the *maghrib* prayers, it's the other side's turn. We call it *waktu geriya*, the hour of the guerrillas."

Suddenly Meng slows down his pick-up to point out a discolouration on the road. "See that patch in the tar? That's where the guerrillas buried their mine that blew up the pick-up carrying members of the special forces. The crater is still there, see?"

I assure Meng that I have been keeping myself updated with the antics of the insurgents in this bloody turf war. The crater, which is about six feet wide, has already been tarred over. We are close to the outskirts of the village of Telaga Sembilan. The mine buried there was detonated just when the pick-up carrying the soldiers was squarely on top of it, crushing the vehicle like a tin can and sending it spinning upwards and forward. Four soldiers were killed instantly in the car, crushed by the impact. The other three who sat at the back were blown out, sent spinning heavenwards before they fell to the ground. But before they could get up and crawl away, the insurgents emerged from the undergrowth, and shot them in the back of the head, one by one. This took place no more than a hundred metres from the coffee shop on the border of the village, in full view of everyone. As expected, nobody came forward to serve as witness for the enquiry later. I hadn't realised before how close the scene of the attack is to the village, and how brazen the guerrillas have become.

While the security condition made it more difficult for me to get to Jala and to do the research that I have come to do, I am equally confused about what is going on and how badly things have deteriorated in the space of two years since I was here last. Driving around the kampong roads I am struck by the familiarity of it all; how so much of Patani and Jala look, sound and feel like Kelantan. The names of villages we pass echo traces of *Jawi*, with family resemblances to Malay. Pa Na Rae (*Panarek*), Te La Go Sem Bi Lan (*Telaga Sembilan*), Lam Phu (*Lampu*), Ka Yomati (*Kayu Mati*). One only has to get past the Patani twang to hear the familiar strains of Malay.

While semantic and phonetic associations and overlapping are of interest to linguists and cultural historians, for those who have to live in these contested spaces conflicts over languages and cultures are not so pleasant or easy. The Southern provinces of Thailand are exactly the kind of shared cultural spaces that academics theorise about, largely because they don't have to live there. But for the folk who reside in these frontier zones, life can be confusing, with tensions negotiated on a daily basis. I need to get a better feel of how the people of Patani, Jala and

Narathiwat feel about their place in the grander scheme of things; and to understand why the insurgency seems to be getting worse. Meng decides that the time has come for me to get a closer glimpse of the reality, so we get off the tarred highway and his pick-up begins to kick up clouds of mud and dust as we go deep into the interior.

The heart of the matter

"Slekooooooong!" Meng calls out as we approach the house at the fringe of the village. *"Slekooooooong!"* comes the reply.

I chuckle at the way the Patanis pronounce '*Assalamualaikum*', with scant regard for transliteration and a distaste for too many vowels. It doesn't even have to sound Arabic in these parts: an approximation will do, for the Patanis are, after all, a pious lot and they don't need some Arab to come and teach them how to be Muslims. No, down here being a Patani Malay means being a Muslim by default, and they're damn proud of that. Meng introduces me to his friends, religious teachers from the *pondok* schools and *madrasah*s of the province, and we get down to the serious business of sipping tea and rolling our *rokok daun*. Now, this is how proper field research is done!

On the wall hangs a framed laminated jigsaw puzzle with the image of the Masjid'ul Haram in Mecca. It looks like the puzzle had never been taken out of the box, and all the pieces are intact and in place. The puzzle I want to understand is somewhat more complex. I look about the living room and notice the many tiny details that I have seen elsewhere; the symbolic paraphernalia and accoutrements of the poor and the low, the home of the underclass and the marginal. From Karachi to Peshawar, from Rantau Panjang to Durban, poor homes all look alike: the odd concession to perceived notions of good taste and pedestrian aesthetics, the sincere attempt to appear presentable to the outsider's gaze. As expected, I find the ubiquitous flower-pot with plastic flowers in them, somewhat dusty. They are orchids this time, white with pink hints on the petals.

Now the rules of fieldwork and the conduct of interviews should be easily understood by anyone with any empathy for his fellow human beings: take your time and don't start by taking out your notebook and asking questions. Apart from protecting the identity of your interviewees (all these names are made up, I hope you realise), one also has to create the comfort zone where communication can take place. This means taking your time to allow the words to flow naturally. So we talk, and talk, and talk about everything under the sun.

The entire day is taken up with long discussions on the history of the southern provinces, so here comes the history lesson: before the modern age and the emergence of nation-states in Asia, there existed a loose federation of Malay-Muslim kingdoms that lined the coastal belt along the Southeastern and Northwestern shores of Thailand and Malaysia, respectively. Historical records clearly indicate that the Kingdom of Patani had been in existence for many centuries, dating back at least to the 17th century, if not earlier. Patani, Jala, Narathiwat and Satun were in turn closely linked to the Malay kingdoms of Kelantan, Trengganu, Perlis and Kedah; and historians of pre-Islamic era have put forth the theory that they were all once linked together in a loose assembly of federated Hindu-Buddhist kingdoms that was called Langkasuka. So strong is this affiliation to the past that the semi-mythical kingdom of Langkasuka remains, to this day, the starting-point for all serious discussion of Patani and its politics. Even the grand ol' Murshid'ul Am of PAS, Tok Guru Nik Aziz Nik Mat, traces his royal genealogy back to the Rajas and Maharajas of Langkasuka.

Then one day some Europeans came along with the bright idea of carving up Southeast Asia for themselves. Artificial boundaries were created and lines were drawn on the map, cutting across the Malacca Straits and dissecting the Malay Peninsula from Sumatra; cutting across the Malay Peninsula and splitting what used to be the domain of Langkasuka in half. Britain's 'forward movement' policy reached as far as the Kelantan-Golok river and stopped at Tak Bai. Following the Anglo-Siamese treaty, Kelantan, Trengganu, Kedah and Perlis came under British indirect rule and were lumped together as the Unfederated Malay States (UFMS), while Patani, Jala, Narathiwat and Satun were left to the advancing forces of the Thais. The history of the latter has been a nasty and bloody one, since. Decades of forced assimilation – first by the monarchs Rama IV and V, and later by less enlightened strongmen like Phibun Songkram, who had a peculiar liking for knee-high leather boots ala' Mussolini – meant that the Malay-Muslims of the south were forced to adapt to Thai ways, whether they liked it or not. Phibun even made it compulsory for the Malays of the south to wear Western hats, and to roll up their sarongs between their knees in the Thai manner; a move not designed to win the hearts and minds of people who preferred to wear their sarongs in their own traditional way, thank you very much. By the 1960s the Patani Malays had had enough and underground movements like the Patani United Liberation Organisation (PULO) was created. Things have been going downhill ever since.

"We are Not migrants!"

The teachers are taken in by the fact that I actually know the history of Patani, Jala and Narathiwat, and that I've written about Patani art and history. Once again the woodcarving book is taken out and shown around, and I promise to send everyone a copy. The teachers lend their weight to the discussion and each one elaborates on his own understanding of Patani's history. Cikgu Nik puts on his historian's hat and opines, "You know that our history goes back centuries. You're the historian, right? You have your old maps and prints, don't you? Now, can you see that Patani was on the map even before Bangkok? We were here during the heydays of Ayudhya. We did not migrate to this place; it was they, the Thais, who came and colonised us! Why is it that when we send our children to the government's Thai schools, they don't even get to learn their own history?"

Cikgu Wan chips in with his contribution to the debate: "You know that we have always been the centre for Islamic teaching here in the Peninsula. There were *pondok* schools here for centuries, and all the Ulama of Kelantan, Trengganu, Aceh, Riau, even Java, came to study in Patani. But now the government tells us that the *pondok* schools are dangerous; that we produce terrorists; that we preach hate against the state. Since when? Why is this a problem now? Why not before?"

Then it's Cikgu Mi's turn to enter the fray and his comments were likewise to the point: "Today, there are more and more migrants from the North and Northeast of Thailand who have settled here. What will happen to us? We, the Malay-Muslims, are no longer the majority in our own province. They tell us to assimilate and to become Thai; but we are not Thai. We are Malay. *Kalao demo nok puja Tuhe' Buda, tok po; tapi kito buke' orghre Buda deh. Kito orghre Patani, orghre Melayu belako. Ngapo demo nok buat kito jadi mace' demo? Ngapo?"*

In the corner I spy the diminutive figure of Cikgu Teacher, the oddest character in the cast. Cikgu Teacher is the oldest teacher of the lot, a retired old man who teaches English to the *pondok* kids using dog-eared copies of Mills & Boon romance novels as his textbooks. His stature is Yoda-like, and he stands at almost half my height when his back is straight. He has two teeth left and they seem to be growing in opposite directions. Itching to vent his spleen, he finally fires his salvo while the rest of us take a drag of our *rokok dauns.* "And do you know whom I hate the most? It's bad enough that we have been taken over by the Thais, that we have lost our culture, our history. But I hate the Americans the most! They don't spell properly! They spell analyse with a 'z'! *Celako Ameriko!*"

The days are spent thus: long walks around the village compounds interspersed by long chats on the verandas of kampong houses till dusk. The plaintive song of Patani has for its lyrics the wonted, recurring appeal for recognition. Why don't they recognise us for what we are? Why is our history not respected? Why do they wish us to be something else? The perils of assimilationist politics are laid bare, and the cost of playing deaf and dumb to the cry for recognition is high: two more civilians are shot in a village the following day, and an alleged insurgent is killed when his house is surrounded by Thai security forces.

By the fourth day I begin to understand how and why things have become so bad over the years. Moved from house to house – ostensibly for my own safety – the same song is sung for me time and again. We cross villages that are now almost exclusively Malay or Thai, the latter recognisable instantly by two things that the Malays hate the most: dogs and pigs. "Don't you communicate with the Thais anymore, Meng? After all, they are your neighbours," I ask as we drive around.

"This is what you don't seem to understand," Meng replies. "In fact, nobody understands us, and nobody ever listens to our side of the story. We don't hate the Thais. We have never hated the Thais. We don't even hate their soldiers and their cops, even though they are abusive to us, even when they insult us in the streets, and even when they bother our women and children. We don't hate them. We just want to be respected and to be left alone."

"But the insurgents are killing everyone these days. They are even killing Muslims when they can. I don't understand this conflict anymore and I don't know what they want. Is this some *jihad* for an Islamic state? Is it, as they say it is on the TV, part of some global Islamist movement?"

"Hahaha! You think we Patanis are so dumb and feeble that we need foreigners to come here to get us worked up?" Meng laughs at me. "That's the problem with you academics: you always look for complicated answers because you think the question is a difficult one. But it's really so easy. Even a child can understand it. There are no foreign militants, no jungle camps, no insurgent army out there in the woods – you saw that yourself. Why do you think the insurgency is taking place? Who do you think the insurgents are? They are all around you in the villages; they walk around and among us, they live in the kampongs with us, and they are just normal people who have lost their patience. We know that the battle is lost, and that there will never be an independent Patani. We have given that up. Nor do we want to become an Afghanistan like it was under the Taliban; we don't want Arabs bringing their Wahhabi Islam here, making things worse. We will be happy to be Thai citizens; but only as long as the Thais accept that being a Thai citizen doesn't mean being a Thai culturally. If you can be a Malaysian citizen and still remain Malay, Chinese or Indian, why can't we be Thai citizens who are still Malays, and Muslims? Is that so difficult to understand?"

And understanding is precisely what is missing in this whole equation; the missing piece in the jigsaw puzzle that is Patani and its quaint little war that hardly makes the headlines anywhere, or even in their own country, for that matter. Deep inside I feel that Meng has stated the truth as bluntly as he can:

there is no insurgent army creeping around in the undergrowth of the jungle; there are no *jihadi* camps in the mountains. All there is are a bunch of frustrated, angry, disenfranchised and marginalised youths who have given up on the political process and have turned their backs to dialogue because they have never been listened to in the first place.

And to make their point, they decide to burn down the school in the village I am staying in on my last night there.

Ashes and embers

Just beyond the tree line, and no further than three kilometres away, the dull red glow from the burning school gives out a curious sensation of warmth and comfort. The government primary school of Kampung Kuruwak is burning nicely, and the kids playing in the compound are quite happy to see it go up in smoke, as school was meant to re-open tomorrow. "Looks like they will get an extended holiday," I smirk to Meng. "Hee hee, kids will be kids, but they still have to attend the religious class at the *pondok,* whether they want to or not!" Meng smirks back.

"How does this solve anything, Meng?" I ask as we hear the sound of the fire engines and police cars racing to the scene, sirens blaring. "It's not a solution, but they, the guerrillas, have made their point, I think." And Meng has made his point too: the sirens are silenced one by one, and the fire engine, ambulance and police cars turn back, fearful of getting any closer to the burning school lest a landmine or ambush has been prepared to welcome them. It is dark, and the *waktu geriya* is here. The night belongs to them, and all the humvees, armoured cars, attack helicopters, infra-red night-vision goggles and submachine guns that the Thai army can muster cannot prevent a group of kampong insurgents from burning down a school with a jerry-can of kerosene and a box of matches.

This is a mass insurgency at its height, and the Thais have lost. And so, sadly, has everyone.

On the road back to Tak Bai for the crossing to Pengkalan Kubur, Kelantan, we drive past the same roadblocks that welcomed me on my arrival. A routine check takes place and I notice that most of those who are stopped are young men either travelling alone on their motorbikes or in groups in pick-ups. During the daytime, the Thai soldiers appear braver in their American-styled uniforms, and one can almost take them seriously.

Then at the ferry crossing of Tak Bai, an incident occurs that is worth recounting here. Waiting for my turn to cross, I sit and smoke on the jetty as the ferry from the Malaysian side comes into view. As is always the case, there is the predictable mad rush to get on board precisely when everyone on board is rushing to get off. (The ferry is, after all, terribly small.) Tucked between two lorries bearing cargo is a tiny motorbike whose driver is equally diminutive. On the bike are some durians, presumably, destined for someone's dinner table on the Malaysian side of the border. For reasons known only to him, the man on the bike is listening to a walkman radio under his helmet that is twice the size of his head. As he inches his way onto the ferry, onlookers shout out: *"Jago! Jago deh! Lori! Lori!"*

In an instant the motorbike, its driver, his walkman and oversized helmet, and the precious cargo of durians, are knocked off the jetty and into the water he falls. With a loud splash. The crowd rushes forward to help him and the tougher-looking lads all jump in, perhaps with the intention of showing off their wet, muscular chests afterwards. The rider is hauled out of the water, but his motorbike is nowhere to be seen; only bubbles rise to the surface. Even the durians are rescued, as everyone comes to the hapless boy's aid.

It is evident that the drenched motorcyclist is Thai, as that is all he speaks at first. Everyone else is Patani-Malay. In the midst of the confusion and the ridiculousness of it all, words are exchanged, and help offered. "Are you all right?" "Where is your passport?" "Did you lose your wallet?" "Can you stand up?" they ask the singular Thai, soaked and embarrassed, amongst a sea of Malays. Then comes the faltering words of Jawi from the cyclist: *"Makaseh, makaseh belako; ambo malu, ambo malu. Lalai tadi, nah habih durie' ambo doh hileng. Tolong ambo deh?"*

And so they do: one by one the durians (there were four in all) are dragged out of the water, dried and accounted for. Having missed the ferry we have to wait for the next one that comes half an hour later. Once on the Malaysian side the Patanis accompany the Thai motorcyclist, durians in hand, to the immigration checkpoint and plead on his behalf to be let through even though his passport and identity papers are soaked. The durians, apparently, have a tryst with destiny that cannot be missed, and have to be delivered no matter what.

Ustaz Meng's words came back to me: "We don't hate the Thais, you see? We have never hated the Thais. That's what you don't understand." Empathy, sympathy, compassion and the ability to recognise that that helpless soaking man in front of you happens to be another human being who has a life, a past, a history of his own that demands your recognition and respect, is perhaps the first condition for any kind of dialogue. I leave Patani with the belief that there is no insurgent army out there, though an insurgency is in full swing and can only get worse as long as both sides do not talk – and talk honestly – to each other. But who has the will to listen?

Bang bang in Patani

Two sides: Wall of a *madrasah* in Patani

Seeking Durga
(Tamil Nadu, Kerala and Karnataka,
Dec 2008-Jan 2009)

"No sir, it's too late. The plane is taking off now, please go back to your seat."

The stewardess is trying out every tone she can muster, from the affectionate nanny to stern matron, but to no avail. Her svelte frame is eclipsed somewhat by the bulk of the passenger whose intention it is to leave the aircraft at all costs – despite the fact that the door has been bolted and the gangway withdrawn. She is soon joined by another lithe member of her uniformed tribe, who likewise tries her best to convince the agitated man of gargantuan proportions that to flatten two air stewardesses in his bid to make good his escape from the craft will get him nowhere, save a prison, where there are not that many pretty stewardesses to serve you a cheese sandwich wrapped in plastic foil. Over the din of the engines and the hum of complicated machinery that blink, whirr and purr, the pilot's voice is heard, yelling from the cockpit: "What's going on back there? Tell the fellow to sit down, dammit! We're taking off now!"

The stalemate goes on for another minute, and while the two stewardesses are trying their best to move the tower of flesh from his present position to the seat where he ought to park his weight, I look around me to survey the faces of the other passengers, eager faces with nervous smiles and eyes turned heavenward. Some are offering their final supplications before their untimely end, convinced that this awkward contraption they have boarded is bound to falter at a crucial moment with the wings snapping off, the fuel igniting, or that a mountain would – for reasons known only to itself – shift to its side and block our path, sending passengers, pretty stewardesses and agitated pilots careening down a rocky mountainside in a million smouldering pieces.

It is only when the plane begins to coast down the runway that the man-mountain relents and grudgingly makes his way back to his seat. It is not fear of sudden death in the stratosphere that has prompted his bid to flee the aircraft, but rather his belated realisation that he has left his cash-stuffed wallet somewhere in the airport terminal.

The other passengers begin muttering their prayers silently, in low, hushed voices, like a collective prayer to a Babelian deity that speaks in many tongues. I sit where I sit and look forward at the pretty stewardesses, who have not lost their composure despite the drama. Closing my eyes, I doze off even before the plane leaves the ground. My only thoughts are of rest, peace, remembrance and longing. Longing to escape again, after another difficult year that has taken its toll on my hairline. Longing to return, to re-connect with the land of my ancestors. Longing for India, and looking forward to visiting her: Durga.

No, this is not a flight to an asylum of unreconstructed nostalgia. And ancestral bonds aside, this is not an attempt to re-connect with my roots in some faraway land either. I am flying to India for the simple reason that I absolutely, and unashamedly, adore the country; and that for the past decade or so, much of my work as a historian has been trained towards that great subcontinent, which we – linen and tweed-clad historians like myself – take for granted.

My destination is southern India, a part of the country I have never visited. I have made my acquaintance with the northern part of the subcontinent, all the way up to Pakistan and to the Kyber pass and beyond, several times. But southern India has always been that precious jewel that I have kept aside as a special treat for myself.

Half asleep but unable to rest, I sit in the semi-darkness of the plane cabin with Majumdar's *History of Ancient India* on my lap. The dog-eared pages of the book have long been sullied by my grubby fingers as I read the chapters again and again, with buttered toast in hand, revisiting the great moments of South Indian history when the Pallavas, Pandyas, Cheras and Cholas were battling it out in their bid to be masters of the South, and midwives to history. Next to me, a passenger nervously chomps on her cheese sandwich that she had just liberated from its plastic wrapper. On her tray is a curious object which turns out to be red wine in a can; an invention, I surmise, that can only have come from Australia, where wine in paper cartons were invented as a joke, and then taken too seriously. Perhaps, in future flights, they will offer wine in tablet form.

Undeterred by all the eating that is going on around me (even the ton of beef, who lost his wallet at the airport, is wolfing down his sandwich, albeit tearfully) I read about the great temples of Tamil Nadu and Kerala, and the men who built them. In a flash, I recall a small discovery I made (purely by chance and certainly not an original breakthrough) while reading late into the night in the library of the School of Oriental and African Studies in London years ago. It occurred to me, while poring over the first colonial maps of Selangor by the Royal Geographical Society in the 1880s, that the place-name

'Cheras' in Kuala Lumpur may well have signified the presence of a significant Indian settlement from Kerala at the time.

That minor revelation that came and went quietly in the dead of night was a key of sorts, a Rosetta stone that opened up a myriad of avenues before me. From that moment on, I could no longer think of India as a far-away country. I began to see Indian influences in everything around me. I waded through the earliest vocabularies compiled by the colonial philologists and found Sanskrit words and phrases aplenty: *keluarga, desa, raja, istana, dewa, satria* and so on. India unfolded like a lotus emerging out of the primordial depth of a memory, the petals unveiling signs and traces, tropes and metaphors that transformed the world I once knew and forced me to look again at the country I have called the home of my ancestors, and yet never recognised it. Good lord, the thought occurred to me: India and Southeast Asia are one and the same.

The breakthrough came like a gentle tap on my overheated forehead. The bridge was complete. Like Hanuman, I knew I had to make the great leap to recover my other half. India, here I come!

Karna returns

Liminality has its advantages and disadvantages, and among the latter one can count the nagging doubt that one belongs anywhere. Perhaps that is why I have always had a particular fondness for the ill-fated character Karna – *Suryaputra*, son of the Sun-God, and the first-born of the Pandawa brothers who was, by a sad twist of fate, destined to live and die among the enemies of his clan, the Korawas. Twice betrayed – first by his mother, and then by his guru – Karna is eventually struck down by his own brother, Arjuna, when he ripped off his golden skin-armour to present it to his mother who abandoned him at birth. Karna's plea to his mother, "Am I not your son as well?" rings with such poignancy that it tugs at my heartstrings, and in him we see the predicament of the complex man-God whose circumstances of birth signalled his end from the very beginning.

Can we escape our fate, our appointed destiny? How were two clans that were one rent asunder; bringing into the battlefield brothers and cousins, locked in mortal combat that would spell the doom of all? In the same vein, how could this great Asian land mass, this vast expanse that stretches from the Thar desert to the mountains and valleys of Timor, be torn apart to the point that we no longer remember our collective history? South and Southeast Asia were once one, with the Indian Ocean as the corridor that connected the two chambers of that grand house. What happened to end this prodigious movement of humanity? How did we become small-minded, parochial, fear-struck strangers to one another, and, by extension, ourselves?

I try to settle these thoughts as they work their way around me. Hoping to find some answers, I hold Majumdar's *History of Ancient India* close to me as I fell asleep in my seat, and soon dreams return to terrorise me.

Seeking Durga

I know not when it happened, and what misfortune occassioned their departure, but it is with a certain reluctance that I lament that fateful moment – its exactitude escapes me – when the guardian angels who stood by me took flight and left me all alone on my journey. Perhaps it was the trepidation of knowing where I was headed, the thought of my destination. I remain ignorant still. Or perhaps it was out of sympathy, and my earnest wish not to witness the crashing of my soul that they knew was bound to happen. Unable to steer me off my path, they abandoned me, like Ahab at the wheel, harpoon clenched in wet, clammy hands with the great whale looming before so large that even the ocean didn't seem big enough to contain the beast.

The year ended with this diagnosis: that ball of hate, wound by threads of anger and knots of despair has grown so big that it is bleeding poison into my fevered skull. Consumed and drowning in bile and venom, I am drinking mouthfuls of the rank poison as I sink into the diseased swamp that floods my interior.

Hate, hate. This fire so hot, it is unseen: a radiating hate that burns so intensely that its flames are invisible to the eye, as if it is so terrible in all its aspects that even sight could not cope with it, and none of the senses would touch it. Hate, burning so deep, like some primordial flame that burns out other flames around it, burrowing deeper and deeper into my caverns. It is into that cavern that I need to venture, vorpal blade in hand to do battle with the demon. And where no angel could come to my aid in its twisted suffocating burrows and crevices, their wings scorched by the heat. Pale and terrified, even they – the immortals – have fled.

I need to slay this demon of hate, to protect that tiny bit of unsullied faith that I have left that good triumphs over evil, that day triumphs over night. Yet, this battle is not fought out of a conviction. There are no brave-hero tales to be recounted. There is life and there is death, kill or be killed; like an animal, cowering, crawling, biting and scratching. A furtive conflict where sweat mixes with sweat, and foul breaths comingle with shameless promiscuity. It is a war with myself, with no one to help me.

Where are my legions? Where stand my allies? No-one, and nothing to help or guide me, save one: Durga, Goddess. Mahishasuramadini, Slayer of Mahishasura. She of the spear-shaft that pierces the heart of the demon. She who wears the garland of skulls. She who wears the skirt of bloodied, severed arms still twitching with life, with blood on her lips, and madness in her eyes. Durga, Mahishasuramadini.

The plane lands, and I wake up. Looking out of the window there is nothing but darkness. In the dead of night, Karna has stolen into his home.

I am in the middle of a traffic jam in dusty, overcrowded Chennai, assaulted by the blaring of a zillion horns, gasping for anything that resembles breathable air.

My eyes burn in the sun's glare, and yet, in the din and chaos of Chennai's bursting streets I feel at home. Chennai, Bangkok, Jakarta – all are one with the sounds and sights of the familiar, irritating, exasperating, confounding, tear-drenched and hysteria-inducing Asian city. Though this is my first day, and Chennai my first port of call, it is already familiar to me. How could I get lost, and why should I worry? I know exactly where I am: Asia. Mother, I am home.

I have not come all the way to spend my time in another bustling metropolis though, and the familiar sights of Chennai – its shopping malls, plazas and grand commercial hotels – jar my aesthetic sensibilities and fill me with the dreaded knowledge that the city shares the same genes with other Asian mega-cities of overflowing cash and misplaced hopes. No, I need to get out of the city as soon as possible, and I need my own chariot. This comes in the form of a rather handsome Ambassador – without doubt one of the best cars ever built and a most trustworthy beast of the road, designed specifically to contest the terrain in India. Backpack safely in the boot and notebook in hand, I travel south in the direction of Thanjavur with an earnest wish to pay my respects to the Pallavas and the Cholas.

En route is the quaint little town of Pondicherry, that curious landmark of France's failed attempt to bring her *mission civilisatrice* to Hind. Caught in its own time warp like a spider trapped in its own web, Pondy is nestled snugly in its little niche of pastiche and clichés, albeit sweet and pretty ones: policemen clad in white uniforms and scarlet *kepis* stand at road crossings as if they have come straight out of a Tamil-dubbed version of *The Pink Panther*; church bells ring as Christmas is approaching, and the street names recall the lives of past French worthies long forgotten elsewhere: *Dumas, Suffren, la Bourdonnais*. The location calls for the right dress, and thankfully I have manage to pack at least three pairs of the identical linen trousers for the occasion.

Strolling down the leafy streets and lanes I watch life pass by, as children shop for toys and trinkets to adorn their Christmas crèches. Plaster statues of the characters of the nativity stand at attention, waiting to be bought and taken home where the baby Jesus would be placed in the centre, flanked by the Virgin Mother and the three wise men. With their own ecumenical touch the vendors also present the public with a host of other local notables: Vishnu, Lakshmi, Rama and Hanuman to take home as well. Now that would be a rather charming nativity, I think, with the infant Jesus cradled in the arms of Vishnu.

Quirkiness aside, I remind myself that the pink-cheeked Jesus is the interloper, and not the other way round. After all, he should be happy if he is given a place beside Vishnu and Lakshmi, for the latter have been around much longer.

The antiquity of the gods is brought home to me at my first place of visit: the temple complex of Mamallapuram, the artistic heart of the Pallava dynasty. At the Mahishasuramadini cave, I gawk at the relief of Durga astride her lion doing battle with the bull-demon Mahishasura. Standing before the bas relief of Arjuna's penance (possibly one of the most photographed spots in all of India) I feel as if the great book of Asian history is open before me. There stands Arjuna on one foot, meditating in the hope that Shiva would consent to give him the magic arrow *pashupatashastra*, with which he intends to slay his nemesis. The river Ganges is represented by a row of serpentine *Nagas*, Snake-gods, writhing as the river coursing its way across the subcontinent. In the corner I can't help but notice the behaviour of a cat, imitating Arjuna in his meditative pose, demonstrating his abstinence by not gobbling up a troop of mice playing at its paws.

Try as I do to prevent it, the art historian's hat falls on my head against my volition. One look at the Nagas reminds me of the *naga* motifs I have seen in Thai, Khmer, and Cambodian art. In a flash a catalogue of familiar images come rushing past: Nagas crowning the meditating Buddha from Cham and Khmer, *nagas* in the Hindu art of Java. I remember the nagas skirting across the lower edges of my antique sarongs from Lasem and Cirebon. All that remains is to connect them all: yes indeed, this is home; this is where it all started.

Step by step, pace by pace, I walk the same earth that has been trod upon by generations of Dravidian stone carvers and architects. My brain is clogged up by too many images and memories as I make my way to the beach for some air, but only to stand right before the temple I have been wanting to see for so long: the Shore Temple of Mamallapuram.

As I make out its silhouette from a distance, the tiny hairs at the back of my neck begin to stand. As I get closer, my heart races with the feeling of certainty I have tried to suppress, for fear of disappointment. "This is it! This is it! The shore temple – and it looks exactly like I imagined it would, the front tower two-thirds the height of the main tower; false storeys, three levels. It can't be true, but it is!"

If proof is ever needed that the development of Hindu-Buddhist art in South and Southeast Asia were contemporaneous between the 7th to 9th centuries, this is it. The shore temple – so-called because of its precarious location so close to the beach, and for the simple reason that nobody knows its original name – bears the most uncanny resemblance to the Hindu temples of Central Java that were built in the same period. While the Pallavas of Southern India were building their very first temples that would later become the prototype of temples across Tamil Nadu right up to the Chola empire, the Javanese Hindus of Holing in Central Java were building identical ones on the Dieng Plateau and the Gedung Songo complex. All of these temples were Hindu, and all of them dedicated to the God Shiva, the primordial God of the first Dravidians and the Javanese. Another piece is slotted into the puzzle, and India feels closer to me than ever.

Our other half

Travelling across southern India is like taking a peek behind the mirror to look at the other side: it is always hidden, yet it is there. My eyes are drowning in a flood of fresh images that are all too new yet all too familiar; place-names that sound strangely like home, and yet alien; faces that look like those of neighbours, but who are strangers nonetheless. Every corner shop looks and feels like the corner shop I hung around in as a kid in Kuala Lumpur, long before the advent of megamalls and cineplexes that flattened the urban landscape into one long, dull, grey pancake of cement and mortar. This is home, yet it is not; so why do I feel as if I belong?

Qur'an and Cricket

My Yohji Yamamotos gather a fine film of yellow dust as I trudge across the narrow streets of Thanjavur, ears deafened by the incessant honking of motorbikes and taxis, and nerves straining to breaking point. Walking beside the Grand Anicut canal I try to imagine what Tanjore felt and looked like a thousand years ago, when it was the heart of the great Chola empire. Here is the capital of the mighty kingdom that Rajaraja I built, a great sprawling maritime power whose fleets crisscrossed the Indian Ocean in search of trade and profit with the Malay and Javanese kingdoms of Sumatra and Java. For decades the Cholas, Malays and Javanese engaged in this conversation about art and philosophy, building temples and developing a common artistic culture that was neither Indian nor Southeast Asian, but rather of the Indian Ocean itself. A civilisation borne by the waves of the sea, its rise and fall alternating like the tide. Then for reasons known only to himself, Rajendra Chola decided one day to flex his muscles and send his fleet eastwards in search of conquest and plunder, decimating (Sri) Langka, Burma, Kadaran (Kedah), Langkasuka and Srivijaya along the way.

Despite the upheavals that occasionally shook the sinews that bound South and Southeast Asia, the two parts of the same world were never far apart, and like siblings who love and hate each other with equal measure, the two halves of this maritime culture remained united by bonds of art, culture and religion. I have come to see the pinnacle of Chola art and architecture, and it is none other than the greatest Chola monument of all, the Brihadishwara temple of Thanjavur.

As I sit on the cool grass and watch the pilgrims shuffle past, I cannot help but be thankful for the gift of sight. Living in an age where the geek is God, we have become jaded with what we see. Our eyes are tired of being lied to, or at least mine are. I cannot take for real the computer-generated towers and palaces that adorn the silver screen any more. No, the armies of orcs and goblins don't move me either. Nor do battle-cruisers or x-wing fighters that zap each other in outer space with tedious predictability. In a world of digitalised images, artificial sweeteners and virtual sex, my senses have gone on holiday. But this, this monument of Rajaraja I; this is real. And this I can believe in. This is the faith of the Cholas carved in stone.

It is then that one truly recognises the power of religious art, when it transcends the superfluous and vainglorious, when even the egos of their builders and architects are dwarfed by the sheer magnitude of such colossal size and ambition. The towering *vimana* of the Brihadishwara temple reaches up, like some gigantic hand made of red stone, to touch infinity and beyond. The perennial song of the human spirit, that longing for God, that need to know, to be sure, to believe, echoes across the sacred precinct, this hallowed ground. Visible from miles away, the great towering *vimana* of the temple was the hand of the Cholas as they caressed the sky, stroking the cheeks of the gods above. Proud yet plaintive, humble despite its ambition: you can only look upon it kneeling.

Over the next three weeks I ply the routes that take me across Tamil Nadu, Kerala and Karnataka, stopping here and there to take in the sights and sounds of this strangely familiar land. The days and nights spent on the rice-barges that sailed up and down the backwaters of Kerala are a welcomed escape from the hustle and bustle of overcrowded city, and I marvel at the development of a state under Communist rule. Not a single fast-food outlet is to be seen, and my eyes are given a rest from the lurid mismatched colours of advertising boards and slogans that have become the norm in Southeast Asia. Paddling along the waterways in my canoe I feel the hushed, unstated joy of being able to pass unseen by local villagers who couldn't care less who I am. Up in the mountains of Ooty, the hill station, it is likewise reclusive and blissfully free of noisome folk; and once again I can play the part of fogey, reading the night away quietly by the fireplace as the eucalyptus faggots fizz, pop and reduce themselves to glowing embers.

But it is in Mysore, capital of the Wadiyar Rajas, that I feel that I have come to the end of my journey. An obligatory tour of the Maharaja's palace is in order, and though the Durbar hall and pavilion are admittedly jaw-dropping and arresting, I cannot help but feel as if I am walking through a grander version of the Kuala Lumpur railway station. No, royal trappings and the finery of rulers are not the flavour of the month for me. I have come here to see something else altogether, and to see her, I have to walk up the Chamundi hills to pay my respects.

Durga revisited

It's not often that one gets to visit a place where a goddess is said to have been born. In Sri Lanka I had a go at Adam's Peak, where local legend has it that Adam fell to earth after he was cast out of paradise. Up in the mountains of Kashmir I was told by the wizened old greybeards that it was the place where Jesus finally came to rest, after he was carried across the Himalayas on a hot-air balloon, of all things. But Mysore is the home of Durga, and right at the top of Chamundi hill, at the end of a thousand slippery steps, is her temple. At daybreak I make my way to say hello amidst the throng of thousands of pilgrims.

As the sun reaches its zenith, the outline of the temple stands out in bold relief. Half-blinded by the glare, I pause to look around me and see the universal dance of humanity in search of answers: one by one, the pilgrims and worshippers kneel and prostrate themselves before the temple gate. The queue is long, and the faces are of varied hues. I spy medicants from Lucknow, fakirs from Hyderabad, peasants from Rajastan. Prayer beads are rubbed and rolled between sweaty fingers. Saffron powder dabbed on foreheads. The sacred thread wound around the wrists of friends and strangers alike. There is an air of merriment about the place, and even the temple Brahmins cannot keep a straight face when a sacred cow decides to chew on a garland a pilgrim tries to hang around her neck. A schoolgirl standing in line to get into the temple tugs at my shirt and asks, "Mister, you come from Japan?" "No, I'm local," is my reply. "Okay, give me a pen then," is her response.

Inside the temple the crowd is hushed, huddled together as they inch their way forward in the cool darkness. Only the chiming of the bells breaks the silence of the faithful. Bathed in the amber glow of oil-lamps, Durga's golden statue radiates a presence that is uncannily warm and inviting.

Is she the one? Are the answers to be found here? I stand quietly by and watch as the pilgrims come forward one by one, in hurried succession, to offer their prayers and lay their garlands and offerings at her feet. I have seen her image many a time before, and in all her avatars. The blood-soaked Kali, sword in hand; the benign Chinamastra, her bloodied head held aloft, feeding her followers with her own life-blood. In all her manifestations she is the embodiment of complexity and contradictions. The pieces fall together, and the riddle answers itself.

The eye of the modern subject recoils at the flagrant disregard for continuity, expecting order even when there should be none. We look upon the ancients and react with incredulity and, pathetically, we attempt to render them cipherable to our simple modern sensibilities and reduce them to the barest of essentials. We do not understand the images of the gods, for we have lost the key to comprehension. Then, that seed of primordial angst; that long-suppressed cry of longing for the divine, slowly claws its way up. In child-like despair we beg, plead and cry out, "Explain yourself to us. Who and what are you?"

In all her manifestations she shatters our settled assumptions and rents the familiar asunder. Durga, Kali, Chinamastra: her demonic countenance shoots bolts of terror into us, but all that is killed is that hollow ego that stands in the path of comprehension. She has come to kill you, but what is slain is nothing more than that shallow conceit that you have, your 'Self'.

Around her neck she wears a garland of severed heads, with faces staring right into ours, and sending us running away for fear of death. But look closely and you will see that on each head is a face that bears a different expression: Lust, Greed, Vanity, Hypocrisy, Hate, Hate, Hate. She has defeated them all, and liberated you from the very same faces that you have worn often.

Around her waist she wears a skirt of severed arms, bleeding and twitching. These are the arms that have committed the sins of your past, the arms that carry our bad karma, the arms that bind you to the karmic cycle of guilt and suffering. She has freed you from your past, offered you a new beginning, breathed new life into you.

And on her face lies the key to understanding her. Amidst the blood and gore, and death and becoming and eternal renewal; between the sharp fangs that drip and the cross brows that speak of murderous intent, rests her smile. And her smile – Durga's smile – is benevolent: "This I do, and your pride I kill, because I love you. I love you."

I recall the saying of the Sufi Muslim mystics, "The distance between you and God is your ego. Kill your ego and step to God." Durga's spear and sword gleam in the sun and I recall the words of my sufi ustaz years ago: 'Faith is the sword that will cut your pride in two, and you will be free.'

After standing there for as long as I can, I make my way out. I offer a final passing glimpse as a sign of respect, and to say, "Thank you, that was worth it." While making my way out I noticed the sign at the oddly-named Museum of Godliness beside the temple that reads: "Five thousand years ago you had visited this place at this time the way you are visiting now. Because the drama of the world repeats itself every five thousand years." Five thousand years ago the peoples of South and Southeast Asia were also one and the same. This land, this sea, this ocean of humanity, was ours together, and remains so still. I have come home, and I shall soon be returning home too. How great it is to be home everywhere.

I pause on my way down to wipe the sweat off my brow.